DEEP THROAT

Also by Time is an Ocean

About the author
Nic Outterside was an award-winning newspaper journalist
and editor for 28 years and currently is the proprietor of
Time is an Ocean, the book publishing arm of **write***ahead*.
Deep Throat is his 53rd paperback book.

DEEP THROAT

Nic Outterside

Time is an Ocean Publications

Time is an Ocean Publications
An Imprint of **write**_ahead_
Lonsdale Road
Wolverhampton, WV3 0DY

Second Printed Edition written and published
by **Time is an Ocean Publications 2022**
Text copyright © **Nic Outterside**
The right of Nic Outterside to be identified as the author of
this work has been asserted by him, in accordance with the
Copyright, Designs and Patents Act 1988.
The front and back cover photographs are
copyright © **Time is an Ocean Publications**
All images within this book are copyright
© **Time is an Ocean** except where
the individual copyright of the owners are accredited.

DEDICATION

For Tom Davison, Jim Seaton and
Fred Bridgland who gave me the freedom,
direction and encouragement.
Also for my investigative colleagues
Sara Brown, Felicity Arbuthnot and
the late Angus MacLeod.

CONTENTS

Foreword

"We live in an unseen world of shadows. Then there are the lies. They start on the very first day. Nobody is as they seem, nothing is what it is made out to be. The truth recedes. Our secret world is beyond the law".
(The Whistle Blower, 1986)

TRUTH is a hollow concept.

After all, what exactly is the truth? What you read in a newspaper, see on the TV, are told by a politician or overhear in the bar of your local pub?

Because, unless you know the real facts you will never know what is true and what is propaganda or just lies.

Highly respected US investigative journalist Caitlin Johnstone once wrote:

"Crazy, stupid conspiracy theorists believe a mature worldview requires scepticism toward power.

Smart upstanding citizens believe the government is your friend, and the media are its helpers.

Crazy, stupid conspiracy theorists believe that government secrecy makes it necessary to discuss possible theories about what might be going on behind that veil of opacity.

Smart upstanding citizens believe that just because a world-dominating government with the most powerful military in the history of civilization has no transparency and zero accountability, that doesn't mean you've got to get all paranoid about it.

Crazy, stupid conspiracy theorists believe the very rich sometimes engage in nefarious behaviour to expand their wealth and power.

Smart upstanding citizens believe billionaires always conduct themselves with the same values that got them their billions in the first place: honesty, morality, and generosity.

Crazy, stupid conspiracy theorists believe it's important to remember the lies that led up to the invasion of Iraq, and the disastrous consequences of blind faith in government claims.

Smart upstanding citizens believe that all you need to do to ensure you're getting all the facts is watch television and run screaming from the room if you accidentally flip past RT.

Crazy, stupid conspiracy theorists believe that the billionaire class which owns the mass media has a natural incentive to prop up the status quo upon which it is built, and so construct an environment where reporters are incentivized to always support the establishment line.

Smart upstanding citizens believe that if that kind of conspiracy were really happening, it would have been in the news."

I have often been called a *"crazy, stupid conspiracy theorist"*.

But I am also an award-winning investigative journalist, who over 37 years has worked across all forms of media, including magazines, weekly and daily newspapers, radio broadcasting, books and online. And I was trained – indeed hard-wired – into dealing with real facts, which, if necessary, could be proved in a court of law.

Among more than a dozen awards to my name are *North of England Daily Journalist of the Year, Scottish Daily Journalist of the Year, Scottish Weekly Journalist of the Year* and a special national award for investigative journalism.

In 1994, 53 MPs signed an Early Day Motion in the British House of Commons praising my investigative research and writing. And in 2016, I was awarded an honorary doctorate in written journalism, triggered by my investigations into the real cause of the 2001 Foot and Mouth Disease epidemic.

The **Oxford English Dictionary** describes investigative journalism as a form of journalism in which reporters deeply investigate a single topic of interest, such as a serious crime, political corruption, or corporate wrongdoing. An investigative journalist may spend months or years researching and preparing a report.

Sometimes the truth is hiding in plain sight. Other times it is hidden under a rock or obscured with lies. My career as an investigative journalist was to find the truth and try to shine a light upon it.

So why title this book **Deep Throat?**

Deep Throat was the pseudonym given to the secret informant who in 1972 provided information about the Watergate Break-ins to **Washington Post** journalist Bob Woodward and fellow scribe Carl Bernstein.

It was only some 30 years later, that *Deep Throat* was revealed to be FBI deputy director Mark Felt.

Woodward and Bernstein's world-shattering revelations would lead to the impeachment and downfall of US president Richard Nixon and the best-selling book and film **All The President's Men.**

Over the past 50 years the term *Deep Throat* has been used to describe other informants, who often under the guise of anonymity, have broken secret information to the press and the wider world. Within this book are 15 of my so-called *Deep Throat* investigations into what others would rather be kept hidden.

They begin with the first in 1990, which uncovered the deadly truth about one of our nuclear power stations, and ending with unanswered questions about the poisoning of two so-called Russian spies Alexander Litvinenko and Sergei Skripal, researched after I had officially retired as an investigative reporter.

In between are my reports of nefarious links between Freemasons and the deselection of a Conservative parliamentary candidate and later the Dunblane Massacre; the real cause of the aforementioned Foot and Mouth Disease outbreak; inconsistencies in the evidence over the death of Princess Diana and Dodi Al Fayed; the corruption of the Fourth Estate and my award-winning inquiry into the link between Depleted Uranium (DU) artillery shells and cancers, immune deficiencies and birth abnormalities.

Deep Throat was first published in a much longer form in 2020, under the title **Contacts** but while revising this book two years later the reality of Establishment cover-up hit home in a shocking, unexpected and personal way.

And what I discovered squared my circle. You can read about this simple twist of fate in Chapter 13.

For now, the key to being a good investigative journalist is having good contacts and being open to the odd Deep Throat phone call or email.

Sometimes those contacts wish to remain anonymous for their own safety or their desire for privacy, other times they are willing to put their heads above the parapet and tell openly of the lies and deceit that their paymasters are peddling. Without them there would be no truth, and I am constantly indebted to all of my contacts.

In 1997, upon being awarded *Scottish Daily Journalist of the Year*, the judges said my contact book *"must be worth well into six figures"*. They went on to say: *"His targets are institutions, governments and politicians – the "system", if you like. All his news features set out to inform and change – and they succeeded magnificently. The judges' minds were "boggled" by his extensive, painstaking research, all undertaken in the public interest."*

I hadn't truly realised until that point just how vital my contacts were to me… I do now!

As for the written word, I have three muses in this life: the writer, singer and poet Patti Smith; the grittiest investigative journalist of our time John Pilger and the late and truly great Paul Foot.

Patti taught me how to write in an open first-person style, John taught me to look beyond the accepted narrative of the Establishment and Paul taught me how to be dogged and not to surrender to bullying or intimidation. Each of them cut a path for others to follow.

I am not worthy to tie any of their bootlaces, but I hope I have stuck to those paths.

Nic Outterside
December 2022

Chapter One
Radioactive

The Dounreay Nuclear Power Station in Caithness, Scotland

IT was the summer of 1990. Like many others, I was held bedazzled as the *Italia 90 World Cup* unfolded on our TV screens, and England found football glory with David Platt, Gary Lineker and the irrepressible Paul (Gazza) Gascoigne.

Earlier that year I had moved to be a reporter on a busy weekly newspaper in North Wales, leaving behind four care-free years working for glossy computer magazines.

So, on the warm evening of Wednesday, 4th July I sat in a large pub near Conwy, with my new pals from the paper to watch a memorable game of football on a large TV screen.

The semi-final of the World Cup: England versus West Germany.

It was a game you couldn't miss. It was a passion.

We were a happy bunch as we forgot work and chatted about football and whether Gascoigne was our new footballing Messiah. We drank beer, cheered loudly as Lineker scored, shouted obscenities when Gazza was booked and then cried into our beer after we lost the game on penalties to the Germans.

More beer was consumed until we wended our ways home.

The next day was press day at my newspaper *The North Wales Weekly News* in nearby Llandudno Junction – the day our weekly work went to press… a hectic morning, followed by feet up and a chance to recharge batteries in the afternoon.

Nursing a hangover (in more ways than one), the morning flew by in a blur, and after a sandwich and a coffee I sat at my desk and began to write a list of stories and tasks for the following week.

The office was empty when the phone on the neighbouring desk suddenly rang loudly.

Out of routine I picked up the call.

"Weekly News, Nic Outterside, can I help you?" I asked.

A woman's voice answered: *"Are you a reporter?"*

"Yes," I replied, and hesitatingly, began to listen.

Within a minute the lady on the phone had me listening like I had never listened before, and I was scribbling notes like there was no tomorrow.

She explained nervously that she was a nurse at the local hospital and her husband had worked for the past 20 years at Trawsfynydd Nuclear Power station, situated some 36 miles away on the outskirts of Snowdonia National Park.

The power station, which takes its name from the nearby village of Trawsfynydd, began construction in July 1959, and both of its reactors were operational by March 1965. The station opened fully in October 1968, at a cost of £103 million.

The previous evening, the lady's husband had planned to come home early to watch the World Cup semi-final and enjoy a few beers.

Instead, she explained, he had arrived home crying and handed her an official letter he had received from his employers, Magnox Ltd. The letter informed him that following monitoring tests, his body had received more than 20 times the safe clinical level of radiation during his years working at the plant. As a result he was to be transferred to another part of the facility for *"his own health"*.

At this point the lady on the phone began to cry uncontrollably.

"I don't know much about radiation or my husband's job, but I do know two of his friends there have recently been diagnosed with cancer, and my husband has been having stomach pains and bleeding from his bowels," she stuttered.

She said she was terrified, as the letter that her husband had brought home was marked *"Confidential"* and he had been told that he and his work colleagues were bound by the Official Secrets Act.

"I can't even tell you my name or where we live" she added, *"Or we could both end up in prison."*

I sat gobsmacked by what I had heard.

This lady – I never did discover her full name – was my first Deep Throat informant.

But I knew that as a journalist I could not do anything with her information unless I had proof (veritas) that this letter existed. I gently informed the lady of my dilemma and suggested we could maybe meet somewhere neutral so I could see the letter for myself.

After a moment's hesitation she agreed and gave me the location of a bus shelter next to a red telephone box on the Penrhyn Road, some three miles from my office. And a meeting time of 4pm was made. I explained I would park near the bus shelter in my black Fiat Uno car.

So, my first *Deep Throat* liaison was arranged.

But as I put down the phone, something worried me… if this information and indeed the letter were bound by the Official Secrets Act (OSA), would that stop me revealing the contents in our newspaper? I knew a little about the OSA as my dad had signed it at least twice on contracts he worked on for the Ministry of Defence, but I needed to know more.

A quick phone call to a legal friend gave me the answer I needed.

"It is a sham and a lie," he told me, *"It is a frightener employed by the company to keep their workers quiet.*

"While the technical data about the reactors may be deemed as being in the national security interest, the health of the reactor workers definitely is not.

"This is a civil nuclear fuel facility, not bloody Faslane," he added.

I was relieved and thanked him.

Two hours later I sat nervously in my car, parked across the road from the arranged meeting place.

A few minutes passed and a lady in her early 50s with dyed blonde hair and wearing a green coat, walked up to the phone box. She looked in the direction of my car. I caught her eye and beckoned her across the road.

She bent down and looked in my open car window.

"Mr Outterside?" she asked nervously.

Her eyes were red from crying as she opened the passenger door and sat next to me.

We started to chat about the sudden change of weather – it had begun to rain – as she hurriedly took a folded letter from her handbag.

"Here it is," she whispered.

I tried to explain that the Official Secrets Act threat was bunkum, but quickly knew her fears did not allow her to believe me.

I read the letter from top to bottom – even glanced at her husband's name and their address which gave me a crucial bona fide – and scribbled a few notes in my reporter's note book.

I no longer have the technical data that was included in that letter, but I was quickly able to ascertain that this poor lady's husband had indeed received something like 23 times the safe recognised level of radioactive contamination during his years working at Trawsfynydd.

Seven days later I made my first exclusive front page splash at my newspaper. The headline rang out: *Workers Health Fears Over Radioactive Poisoning.*

I was delighted to break some news that the nuclear industry did not want to become public.

Inside I felt my first buzz as a proper journalist.

But I also thought deeply about the man – and his colleagues – who had had their lives ruined by their toxic work environment.

Some years later I discovered that the man died in 1991, *"after a long illness"*.

In 2015 it was reported that the now partially decommissioned Trawsfynydd Nuclear Power Station may also have been responsible for elevated levels of cancer found in villages and other communities downwind of it.

Research supervised by Dr Chris Busby, attached to the Latvian Academy of Sciences in Riga, showed the incidence of breast cancer was five times higher downwind from the power station than would have been expected. Some other kinds of cancer were found at around double the expected rate.

Trawsfynydd is the only inland nuclear power station in the UK. It has two Magnox type CO2 cooled graphite moderated reactors and is situated on a lake, Llyn Trawsfynydd, which acts as a cooling water source and is also a sink for radioactivity released from the plant.

A significant amount of radioactive material now exists in the lake bed sediment.

The prevailing winds at the site are south westerly and more than 90% of those living downwind of the power station were surveyed by researchers working for Dr Busby.

A paper, published by **Jacobs Journal of Epidemiology and Preventive Medicine**, states: *"Trawsfynydd is a 'dirty' nuclear power station. As it has carbon dioxide, gas-cooled graphite block reactors, its releases to the air are higher than most other types of nuclear reactor.*

"In addition, all the liquid releases are discharged to the lake, where they have accumulated to the lake body sediment.

"Results show very clearly that the downwind population has suffered because of these exposures. This is most clear in breast cancer in the younger women below 60, where the rates were almost five times the expected.

"Additionally we see a doubling of risk in those who ate fish from Trawsfynydd Lake, which supports the conclusion that it is mainly a nuclear power station effect that is being seen."

Other forms of cancer showing elevated levels included prostate, leukaemia, mesothelioma and pancreas. Altogether, 38 people in the area researched were diagnosed with cancer between 2003 and 2005, against an expected level of 19.5.

A spokesman for Magnox Ltd refused to detail the concerns and simply said: *"Comment on the details of the study is a matter for experts in public health. However the radiation exposures of our workforce, and that of the general public, from authorised discharges from the nuclear industry, are well below the maximum levels authorised by independent regulatory bodies."*

Dr Jill Meara, director of Public Health England's Centre for Radiation, Chemical and Environmental Hazards (CRCE), said: *"Identification of disease clusters are matters for local public health teams. If those teams need specialist support, such as in radiation epidemiology, they can talk to CRCE for assistance."*

My first investigative scoop in North Wales in 1990 came back to me six years later, while I was working at **The Scotsman** daily newspaper in Edinburgh and investigating a series of radioactive leaks at the Dounreay nuclear power plant on the north coast in Caithness.

The experimental nuclear facility was first commissioned in 1955 and by 1996 it was old and decrepit by late 20th century standards.

In September 1996, I started to receive tip-offs and a series of leaked secret documents from three trusted contacts… all experts on the nuclear industry. One was a Scottish environmental campaigner, another was a professor at an English university and the last was a scientific advisor to Labour shadow cabinet minister Michael Meacher MP.

Each told me independently that radioactive leakage problems which were plaguing the Dounreay plant at the time could all be traced back to the 1960s and 1970s.

It was hard to ignore this body of expertise and the evidence they provided.

The story goes something like this:

On the morning of Tuesday 10th May 1977, there was a loud explosion at the Dounreay plant. The UK Atomic Energy Authority, which ran the plant, had dumped at least 2 kilograms of sodium and potassium down a 65-metre shaft in the underlying rock, already packed with radioactive waste and flooded with seawater.

The results were dramatic. The sodium and potassium reacted violently with the water. The explosion blew off the shaft's huge concrete lid, threw its steel top plate 12 metres to one side, badly damaged the 5-tonne concrete blocks at the mouth of the shaft, and blasted scaffold poles up to 40 metres away.

An eyewitness reported a plume of white smoke blowing out to sea.

The ground around the shaft was littered with radioactive particles hot enough to injure and kill. Over the next 18 years, almost 150 such particles were found on Dounreay's beaches.

Officially the accident was the most serious ever at Dounreay, and the particles it spewed out perhaps the most dangerous ever released by the British nuclear industry.

Despite this, the Scottish Office's Industrial Pollution Inspectorate was reluctant to prosecute Dounreay because it feared it may not be able to prove that the plant was the source of the particles, even though the UKAEA itself did not deny it.

In 1987, the UKAEA was asked by the Committee on the Medical Aspects of Radiation in the Environment (COMARE), which advises the Department of Health, to list all its *"unplanned discharges"* from Dounreay. This was part of its investigation into a cluster of cases of childhood leukaemia in communities around the Dounreay plant.

However the UKAEA made no mention of the explosion, on the grounds that nothing dangerous had ended up beyond its fence. But the UKAEA's internal incident reports immediately after the explosion say that contaminated *"items"* were indeed retrieved from outside the site boundary.

In 1987, COMARE also asked where the radioactive particles found on the foreshore had come from. The UKAEA claimed that they had leaked from a damaged storm drain containing the remains of a small radiation spillage from 1965.

They also told COMARE that the Industrial Pollution Inspectorate had concluded that *"in radiological terms the protocols gave no grounds for concern"*.

But according to Tom Wheldon, head of COMARE's special beach contamination working group: *"If you ingested one of the hottest particles and it lodged in your gut, you would probably be dead from gastrointestinal burns within the week."* Elsewhere in the body, most of the particles could irradiate the bone marrow enough to significantly increase the risk of leukaemia.

One of the particles that was found contained 200 million becquerels of radioactivity, while the majority ranged between 1 and 10 million becquerels.

In a report published jointly with the Radioactive Waste Management Advisory Committee (RWMAC) COMARE said that a single particle contained as much radioactivity as the total that the UKAEA originally claimed had leaked.

For its part, the RWMAC concluded that the waste shaft, which was used between 1959 and 1977 to dump unknown amounts of debris such as irradiated fuel elements and contaminated glove boxes, was *"not an acceptable model for the disposal of radioactive waste"*. The committee suggested that the UKAEA should retrieve, repackage and dispose of the waste elsewhere *"over a relatively short timescale"*.

This conflicted with a report commissioned by the Scottish Office in 1990 from RM Consultants of Abingdon, which said that such an operation would be *"without precedent, costly and potentially dangerous"*.

The UKAEA reacted urgently and said such a procedure could cost up to £200 million and take more than 10 years to complete. The consultants' report also warned that the possibility of another sodium-potassium-water reaction *"cannot be ruled out"*.

The particles found on the beach were typically a millimetre across and contained uranium, aluminium, caesium and plutonium. They were identified as originally part of fuel elements used in Dounreay's Materials Testing Reactor in the 1960s.

Swarf from milling the elements was poured into small screw-top aluminium cans, which were then dropped down the waste shaft.

Every year since 1983, the UKAEA had found an average of 12 radioactive particles on the Dounreay foreshore, a rocky area which was accessible to the public.

Then in 1984, one particle containing 100,000 becquerels of radioactivity was found on the adjoining Sandside Beach, an attractive bay west of Dounreay often visited by the public.

Although COMARE believed that there could be more particles there, it regarded the likelihood of any member of the public coming in contact with them as *"very small"*. It concluded that the particles are *"most unlikely to explain the observed excess of childhood leukaemia in the Dounreay area"*.

Dr Wheldon pointed out that if the kind of particles found on the Dounreay foreshore had been present on Sandside Beach, they would easily explain the excess in the number of cases of childhood leukaemia. It is, he said, *"a horrifying scenario"*.

My own investigations were to dig a lot deeper and the discoveries were quite terrifying.

I discovered via unreleased classified reports that Dounreay had suffered more than a dozen radioactive *"losses"* and many previously unreported *"serious"* radiological incidents.

Among documents leaked to me, one showed a *"critical"* condition of one of the plant's nuclear reactors.

When I confronted the UKAEA about the find, they squirmed and replied that tackling the problem could cause a reactor fire and *"release radioactivity into the environment."*

This type of inaction I found to be typical of the management of the plant.

One unpublished UKAEA safety report disclosed 10 incidents which were regarded as *"serious"* (the highest level for nuclear accidents) with the potential to cause *"death or serious physical impairment"*.

- In 1982, two men were *"exposed to substantial fractions of the annual limit of intake of a plutonium isotope mixture, while a third person was exposed at three times the annual limit"*.

- In 1984, there were two serious incidents in which one worker was contaminated with radiation to 150% the annual dose limit.

- In 1995, there was a plutonium blow-out in a reprocessing plant. The unit was evacuated as radioactivity levels reached 20 megabecquerels – 10,000 times the safe working level.

Another document revealed that the level caused by the explosion in the waste shaft in 1977 was more than six times that admitted by the UKAEA.

But it was classified documents detailing the losses of radioactive material from the plant which were perhaps more sinister.

- In 1980, the UKAEA had waited more than four years to admit the loss of two 4ft fuel pins from the heart of the reactor, containing 10 and 25 grammes of plutonium in 1973 and 1976. The UKAEA blamed the losses on *"anomalies in the paperwork"*.

- In 1983, more than 1.4kg of plutonium and a similar quantity of highly enriched uranium could not be accounted for. The UKAEA tried to explain the loss as due to *"uncertainties"* in measurements.

- In 1989, Dounreay's health and safety report revealed that a 32 megabecquerel sealed source of Caesium-137 was reported missing from its storage cabinet. Despite an internal investigation the UKAEA could not establish how it might have been lost.

- In 1991, Dounreay's D1203 uranium reprocessing plant was closed after a reported loss of a staggering 19.5kg of uranium during a routine stock-take. After an internal audit, it was admitted than only 1.8kg of highly enriched uranium-235 could not be accounted for, while the UKAEA claimed that 3kg of the material had been washed out to sea.

- In 1995, a further 4kg of plutonium and 1kg of highly enriched uranium was lost from the D1206 plant.

If these were genuine losses then the environmental and health risks were extremely serious, not only to the Caithness area but to the whole of coastal Britain and other countries bordering the North Sea.

But perhaps more worrying was that if the losses were due to theft, these materials could provide another country or terrorist organization with the ingredients for a nuclear bomb.

However horrifying these discoveries were, it was what I found from a decade earlier which was truly terrifying and shook all my trust in the entire nuclear industry.

Further confidential UKAEA reports revealed that in 1964-65, overheating of the Dounreay fast reactor damaged its breeder blanket and fuel pins. Several *"outer zone breeder"* elements became jammed. The reason for the jamming was *"swelling of the elements under high temperature"* and this was putting pressure on the reactor core.

"It was approaching a Chernobyl type situation of a possible meltdown," explained one of my contacts.

"They had to free the radioactive rods, the fuel pins and damaged blanket... and it appears that they did... but where did they put all this highly radioactive material?" he mused.

My investigative journalist friend Sara Brown ironically found the answer in the classified inventory of the controversial waste shaft.

It revealed that between 1959 and 1963 huge amounts of nuclear material and fuel elements had been dumped in the shaft.

Suddenly in 1964, more than 34 highly radioactive steel reactor breeder elements were dumped in one phase and a reactor Hex block was also deposited among so-called intermediate waste.

Then between 1965 and 1967 mixed plutonium/uranium oxides, sealed high active plutonium waste and more than 40 cans of DFR reactor waste and solid fissile waste were also dumped in the shaft. It was a nuclear time bomb which partly exploded 10 years later, while the remainder remained buried.

It was small wonder that the government began decommissioning the whole of the Dounreay complex in 1994, and that after my investigation the process was given greater urgency. In 1996 the then Conservative government claimed the decommissioning would continue until at least 2025.

But the story was far from over. In 2002, it was revealed that the decommissioning of Dounreay was going to cost more than £4 billion in an operation lasting 60 years.

16

Dounreay's nuclear losses over the years revealed

EXCLUSIVE: *Missing material could have been used to make bombs, say environmentalists*

NIC OUTTERSIDE

Chief Investigative Reporter

DOUNREAY has lost substantial amounts of radioactive material seven times in the past 23 years, according to confidential documents.

Environmentalists claim that the material could be used by terrorists to make nuclear bombs. But the United Kingdom Atomic Energy Authority, which manages Dounreay, says the losses are due to auditing mistakes and innocent glitches.

The revelations come after *The Scotsman* disclosed yesterday that Dounreay has suffered ten previously unreported "serious" radiological incidents.

Health and safety reports and confidential UKAEA documents reveal a series of losses of nuclear materials from Dounreay.

● In 1980 the UKAEA admitted the loss of two 4ft "fuel pins" for the heart of the reactor containing 10 and 25 grammes of plutonium, in 1973 and 1976. The UKAEA failed to find them and Clifford Blumfield, Dounreay's director in 1980, blamed the loss on "anomalies in the paperwork".

● In 1983 more than 1.4kg of plutonium and a similar quantity of highly enriched uranium could not be accounted for.

The UKAEA said the loss was probably due to "uncertainties" in measurements and added:

"Irradiated fuel elements are highly radioactive and can only be safely handled remotely behind heavy shielding. Their illicit removal and the subsequent extraction of the plutonium they contain are consequently virtually impossible."

● On Dounreay's health and safety report for 1989 reveals that a 32 Megabecquerel sealed source of caesium-137 was reported missing from its storage cabinet. Despite an internal investigation the UKAEA could not establish how it might have been lost.

● On 4 December, 1991, Dounreay's D1203 uranium reprocessing plant was closed after the reported loss of 19.5kg of uranium during a routine stocktake. After an internal audit, it was admitted that only 1.8kg of highly enriched uranium-235 could not be accounted for, while the UKAEA claimed that 3kg of the material had been washed out to sea.

Two months later the European Commission charged the UKAEA with breaching EC regulations over the control of radioactive materials at Dounreay and ruled that the D1203 plant stay shut until adequate stock controls were introduced.

● But last year a further 4kg of plutonium and 1kg of highly enriched uranium was "lost" from the D1206 plant.

The UKAEA claimed the dis-

crepancy was due to a new technique for measuring the weight of plutonium.

Last night, Friends of the Earth warned that the lost plutonium could be used to construct a hydrogen bomb. A spokesman said: "To prove a point, the US built a nuclear bomb using British reactor-grade plutonium and exploded it in Nevada in 1962.

"Such a degree of lost or unaccounted for material from Dounreay is another example of the gross mismanagement and is exceedingly worrying."

Labour called for an inquiry into Dounreay. Michael Meacher, Labour's environment protection spokesman, has written to John Gummer, the Environment Secretary, and Michael Forsyth, the Scottish Secretary, demanding action.

Last night, the UKAEA said it would respond "fully" to the issues raised by *The Scotsman* "within the next few days". It also denied that its health and safety reports were "secret".

Local reaction, Page 6

9 770307 585036

No.47,749

Revealing the radioactive cover-up at Dounreay (*The Scotsman*)

But more pressing was the persistent threat to the health of local people and workers, who had been exposed to a catalogue of near disasters at the facility.

17

Since the first granular sand-sized specks of plutonium were found to be leaking out of the plant in 1984 and on to the beaches of Caithness, several hundred particles had been discovered since, with one government report concluding that *"fatalities might occur"*, and that such hot spots *"present a real hazard to health"*.

In 1997, the discovery of a particle offshore led to a fishing ban within 2km of Dounreay.

No-one will ever know for sure the extent of the contamination, but as the controversy raged, pressure from the public led to investigations.

In 1994, in a scene reminiscent of the Hollywood movie **Silkwood**, a UKAEA study revealed levels of plutonium in the homes of Dounreay workers were *"significantly"* higher than in other homes in Thurso.

In a situation more acute than the one I discovered at Trawsfynydd, workers at the Dounreay plant had been carrying home plutonium particles – readings were 50 times higher in 21 out of 34 homes monitored. By then, Dounreay had absorbed its second generation of local workers.

In 1998, the Health and Safety Executive made 143 recommendations on safety, quality, environmental systems and an integrated management system.

Safety had been the most contentious issue surrounding the reactor, with the UKAEA fined £101,000 in 2000 on three charges of contaminating three workers in 1995.

Today's safety concerns are a far cry from the optimism and faith placed in the all-powerful fast breeder reactors in the 1950s and early 1960s.

Hundreds of scientists and engineers had moved to the remote northern town of Thurso to be part of a bold and appealing venture aimed at providing limitless amounts of electricity at negligible cost, by using plutonium instead of uranium as a fuel, extracting energy with 60 times more efficiency.

However, what is clear is that the scientists of those early days of nuclear power did not always take the proper precautions, and the 1,000 tonnes of radioactive junk thrown down the waste shaft, dug

65 metres into the cliff-top, would later provide the fuel for the 1977 explosion.

In 2012, tests were carried out to determine the potential hazard of what was believed to be the most radioactive particle ever found on a public beach in the UK.

Initial laboratory analysis carried out at Dounreay showed that the *"significant"* particle has an estimated radioactivity of up to two mega-Becquerels – a level that could cause serious health effects.

The radioactive hotspot was discovered at Sandside beach.

A spokesman for Dounreay Site Restoration Ltd (DSRL), the company responsible for the closure and decommissioning programme, said: *"The particle was detected in the water's edge at Sandside.*

"Checks carried out on the beach indicated that the particle had higher than normal beta dose rate.

"Initial analysis carried out at Dounreay showed low caesium-137 content, niobium-94 and a high beta dose rate suspected to be from strontium-90.

"Further non-destructive testing indicated that the estimated radioactivity of the strontium-90 is one to two mega-becquerels, which is equivalent to a 'significant' particle."

Until then, the most radioactive particle found at Sandside was one discovered in 2007, which had a reading of 500,000 becquerels (Bq). In March 2010, a particle measuring 270,000 Bq was also detected.

The spokesman said that the company had informed the Scottish Environment Protection Agency (SEPA) of its initial findings and the need for additional tests to *"understand the chemistry of the particle and verify its potential hazard".*

He added: *"The particle was the 208th to be recovered from the beach at Sandside."*

Stan Blackley, chief executive of Friends of the Earth Scotland, said: *"The depressing thing about this is that the more we look at this site, the more and worse we seem to find. We are now several hundred particles down the line and still they keep coming and getting hotter and hotter."*

Leading UK nuclear expert Dr John Large said this first recorded presence of the so-called *"daughter of plutonium"* and the nuclear waste washed up on Sandside beach was probably discharged into the sea decades earlier.

The 1996 UKAEA background brief began to shed new light on Dounreay

He added: *"The trouble is that 20 or 30 or so years later it has turned up on a beach. If it reaches the surface — which is quite possible given natural disturbance by the tide and gets dried out it can become airborne, thus threatening local communities. It is alarming. This is serious... because there is a real risk these particles could end up in areas of mass population."*

Seven years later, in 2019, SEPA admitted that the radioactive contamination that leaked for more than two decades from Dounreay will never be completely cleaned up.

SEPA decided to give up on its aim of returning the seabed near the plant to a *"pristine condition".* To do so, could cause *"more harm than good".*

So, the Scottish government's environmental watchdog opted to encourage remediation *"as far as is practically achievable"* but to abandon any hope of removing all the radioactive pollution from the seabed.

Tens of thousands of radioactive fuel fragments escaped from the Dounreay plant between 1963 and 1984, polluting local beaches, and the seabed, it declared.

SEPA pointed out that the contamination had been extensively investigated.

"It is now widely accepted that a literal return to a pristine condition is a far from simple or even achievable concept," said its spokesman.

"Trying to achieve it might also cause more harm than good. There is the potential that ecosystems may be destroyed on trying to get to something which does not pose a significant hazard."

An expert committee set up by SEPA warned in 2006 that disturbing the seabed could cause particles to escape and be swept ashore, putting members of the public at risk.

The most radioactive particle found *"could have had life-threatening consequences if it had been ingested,"* they said.

SEPA's board agreed to change its policy to encourage further remediation.

Scientists now believe that the land around the Dounreay site at Caithness could remain out of bounds to humans and other animals for more than 300 years.

- **Appendix A**

Chapter Two
Dodgy Handshakes

The secret brotherhood of the Freemasons

MOST people who pick up this book will have their own
opinions on Freemasonry, either from things they may have
read, or from personal dealings they might have had with the
men of the funny handshakes, bared chests and a dangling
hangman's noose.

Many will also have heard stories of Freemasons exchanging favours over everyday matters such as planning permission for a dwelling or building extension or even favourable treatment from the police and judiciary.

In my own background I had an Uncle Rick who was a Freemason. He died 25 years ago, and my knowledge of his Masonic activities never stretched beyond his golfing tournaments and formal dinner dances at his local Lodge in West Sussex.

On the other hand (sorry for the pun) my former father-in-law Wilf took Masonic activities much more seriously and was a regular at his Temple in Sunderland. Three days after he died from cancer in 1987, two unknown gentlemen turned up at my mother-in-law's front door to speedily take away his Masonic case and regalia, stating they were the *"property of the Lodge"*. They disappeared like characters from the movie **Men in Black**, as quickly as they came.

But let me begin this chapter by introducing you to Tom Minogue, who is 80 years old at the time of writing this book, and someone who shares my own peculiar interest in Freemasonry.

Tom moved to Dunfermline, a small textile town in Fife in the 1980s to start a business and quickly became aware that the local Freemasons had a strange and *"all-pervading"* influence over the town.

"Local people told me that this was the way things had always been done and I was told that I would get nowhere in business 'unless I went along to the Lodge'," he said.

"The real effect of Freemasonry came to my attention when a man I knew joined the cartel of local Freemason builders who tendered for council contracts.

"I built new business premises on land close to his premises and I began to notice building materials were being delivered before the council tenders were opened and decided upon.

"In a later incident, a complete renovation was being carried out on the Masonic Lodge and I watched as Masons removed materials from the sheds for council renovations and took them directly to the Lodge."

What happened next to Tom casts a light on the power of the Freemasons.

"Until that point although the local Lodge had a bar and was very busy with its weekly evening harmonies it did not have a drinks licence because of the

over-provision of licences in the area. One non-Masonic club had an application for a drinks license refused for this very reason," he explained.

"When I phoned the police to report illegal drinking at the Masonic lodge, a drinks licence was granted almost immediately."

And it was here, after making his complaint that Tom felt the malice of the Masons.

"I soon became a target of the Masons and began to have almost weekly problems. I had a dispute with one Mason over the boundary of my premises when my drains were deliberately blocked, my water pipe cut and trenches dug to prevent access. There was then an altercation during which this man attacked me.

"The policeman who came round to investigate the incident I knew was a Mason because I had seen him regularly going in and out of the Lodge. He suggested it would be better all-round if I left town.

"I was charged with breach of the peace and found guilty. I later discovered a passer-by had seen the incident but the police did not take a statement and told him to go away. I later discovered his version of events was the same as mine, but he was not prepared to make a statement because he had to live in the town," he added.

Tom has been a thorn in the side of Scottish Freemasonry for more than 35 years as he sought to uncover more and more about the secret society.

Bill Hodgson's tale is much more sinister and reaches to the very top of British society, including a first cousin to the Queen. And it proves beyond any doubt Tom's assertion: *"The Masons are not to be messed with."*

I first met Bill in February 1991, just four months after taking up my initial newspaper editorship at the **Argyllshire Advertiser** on the west coast of Scotland.

Bill, a former farmer and wine importer, had been selected in September 1989 as the Conservative parliamentary candidate in the Tory/Lib Dem marginal seat of Argyll and Bute.

In 1979, he had achieved the largest Conservative swing in Scotland in the safe Labour seat of East Kilbride. Eight years later he came within 916 votes of ousting Labour in Carlisle, after what supporters called: *"the best political campaign the city has ever seen."*

24

Bill was now touted to do well in Argyll against the incumbent Lib Dem MP Rae Michie.

He had already moved his family to a spacious detached villa in Campbeltown – at the southern end of this vast rural constituency which takes in Oban, Lochgilphead, Inveraray, Dunoon and Bute and the Inner Hebridean islands of Islay, Jura and Mull.

Although I was a Tory activist as a teenager, my personal politics at the time were well to the left of Bill, and I had no natural affinity for a Thatcherite Conservative government which in my opinion had ruined our country over the previous 11 years.

But Bill, 54, and his politically astute wife Eelan, were gregarious, self-effacing and above all, seemingly totally honest – rare in any politician.

After an initial meeting, both the Hodgsons were regular visitors to my newspaper office, usually sharing a newsworthy story or a tip-off over a cup of tea and a biscuit.

It soon became obvious that Bill was a bit of a maverick – a go-getting politician who was not afraid to speak his mind.

And I quickly became aware of his no-nonsense track record.

Within two months of his selection, Bill became involved in a bitter row with one of Argyll's biggest landowners, Douglas Campbell, who had brazenly flouted planning orders and felled a forest of trees in order to build 40 luxury holiday chalets.

In the ***Dunoon Observer*** – my competition paper in the south of the constituency – nature-loving Bill was reported as saying the tree felling was the *"misconduct of a barbaric Philistine".*

Mr Campbell was one of 13 applicants who had earlier stood against Bill for the Conservative nomination for Argyll and Bute. He was also a prominent Freemason and close friend of Ian Campbell, the 12th Duke of Argyll, first cousin to the Queen and Master Freemason in Scotland.

Bill's words were ones which Douglas Campbell did not forget.

Just before my own arrival in Argyll, Bill had also fallen out with the Conservative Party's constituency secretary, Noel Facenda.

The bungling Facenda had placed politically charged Christmas adverts in the local press (including my own paper) which were a flagrant breach of UK electoral law and potentially threatened Bill's candidacy.

Bill was livid with what he regarded as gross incompetence by his agent.

Then soon after my first meeting with the Hodgsons, Bill verbally attacked Argyll and Bute District Council – in which the Tories shared power – for overspending and publicly called for the council to be replaced.

This ruffled the feathers of some prominent Tories and a shadowy campaign to *"Get Bill out"* began.

On 25th May, the simmering row began to spill into open warfare with the resignation of the constituency chairwoman - and close friend of Douglas Campbell – Margaret Forrest, who claimed that she had been subjected to *"verbal assaults"* from Mr Hodgson.

It was at this point Bill began briefing me weekly about the shenanigans and moves to unseat him by some of his own party officials. This was despite that among party members in Argyll and voters at large, Bill was seen as increasingly popular and positively electable… a Tory closer to the people than to the landowners who dominated the power plays in Argyll.

But on 16th August 1991, Bill suffered a minor heart attack and was rushed to hospital. However, he was assured by his doctors that a simple heart-by-pass operation would ensure a return to perfect health. But while he awaited the operation, rumours about his status as a candidate began to circulate more openly and widely.

His Labour opponent Des Browne (later to become Secretary of State for Scotland and a good friend) went on the record as saying: *"Bill Hodgson won't last long, his own party are out to get him."*

At a small dinner party at his home, Bill told me he had taken enough knives in the back and needed to fight back.

Then on 9th September, rumours of a coup against him began to emerge. Indeed, Bill told 40 supporters at a meeting in Campbeltown that the perpetrators were using his health as a smokescreen to unseat him.

"There has been an energetic commitment to apathy, disloyalty and the worship of incompetence," he said. *"And because I have dared to draw attention to this mess and the clique behind it, they want to get rid of me."*

He was pouring oil onto a smouldering fire.

His statement was discussed at a constituency meeting called the very next day. Tempers were roused.

But Campbeltown councillor Archie McCallum, who had replaced Margaret Forrest as chairman, robustly denied there was any plot to oust Bill as their candidate.

"We are only interested in his health," lied Mr McCallum, who along with Mr Facenda were also active Freemasons.

Then came an unexpected Deep Throat phone call from a Conservative Party official to tell me that on 23rd September, three days after Bill's scheduled heart by-pass operation in Glasgow, the local executive held an emergency meeting in his absence to discuss his future. The informant went on to tell me that the Duke of Argyll – prompted by Douglas Campbell – proposed a motion calling for Bill's resignation. It was passed by 27 to 17, despite that many members who were entitled to vote were given late notice of the meeting and had been unable to attend due to the vast geographical nature of the constituency.

I rang Bill the next day to get his reaction to the events, and from his hospital bed he issued a press statement in which he said: *"What has really annoyed me has been the sneaky, chicken-livered way in which the plotters have behaved... I am not going to resign to satisfy their egos."*

Open political warfare had been declared.

The local Conservative Party was now about to split sharply down the middle.

At the executive meeting, Michael MacRoberts, chairman of the Colintraive branch of the party, demanded that no-one should speak to the press about what had been discussed as they tried to find a compromise. But within 24 hours, more than half a dozen of those present at the meeting breached the ruling and began feeding information to the press.

The fight was about to escalate to the highest echelons of British politics.

Bill was rarely off the phone to me with updates and it was here that for the first time in my career as a journalist that my home telephone was bugged and my calls with Bill were intercepted and recorded. I have never found by whom, but the machinations which I am now about to tell may give powerful clues.

The first to show his true colours was Archie McCallum.

In a private letter dated 1st November to a party member, McCallum detailed the jaundiced case against Bill. *"The whole blame lies with Bill for sending out that press release,"* he wrote.

At another executive meeting on 9th November, it was decided to try and take some heat out of the situation which was by now being reported by Scotland's national press.

Meanwhile at my small newspaper office in Lochgilphead I was suddenly visited by the Scottish Conservative Party's director of communications, Brian Townsend.

Brian was clearly on a fishing expedition to find out how much I knew about the activities within the local party.

But he also tried to put pressure on me by suggesting that Bill Hodgson was a rogue candidate and was becoming increasingly unpopular.

Then the executive meeting decision of 23rd September was rescinded, and members decided to ask Bill to account for himself at the next meeting on 7th December.

But McCallum, feeling the tide might be turning, was quick to up the ante. He claimed that at a private meeting in late November Lord Willie Whitelaw, former Conservative Party Chairman and Home Secretary, and leading Freemason, had recommended that the constituency *"ditch Bill Hodgson",* claiming he had run into problems in Carlisle in 1987.

Of course, nothing could be further from the truth. Bill had fought an outstanding campaign in Carlisle, recognised by many in the party, including the then Prime Minister Margaret Thatcher.

Later it was established that the private meeting with Whitelaw was at Inveraray Castle – home of the Duke of Argyll - with the duke and Douglas Campbell also present.

The Masonic plot against Bill Hodgson was almost complete with a cousin of the Queen and a former Tory Home Secretary at the hub.

The late Bill Hodgson

So, with the power brokers stacked against him, Bill appeared before the constituency executive on 7th December 1991. He was voted down by 36 votes to 33 and his resignation demanded immediately, or his enemies would pursue his deselection.

McCallum defended the move saying: *"I'm afraid that Bill has shot his bolt."*

But Bill's supporters said the meeting had been rigged to exclude delegates who supported him. In a letter to Scottish Conservative Party Chairman Lord Sanderson, John Maclean, an executive member, claimed that branches likely to have backed Bill had been excluded from the vote. Asking Sanderson to conduct a secret postal ballot, Maclean also alleged that other pro-Hodgson party members had been excluded on *"various flimsy grounds"*. Had those branches and individuals been allowed to attend, there would have been an eight-vote majority for Bill.

Then during a hastily called meeting with Lord Sanderson – another leading Scottish Freemason – and Michael Hirst, President of the Scottish Conservative Association, Bill refused to resign. He had public opinion with him and was backed by four branches and hundreds of members who threatened to leave the party if he was forced to stand down.

Two weeks later, 205 party members signed a petition demanding a general meeting to discuss Bill's candidacy. It was clear that they would win the day.

But always expect the unexpected when the Masons are involved. Less than 24 hours after the demand for the meeting was tabled and with orders from Central Office, the Scottish Conservative Association stepped in and dissolved the entire constituency association in Argyll. In doing so they deselected Bill as parliamentary candidate and excommunicated hundreds of Tory party members in one blow.

Michael Hirst said that the decision to disaffiliate the Argyll association was made with *"considerable reluctance"*.

"Not in living memory of those here has this ever happened before," he added.

Donald Nicholson, chairman of the Ardchattan branch said: *"What happened to Bill is a travesty. These things will never be forgotten as long as Argyll is a constituency."*

Argyll constituency vice chairwoman Sheena Dixon said: *"Bill was a professional and worked incredibly hard in the two years he was here. It seemed he worked too hard for some and upset others whose power will not be upset."*

Another party executive member added: *"Bill's future was decided by a cabal of powerful people within our party. The one thing that unites them, other than being Conservatives, is they all belong to one secret society."*

Bill's final words on the matter were: *"I have a feeling of sickness for those who have campaigned so venomously for my deselection using lies, libels and vile innuendo as their weapons."*

Bill's successor as Conservative candidate for Argyll and Bute, John Corrie, failed to unseat Lib Dem MP Rae Michie in the 1992 General Election taking just 27% of the vote. By the General

Election of 2015, the Tory vote in the constituency had fallen to just 15%.

Bill sadly died in October 2010. But he left me with many memories of wine-fuelled chats by his fireside and his wonderful sense of humour.

Lord Whitelaw died at his home near Penrith, in 1999, aged 81. Like many other leading Conservative politicians of his generation, including former Prime Minister Edward Heath, Geoffrey Rippon, Reginald Maudling, Lord Carrington, Douglas Hurd and Keith Joseph he was recognised as a prominent and active Freemason.

Ian Campbell, the 12th Duke of Argyll died of heart failure during surgery at a London hospital in 2001, aged 63.

Douglas Campbell died in May 2015 aged 79.

My next collision with Freemasonry took *sinister* to a whole other level.

Wednesday 13th March 1996 will stay etched in my memory for every day of my life.

It was a typically dreich spring day in Edinburgh as I settled down to a diary of interviews and enquiries in my job as an investigative reporter at **The Scotsman** – at the time Scotland's most pre-eminent broadsheet newspaper, with a daily circulation of about 90,000.

Back home in Perth – some 33 miles north of my office - I had left my partner to go shoe shopping for our two young daughters Rhia and Shannon. Over a rushed slice of toast she planned to browse a few shops in our fair city and maybe venture out to Dunblane or Stirling later in the day.

At **The Scotsman** offices I looked out over the grey North Bridge towards Princes Street, checked my diary and clocked a quick coffee before a long-awaited telephone interview with Scottish born actor Tom Conti.

Tom was a champion of the London based organisation Justice, which campaigned on behalf of those imprisoned as a result of miscarriages of justice by the Scottish and English courts. At the time I was running a newspaper campaign on behalf of a young man named Craig MacKenzie, who had - in my opinion - been wrongly convicted of murder of a fellow Edinburgh teenager David Edwards. My campaign had been running over three months with little movement from the Scottish legal system to intervene.

I saw the interview with Tom Conti as a key move to add weight to the campaign.

The newsroom was quiet and I sipped my coffee. Outside the morning remained grey.

The phone rang at the arranged time and the unmistakable burr of Mr Conti's voice greeted me at the other end. The star of **Shirley Valentine** was relaxed as we shared notes on the weather in Edinburgh and London. It was like meeting an old friend for a coffee as we progressed to discuss our work and recent challenges.

Eventually after what seemed about 20 minutes we began to talk about the Craig MacKenzie case, suddenly the Press Association updates on my monitor began to flicker an instantly disturbing piece of news: *"Six children believed shot in Dunblane".*

I reported the news immediately to Tom, just as a clamour of noise erupted around me in the newsroom. And with it came a further update from the PA wires: *"Ten children shot".*

I quickly relayed the information to Tom as a familiar voice from the newsdesk was shouting in my direction. Tom and I politely suggested to each other that we leave the interview for another day. As he rushed to his TV to watch the rolling news, I glanced once more at my monitor to see the horror of Dunblane unfolding before my eyes.

Ian Stewart, the news editor ordered my friend Stephen and fellow colleagues Jenny and Lynn to get to Dunblane as quickly as they could.

"And be safe," he added, as they scurried out of the newsroom, notebooks in hand. He turned to me and asked me to stay at my desk and collate information as it came in and try to make some sense of it all.

But my mind was in panic. Which children had been killed and exactly where in Dunblane? And where was my partner and my two gorgeous daughters?

This was 1996 and very few people had the luxury of mobile phones, least of all newspaper journalists and their families.

I tried our home phone vainly for an answer.

Had she gone to Dunblane?

My heart was racing.

Then the PA reported the shooting was confined to the town's primary school, but there was no word as to whether the gunman had gone on a rampage elsewhere.

Within an hour, the death toll had risen again before my partner telephoned me to ask if I had heard the news about Dunblane.

I think my barked reply was something akin to: *"Of course I have, where have you been?"* She calmly told me she had heard the news on a radio in a shoe shop in Perth!

Back in the fray by mid-afternoon it was clear the gunman was also dead.

The day had become a blur of adrenalin. By early evening a couple of my colleagues had returned visibly shell-shocked from Dunblane and I had pieced together information about the shootings from many different contacts...

After gaining entry to Dunblane Primary School, 43-year-old former shopkeeper Thomas Hamilton made his way to the gymnasium and opened fire on a Primary One class of five and six-year-olds, killing or wounding all but one. Fifteen children died together with their class teacher, Gwen Mayor, who was killed trying to protect them.

Hamilton then left the gym through the emergency exit. In the playground outside he began shooting into a mobile classroom. A teacher in a mobile classroom realised that something was seriously wrong and told the children to hide under the tables.

Most of the bullets became embedded in books and equipment, though one passed through a chair which seconds before had been used by a child. He also fired at a group of children walking in a corridor, injuring one teacher.

It later transpired that Hamilton returned to the gym and with one of his two revolvers fired one shot pointing upwards into his mouth, killing himself instantly.

A further eleven children and three adults were rushed to hospital as soon as the emergency services arrived. One further child was pronounced dead on arrival.

Along with my colleagues I worked until 9pm that evening and turned in a 12 hour shift the following day, trying to keep a clear head and report calmly the events which had transpired on that fateful Wednesday.

Sleep on the Wednesday and Thursday nights was impossible as my mind ran overtime. It was like being on speed in something akin to the movie ***Jacob's Ladder***.

Friday morning dawned and I grabbed my toast, kissed my sleeping daughters and again drove the 33 miles to Edinburgh.

While the families and friends of the bereaved were going through their own personal hell, the Friday at work was all about investigating what had gone on at Dunblane, how Hamilton had acquired such an arsenal of guns and, I suppose, who else might be to blame.

We needed some lines of enquiry for our Saturday and Monday editions.

I had to keep my head engaged and soon stories of police complicity and Masonic cover-up began to emerge.

Ironically, my colleague Stephen Breen and I were in the throes of a month-long investigation into the role that Freemasonry had in Scottish society.

Within days of the Dunblane massacre we were receiving telephone calls from contacts in that investigation, suggesting we should look into the masonic background of Thomas Hamilton and the police officers who had granted his firearms licences.

Questions were asked whether he had abused a position as a Freemason for over 20 years prior to the shooting.

One Labour MP who had campaigned against secret societies said that Hamilton's membership of the Freemasons could explain his *"apparently charmed life"* and should be investigated by a public inquiry into the massacre.

A senior Scottish Freemason also told me that Hamilton had visited functions at different Lodges where he would have come into contact with people of influence in both the police and other avenues of public service. *"Although I believe his own Lodge didn't knowingly protect him, I am sure that favours between individual brothers would have been exchanged,"* he said.

Masonic link may explain Hamilton's 'charmed life'

Dunblane massacre: Suspicions grow that killer followed grandfather into the Freemasons

QUESTIONS are being asked whether the Dunblane primary school killer Thomas Hamilton abused a position as a Freemason for almost 20 years in order to gain influence with people in authority.

A Labour MP who has campaigned against secret societies said last night that Hamilton's membership of the Freemasons could explain his 'apparently charmed life' and should be investigated by Lord Cullen's inquiry into the massacre.

People have claimed that Hamilton was a Freemason and may have socialised with people in positions of influence while attending Masonic meetings and functions.

A senior Scottish Freemason told The Scotsman that Hamilton had been a Mason for a number of years and had visited functions at different lodges.

"Although I believe his lodge didn't knowingly protect him, I am sure favours between individual brothers would have been exchanged," he said.

The Scotsman has obtained a list of more than 100 senior Freemasons in the Central Belt of Scotland in an effort to trace Hamilton's own lodge membership. Of the names we contacted most refused to confirm or categorically deny that Hamilton was a Freemason.

The Scotsman has also discovered that Hamilton's grandfather Jimmy – who raised him after his natural parents separated – has been a Freemason for more than 40 years, and that Hamilton had probably followed the natural course into the lodge.

One past master of a Stirlingshire lodge said that Jimmy, now aged 88, had often attended functions at his lodge. He had not met Thomas Hamilton, but thought that he would have followed his grandfather into Freemasonry.

A grand master of another Stirlingshire lodge said he was "wary about saying too much" because of the sensitivity surrounding the massacre.

However, he added: "I've known old Jimmy for many years and he was a member of a Glasgow lodge. I don't know about [Thomas], but it is likely he would have followed Jimmy into his lodge."

Although Freemasonry is virtually unknown at the top of Scottish business, many of its members are shopkeepers such as Hamilton – lawyers, middle managers and police officers. As the owner of a DIY shop, Hamilton would have been a natural Freemason.

Martin Short, the author of Inside the Brotherhood, a book on Freemasonry, says the most common form of entry into Freemasonry is for a father to sponsor the son into the apprenticeship. He adds that "an astonishing" 20 per cent of police officers are currently Freemasons.

Chris Mullin, the Labour MP who has campaigned against secret societies, said he found the alleged Masonic link with Hamilton "very interesting".

"It certainly provides a possible explanation of the apparently charmed life that Hamilton led," he said.

"This is obviously a matter that Lord Cullen will wish to explore as part of his inquiry."

Last night, a spokesman for the Grand Lodge of Scotland in Edinburgh admitted that it did not have a collated database of its members and could not be certain whether or not Hamilton was a Freemason.

Another spokesman for the Grand Lodge said if a lodge became aware that one of its members was trying to misuse masonship, then they had the powers to throw them out.

In the past year, 20 people have been thrown out nationally after being convicted of criminal offences, but no figures are kept centrally of those expelled for misuse of their membership.

Dunblane Primary, the scene of the killings by Thomas Hamilton (above). Questions are being asked about possible links with Masons. Picture Robert Perry

Secret brotherhood which protects its own

FRED BRIDGLAND

THE Freemasons of Britain are strongly protective of their fellow Masons. They rarely punish brethren who break the criminal law of the land, Martin Short, author of a best-selling investigation into Freemasonry, last night told The Scotsman.

"Scotland is a place where one Mason looks after another," said Mr Short. "If Thomas Hamilton was one of the brethren it is pretty bad news for the Masons because one is inclined to assume he may well have received favours. They would not allow one of their own brethren to be exposed to public ridicule and would do everything to avoid his membership being known.

Short, whose book Inside the Brotherhood: Further Secrets of the Freemasons was first published in 1989, referred to a local government ombudsman decision in Hamilton's favour in 1983. The ombudsman overturned a decision by Central Regional Council to end his lease of Dunblane High School premises for his boys' club, the Dunblane Rover Group.

"The fact that he managed to bamboozle the ombudsman suggests that the ombudsman from the judge.

Mr Short and Masonry was an organisation of men only convince the ombudsman that he was OK, you can be pretty sure that his lodge would have felt at least equally strongly. The Masons in the lodge would not have wanted to think ill of him and would therefore have tried to protect him from all-comers.

"Social pressures make it difficult for an honest Mason to complain about criminal or immoral conduct by his brothers," said Mr Short. In fact, it would be the complainant, not the wrongdoers, who faced ostracism and probable exclusion from the lodge.

Mr Short said Masonry was who voluntarily swear mutual aid and to guard each other's secrets: it has its own strict rules, inquiry systems, punishments and courts of appeal. He said that when it became known he was miscarrying his book he lost count of the brethren who cautioned him to "watch out" or "take care".

Mr Short went on: "One man whose evidence sent a fellow Mason to jail told me of the fears during that trial and the extreme precautions he had taken to stay alive. He advised me to do the same."

Mr Short's 711-page book lists some of the reasons why he was inclined to take the advice seriously. It also lists some of the bizarre initiation ceremonies of Masonry. Mr Short, for example, describes a Masonic lodge in Lincolnshire where a candidate Mason is lowered into a trap below the temple floor on the Friday before full moon to confront a female skeleton as a symbol of mortality.

Several traditional crafts and professions are bastions of Freemasonry. Mr Short argues in his book, for instance, is the example of the Metropolitan Police where, in 1987, he identified one assistant commissioner, two deputy assistant commissioners, 12 commanders, 23 chief superintendents, ten superintendents and seven chief inspectors as members of a single Masonic lodge.

Mr Short argues that Freemasonry extends into local government, the armed services, industry and the intelligence services to an extent which would astonish anti-Masons. He says 100,000, or one in 14 of Scotland's working population, are Freemasons.

The Masonic link to killer Thomas Hamilton revealed in The Scotsman

I quickly discovered that Hamilton's grandfather Jimmy – who raised him after his natural parents separated – had been a Freemason for more than 40 years rising to Lodge secretary. Hamilton would have followed the natural progression into Freemasonry courtesy of backing from his grandfather.

35

One past master of a Stirlingshire lodge told me that Jimmy, then aged 88, had often attended functions at different lodges and it was likely that Hamilton had followed his grandfather into Freemasonry. A grand master of another Stirlingshire lodge confirmed this likelihood to me a couple of days later.

Martin Short, the author of **Inside the Brotherhood** – a seminal book on Freemasonry published in 1989 - said the most common form of entry is for a father to sponsor a son into a Masonic Apprenticeship. He said that an astonishing 20 per cent of police officers above the rank of sergeant were Freemasons. He also told me that Freemasons are strongly protective of their fellow Masons and rarely punish brethren who break the law of the land.

"Scotland is a place where one Mason looks after another," he told me. *"If Thomas Hamilton was one of the brethren it is bad news for the Masons, because one is inclined to assume he may well have received favours."*

They would not allow one of their own brethren to be exposed to public ridicule and would do everything to avoid his membership being known.

Mr Short then referred to a local government ombudsman decision in Hamilton's favour in 1983. The ombudsman over-turned a decision by Central Regional Council to end his lease of Dunblane High School premises for his boys' club The Dunblane Rover Group.

"The fact that he managed to bamboozle the ombudsman suggests that the ombudsman was bombarded by letters," added Mr Short. *"If he managed to convince that ombudsman that he was okay, you can be pretty sure that his Lodge would have felt equally strongly. Masons in the Lodge would not have wanted to think ill of him and would therefore have tried to protect him and indeed help him."*

But then as our enquiries into Hamilton's Freemasonry links to senior police officers began to piece together a conspiracy, three events occurred in quick succession.

Ten days after the Dunblane Massacre we discovered that my and Stephen's telephones and that of our Stirling reporter John Smith were all being bugged by Scottish Police, as we were able to intercept their listening devices on our lines.

Next, the Tory government appointed Lord William Douglas Cullen of Whitekirk to head up a public inquiry into *"the circumstances leading up to and surrounding"* the Dunblane Massacre, paying due note to the *"licensing of firearms and ammunition."*

Then came the most shocking and unprecedented move which scuppered all press scrutiny of Thomas Hamilton until *"after"* the inquiry concluded in October of that year. On Thursday 4th April, Lord MacKay of Drumadoon, the Lord Advocate and Scotland's highest law lord demanded the attendance at his Edinburgh chambers of all editors of Scottish national and regional newspapers. Some travelling from as far as Glasgow, Dundee and Aberdeen quickly attended this peculiar summit. And all left the meeting with their tails between their legs after being instructed that any further reporting into Thomas Hamilton and the events surrounding the Dunblane Massacre would be considered subjudicy and prejudicial to Lord Cullen's inquiry.

Quite how any member of the press could prejudice a top judge and QC is still beyond my understanding, some 26 years later!

The Cullen Inquiry report of 16th October 1996 dismissed all links between Thomas Hamilton and Freemasonry as unproven conjecture.

But nine years later in 2005 the full scale of official incompetence or cover-up that left Thomas Hamilton free to kill 16 children and their teacher in the Dunblane massacre began to be revealed in a raft of secret documents.

Testimony, police reports and profiles in the 106 documents endorsed claims of cover-up and conspiracy in the aftermath of the shootings.

Mick North, whose only daughter Sophie, five, was killed by Hamilton said the documents showed that police and crown prosecutors had failed to take proper action against Hamilton despite a series of incidents that demonstrated he posed a serious threat to children.

"The documents ... in many ways confirmed what I already believed I knew about the role of the police and the involvement of the procurator fiscal service. There was incompetence," said Dr North.

The documents from the police investigation into the shooting were submitted to Lord Cullen's inquiry but were placed under a 100-year-rule to keep them secret.

The papers also included letters raising the theory that prominent figures connected with Hamilton were Freemasons.

Further documents included a statement from a firearms expert saying that, on 7th March 1996, Hamilton asked for instruction in close-range instinctive shooting and gave testimony that, for two years prior to the massacre, Hamilton had questioned boys about the layout of the gym at Dunblane primary school.

One of the most persistent claims was that Hamilton had received favours from friends in the Central Scotland police force to enable him to keep his gun licence.

Later the same month in 2005 award-winning journalist and author Fidelma Cook revealed in the **Mail on Sunday** claims that some senior police officers had covered up abuse allegations against Thomas Hamilton.

In something of an ironic twist, the claims were made by Sandra Uttley, Mick North's estranged ex-partner, who petitioned the European Court of Human Rights to demand a new inquiry into the tragedy. The then 45-year-old, who dealt with the aftermath of the killings in her job as a paramedic, said: *"There are glaring anomalies in the inquiry – inconsistencies in witness testimony, incorrect information given on oath and the absence of vital witnesses.*

"It is also blatantly obvious that Central Scotland Police, who were chosen to investigate the background to the murders, should never have been involved in a so-called independent inquiry.

"They were implicated in the events under scrutiny and continually provided Hamilton with renewals of his gun licence despite long-term and repeated warnings that this should not happen. It was known that Hamilton had friends in the police force, including one highly placed officer.

"Lord Cullen read none of the preparatory material before the inquiry. That material has now been sealed and locked away for 100 years despite the public never having had the chance to see those documents," she added.

"I believe that Hamilton was a major provider of pornographic photographs and videos to a ring of men prominent in Central Scotland, including police

officers who protected him from numerous allegations of physical abuse at boys' camps and clubs he ran.

"They protected themselves after the massacre which conveniently ended in his suicide."

The existence of the secret dossier of evidence which was withheld from the Cullen inquiry revealed why prosecutors failed to bring the gunman to court before the massacre despite more than 20 complaints, mostly about his running of sports clubs and a summer camp at Loch Lomond in 1991.

The existence of the report was mentioned at the inquiry but never seen. In fact, Lord Cullen ruled in favour of a motion that the prosecutors who decided not to take legal proceedings against Hamilton should not have to justify their decision.

Among the sealed documents was a report revealing that a senior prosecutor ordered pictures of semi-naked children, seized as evidence before the tragedy, to be returned to Hamilton. Others linked the gunman to the Freemasons.

But it didn't end there!

Extracts published during the Cullen Inquiry showed a 1991 police report recommended Hamilton should be prosecuted for his activities at the summer camp and have his gun licence revoked, but no further action was taken.

Scottish Executive Cabinet minutes from February 2003 stated: *"The Lord Advocate said the 100 years closure to the police reports on Thomas Hamilton had been applied to protect the children concerned and their siblings.*

"If the documents were released earlier into the public domain, there would be a possibility that individuals who were still alive could be identified."

They continued: *"There was a strong public perception of a cover-up. A 100 years' closure seemed incomprehensibly lengthy to the public … What mattered was to close the story down."*

In 2018, it emerged a military boarding school with alleged links to Hamilton was to be investigated by the Scottish Child Abuse Inquiry. Queen Victoria School was one of 17 additional institutions to be included in the national inquiry led by Judge Lady Smith.

The Dunblane school, which serves the families of military personnel, had previously been linked to Hamilton.

Glen Harrison, a former housemaster, claimed pupils were abused by a paedophile ring at the school in the 1980s and 1990s. He said he first raised his concerns with police in 1991.

From November 1981, Hamilton hired school halls for 15 boys' clubs from local authorities across the Central, Fife and Lothian regions. He held a Grade 5 certificate from the British Amateur Gymnastics Association, which permitted him to coach under supervision, but most of the activity was football.

A summer camp run by Hamilton on Inchmoan Island on Loch Lomond was visited by police in July 1988, after one boy had returned home unhappy.

The 13 boys appeared cold and inadequately dressed and the sleeping bags were damp. Although some said they were homesick and Hamilton would not allow them to phone their parents, none wished to leave with the officers. The procurator fiscal investigated stories from the boys that Hamilton had slapped them, but no legal action was taken.

However, it is the complaints about another summer camp run by Hamilton, in Mullarochy Bay, Loch Lomond, in July 1991, that are believed to form the backbone of a police report, ordered by Lord Cullen to be protected from public view for a century.

The report, written by Detective Sergeant Paul Hughes, the former head of Central Scotland Police's child protection unit, was damning, but only extracts of his investigation were revealed during the Cullen inquiry.

Part of the report contained a passage from Mr Hughes recommending in 1991 that Hamilton's gun licence be revoked. He wrote: *"I am firmly of the opinion that Hamilton is an unsavoury character and an unstable personality. I would contend that Hamilton will be a risk to children whenever he has access to them and he appears to me to be an unsuitable person to possess a firearms certificate. It is my opinion that he is a devious and deceitful individual who is not to be trusted."*

The question now is whether the report did more than list abused children.

Did it, as alleged, also contain damning evidence that Hamilton had friends in high places, or even that he was being protected by politicians in a Masonic network involving senior police officers and members of the country's judiciary?

Lord Cullen has been asked formally on a number of occasions since 1996 whether he was or had been a Freemason. On each occasion he has either obfuscated or answered through a third party that he has not.

- **Appendix C**

Chapter Three
Bitter Rendition

Terror suspects rendered and on a flight to who knows where?

THE November 2015 terror attacks in Paris shook the Western world and hardened a right wing resolve against so-called Islamic fundamentalists.

But like many other terror incidents over the past 50 years, all was not as it seemed and gave the West another pretext to invade countries it deemed *"a problem"*.

To remind readers, there were a series of co-ordinated attacks that took place on 13th November 2015 in Paris and the city's northern suburb, Saint-Denis. Three suicide bombers struck outside the Stade de France in Saint-Denis, during a football match. This was followed by several mass shootings and a suicide bombing at cafés and restaurants in the city centre. Gunmen carried out another mass shooting and took hostages at an *Eagles of Death Metal* concert in the Bataclan Theatre, leading to a stand-off with police. The attackers were shot or blew themselves up when police raided the theatre. They killed 130 people, including 90 at the Bataclan. One traumatised survivor committed suicide in November 2017, two years after the event, and was later recognized as the 131st victim.

Another 413 people were injured. Seven of the attackers also died while the authorities continued to search for accomplices.

The attacks were the deadliest in France since World War 2.

But Western governments' strongest efforts to pin the blame solely on radical ISIS jihadists did not go to plan. Increasing numbers of observers questioned the role that the USA's CIA and Israel's Mossad may or may not have had in the killing of 130 people on that fateful night in the French capital.

Maybe as we are in the third decade of our century, the time is right to look in depth at the USA's murky interference in the Middle East. In one of the fiery oratories for which he was well-known, the late Hugo Chávez once stated that: *"the American empire is the greatest menace to our planet."*

Looking at the history of US engagement in Latin America, it is easy to see why Chávez made such a claim. From overthrowing democratically elected leaders, operating death squads, and torturing civilians, the history of US involvement in the region helped create a widespread popular backlash that persists to this day.

Since the late 1980s the USA's theatre of war has switched from Latin America to the Middle East, and many of the same tactics of that period were redeployed on the other side of the world.

The UK Sunday newspaper ***The Observer*** revealed that Pentagon officials at the highest levels oversaw torture facilities during the war in Iraq in 2003. The evidence includes: rooms used for interrogating detainees stained with blood; children tied into extreme stress positions with their bodies beaten to discoloration and others tortured with high voltage electricity or by waterboarding.

Most chillingly, a veteran of the United States' *"dirty war"* in El Salvador was reported to have been brought in to personally oversee the interrogation facilities.

This programme was condoned at the highest levels of the US military and utilised *"all means of torture to make the detainee confess … using electricity, hanging him upside down, pulling out their nails"*.

At the now infamous *School of the Americas*, thousands of Latin American *"special forces"* were explicitly trained in torture techniques by US handlers. Many of those SOA graduates took their new training home to El Salvador, where they waged a war that killed an estimated 80,000 Salvadoran civilians.

The creation and patronage of locally trained indigenous militias – such as we later saw with ISIS – was to wreak havoc among subject populations in pursuit of American military objectives.

The USA's most prominent trained paramilitaries were the Iraqi Special Operations Forces (ISOF), an elite counterterrorism force referred to as *"the dirty brigade"*.

Trained and guided by US military advisers at every level of its hierarchy, the ISOF was structured so as to place it outside the confines of normal oversight by international observers.

The use of torture, the patronage of proxy forces, and the facilitation of widespread human rights abuses all characterise US policy in the so-called *"war on terror."*

Evidence has emerged that ISIS and its military advances in northern Iraq and Syria had been shaped and controlled out of Langley, Virginia, and other CIA and Pentagon outposts to help spread chaos in the world's second-largest oil state, Iraq, as well as weakening Syrian stabilisation efforts.

There is widely corroborated evidence that MI6 cooperated with the CIA on a rat line of arms transfers from Libyan stockpiles to the Syrian rebels in 2012 after the fall of the Gaddafi regime.

So, the US and its allies weren't only supporting and arming an opposition they knew to be dominated by extreme sectarian groups; they were prepared to countenance the creation of some sort of *"Islamic state"* – despite the *"grave danger"* to Iraq's unity – as a Sunni buffer to weaken Syria.

But all is not as it seems. According to well-informed Iraqi journalists, ISIS overran the strategic Mosul region, site of some of the world's most prolific oilfields, with barely a shot fired in resistance.

In one report, residents of Tikrit reported remarkable displays of *"soldiers handing over their weapons and uniforms peacefully to militants who ordinarily would have been expected to kill government soldiers on the spot."*

The offensive coincided with a successful campaign by ISIS in eastern Syria.

And according to Iraqi journalists, Sunni tribal chiefs in the region had been convinced to side with ISIS against the Shiite Al-Maliki government in Baghdad. They were promised a better deal under ISIS Sunni Sharia than with Baghdad anti-Sunni rule.

Key members of ISIS were trained by US CIA and Special Forces command at a secret camp in Jordan in 2012, according to informed Jordanian officials. The US, Turkish and Jordanian intelligence ran a training base for the Syrian rebels in the Jordanian town of Safawi in the country's northern desert region, conveniently near the borders to both Syria and Iraq. Saudi Arabia and Qatar, the two Gulf monarchies most involved in funding the war against Syria's Assad, financed the Jordan ISIS training.

Advertised publicly as training of *'non-extremist'* Muslim jihadists to wage war against the Syrian Bashar Assad regime, the secret US training camps in Jordan and elsewhere trained perhaps several thousand Muslim fighters in techniques of irregular warfare, sabotage and general terror.

Former US State Department official Andrew Doran wrote in the conservative **National Review** magazine that some ISIS warriors also held US passports.

Iranian journalist Sabah Zanganeh noted: *"ISIS did not have the power to occupy and conquer Mosul by itself. What has happened is the result of security-intelligence collaborations of some regional countries with some extremist groups inside the Iraqi government."*

What is clear in the days since the fall of Mosul is that some of the world's largest oilfields in Iraq were suddenly held by Jihadists and no longer by an Iraqi government determined to increase the oil export significantly.

Today those who finance and arm the sectarian groups have slaughtered hundreds of thousands of innocent people in the wars in Afghanistan, Iraq and Syria. We now know that the air campaign against Islamic State in Iraq and Syria killed more than 450 innocent civilians, even though the US-led coalition acknowledged just two non-combatant deaths.

Airwars, a project by a team of independent journalists, has published details of 52 air strikes with what it believes are credible reports of at least 459 non-combatant deaths, including those of more than 100 children. One of the attacks investigated was on Fadhiliya, Iraq, where witnesses and local politicians said a family of five had died, including a pregnant woman and an eight-year-old girl.

In the summer of 2018, the **Guardian** newspaper shone a mainstream media spotlight on the true scale of the UK's role in the rendition and torture of many innocent suspects following the 9/11 atrocities in 2001 and the conflicts that ensued.

Two government reports published on 28th June that year revealed British intelligence's treatment of terrorism suspects. The reports by the parliamentary intelligence and security committee amount to one of the most damning indictments ever of UK intelligence, revealing links to torture and rendition were much more widespread than previously reported.

While there was no evidence of officers directly carrying out physical mistreatment of detainees, the reports say the overseas agency MI6 and the domestic service MI5 were involved in hundreds of torture cases and scores of rendition cases.

The reports were published despite the US government demanding last-minute changes and say the British secret service agencies were aware *"at an early point"* of the mistreatment of detainees by the US and others.

There were two cases in which UK personnel were *"party to mistreatment administered by others"*.

The report dealing with the treatment of detainees, which was leaked to me in 2018, details a litany of cases of concern, saying: *"We have found 13 incidents where UK personnel witnessed at first hand a detainee being mistreated by others, 25 where UK personnel were told by detainees that they had been mistreated by others and 128 incidents recorded where agency officers were told by foreign liaison services about instances of mistreatment. In some cases, these were correctly investigated but this was not consistent."*

It says that in 232 cases UK personnel continued to supply questions or intelligence to other services despite knowledge or suspicion of mistreatment, as well as *"198 cases where UK personnel received intelligence from liaison services which had been obtained from detainees who knew they had been mistreated – or with no indication as to how the detainee had been treated but where we consider they should have suspected mistreatment."*

The committee found three individual cases where MI6 or MI5 made or offered to make a financial contribution to others to conduct a rendition operation. In 28 cases, the agencies either suggested, planned or agreed to rendition operations proposed by others.

In a further 22 cases, MI6 or MI5 provided intelligence to enable a rendition operation to take place. In 23 cases they failed to take action to prevent rendition. The report says those at headquarters were aware of reports of mistreatment by the US – including 38 cases in 2002 alone – but did not take them seriously.

"That the US, and others, were mistreating detainees is beyond doubt, as is the fact that the agencies and defence intelligence were aware of this at an early point," the report says.

"The same is true of rendition: there was no attempt to identify the risks involved and formulate the UK's response. There was no understanding in HMG of rendition and no clear policy – or even recognition of the need for one."

After the attacks of 11th September 2001 against the United States, the Central Intelligence Agency (CIA) conspired with dozens of governments to build a secret extraordinary rendition and detention programme that spanned the globe.

Extraordinary rendition is the transfer - without legal process - of a detainee to the custody of a foreign government for purposes of detention and interrogation.

The programme, started under President George W Bush, was intended to *"protect America"*. But instead, it stripped people of their most basic rights, facilitated gruesome forms of torture, at times captured the wrong people, and debased the United States' human rights reputation world-wide. Until today, the United States and the majority of the other governments involved - more than 50 in all - have refused to acknowledge their participation, compensate the victims, or hold accountable those most responsible for the programme and its abuses.

Now additional facts expose just how brutal and mistaken the programme was:

- At least 136 individuals were extraordinarily rendered or secretly detained by the CIA and at least 54 governments participated in the CIA's secret detention and extraordinary rendition programme.

- A series of US Department of Justice memoranda authorized torture methods that the CIA applied on detainees. The Bush Administration referred to these methods as *"enhanced interrogation techniques"* which included: *walling, water dousing, waterboarding, stress positions, wall standing, cramped confinement, insult slaps, facial hold, attention grasp, forced nudity, sleep deprivation and dietary manipulation.*

- The CIA's Office of Inspector General reportedly investigated a number of *"erroneous renditions"* in which the CIA had abducted and detained the wrong people. A CIA officer told the **Washington Post**: *"They picked up the wrong people, who had no information. In many, many cases there was only some vague association with terrorism".*

- German national Khaled El-Masri was seized in Macedonia because he had been mistaken for an Al Qaeda suspect with a similar name. He was held incommunicado and abused in Macedonia and in secret CIA detention in Afghanistan. On 13th December 2012, the European Court of Human Rights held that Macedonia had violated El-Masri's rights under the European Convention on Human Rights, and his ill-treatment by the CIA at Skopje airport in Macedonia amounted to torture.

- Wesam Abdulrahman Ahmed al-Deemawi was seized in Iran and held for 77 days in the CIA's *"Dark Prison"* in Afghanistan. He was later held in Bagram for 40 days and subjected to sleep deprivation, hung from the ceiling by his arms in the *"strappado"* position (a victim's hands are tied behind his back and is then hung by a rope to a beam), threatened by dogs, made to watch torture videos, and subjected to sounds of electric sawing accompanied by cries of pain.

- After being extraordinarily rendered (taken) by the United States to Egypt in 2002, Ibn al-Shaykh al-Libi, under threat of torture at the hands of Egyptian officials, fabricated information relating to Iraq's provision of chemical and biological weapons training to Al Qaeda. In 2003, then Secretary of State Colin Powell relied on this fabricated information in his speech to the United Nations that made the case for war against Iraq.

- Abu Zubaydah was waterboarded at least 83 times by the CIA. FBI interrogator Ali Soufan testified before Congress that he elicited *"actionable intelligence"* from Zubaydah using rapport-building techniques but that Zubaydah shut down after he was waterboarded.

- On 20th November 2002, Gul Rahman froze to death in a secret CIA prison in Afghanistan called the *"Salt Pit,"* after a CIA case officer ordered guards to strip him naked, chain him to the concrete floor, and leave him there overnight without blankets.

- Fatima Bouchar was abused by the CIA for several days in the Bangkok airport. Bouchar reported she was chained to a wall and not fed for five days, at a time when she was four-and-a-half months pregnant. After that she was extraordinarily rendered to Libya.

- Syria was one of the *"most common destinations for rendered suspects,"* as were Egypt and Jordan. One Syrian prison facility contained individual cells that were roughly the size of coffins. Detainees report incidents of torture involving a chair frame used to stretch the spine (the so-called *German Chair*) and beatings.

- Muhammed al-Zery and Ahmed Agiza, while seeking asylum in Sweden, were extraordinarily rendered to Egypt where they were tortured with shocks to their genitals.

- Abu Omar, an Italian resident, was abducted from the streets of Milan, extraordinarily rendered to Egypt, and secretly detained for 14 months while Egyptian agents interrogated and tortured him by subjecting him to electric shocks. An Italian court convicted in absentia 22 CIA agents and one Air Force pilot for their roles in the extraordinary rendition of Abu Omar.

- Known black sites - secret prisons run by the CIA on foreign soil - existed in Afghanistan, Lithuania, Morocco, Poland, Romania, and Thailand.

The Senate Select Intelligence Committee completed a 6,000 page report that further details the CIA detention and interrogation operations with access to classified sources. In December 2014, the committee released a heavily redacted 525-page portion of the report.

But this is only the tip of the torture and rendition story.

A full 13 years earlier, in February 2005, Jane Mayer reported the Maher Arar case and shone a spotlight on the extent of the rendition processes in the *New Yorker* magazine:

*On 27th January, President Bush, in an interview with **The Times**, assured the world that "torture is never acceptable, nor do we hand over people to countries that do torture."*

Maher Arar, a Canadian engineer who was born in Syria, was surprised to learn of Bush's statement. American officials, suspecting Arar of being a terrorist, apprehended him in New York and sent him back to Syria, where he endured months of brutal interrogation, including torture.

When Arar described his experience, he said the pain was so unbearable, so that "you forget the milk that you have been fed from the breast of your mother."

Arar, a 34-year-old graduate of McGill University, whose family emigrated to Canada when he was a teenager, was arrested on 26th September 2002, at John F Kennedy Airport.

Arar was detained because his name had been placed on the United States Watch List of terrorist suspects.

He was held for the next 13 days, as American officials questioned him about possible links to another suspected terrorist. Arar said that he barely knew the suspect, although he had worked with the man's brother.

Arar, who was not formally charged, was placed in handcuffs and leg irons by plainclothes officials and transferred to an executive jet.

The plane flew to Washington, continued to Portland, Maine, stopped in Rome, Italy, then landed in Amman, Jordan.

During the flight, Arar said, he heard the pilots and crew identify themselves in radio communications as members of "the Special Removal Unit".

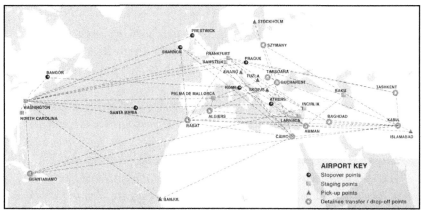

The spider's web of rendition flights

The Americans, he learned, planned to take him next to Syria.

Ten hours after landing in Jordan, Arar said, he was driven to Syria, where interrogators, after a day of threats, "just began beating on me." They whipped his hands repeatedly with two-inch-thick electrical cables and kept him in a windowless underground cell that he likened to a grave. "Not even animals could withstand it," he said.

Although he initially tried to assert his innocence, he eventually confessed to anything his tormentors wanted him to say. "You just give up," he said. "You become like an animal."

A year later, in October 2003, Arar was released without charge, after the Canadian government took up his cause.

Imad Moustapha, the Syrian Ambassador in Washington, announced that his country had found no links between Arar and terrorism.

Arar began suing the US government for his mistreatment.

"They are outsourcing torture because they know it's illegal," he said. "Why, if they have suspicions, don't they question people within the boundary of the law?"

Rendition was originally carried out on a limited basis, but after 9/11 when President Bush declared a global war on terrorism, the programme expanded beyond recognition - becoming, according to a former CIA official, "an abomination."

What began as a programme aimed at a small, discrete set of suspects - people against whom there were outstanding foreign arrest warrants - came to include a wide and ill-defined population that the Administration terms "illegal enemy combatants."

Many of them have never been publicly charged with any crime.

Five days after the attacks on the World Trade Centre and the Pentagon in 2001, Vice-President Dick Cheney argued that the government needed to "work through the dark side."

Cheney went on: "A lot of what needs to be done here will have to be done quietly, without any discussion, using sources and methods that are available to our intelligence agencies, if we're going to be successful... it's going to be vital for us to use any means at our disposal, basically, to achieve our objective."

Terrorism suspects in Europe, Africa, Asia, and the Middle East have often been abducted by hooded or masked American agents, then forced onto a Gulfstream V jet, like the one described by Arar.

This jet, which has been registered to a series of dummy American corporations has clearance to land at US military bases.

Upon arriving in foreign countries, rendered suspects often vanish. Detainees are not provided with lawyers, and many families are not informed of their whereabouts.

The most common destinations for rendered suspects are Egypt, Morocco, Syria, and Jordan, all of which have been cited for human-rights violations by the State Department and are known to torture suspects.

To justify sending detainees to these countries, the Administration appears to be relying on a very fine reading of an imprecise clause in the United Nations Convention Against Torture requiring "substantial grounds for believing" that a detainee will be tortured abroad.

The CIA itself is holding dozens of "high value" terrorist suspects outside of the territorial jurisdiction of the US, in addition to the estimated 550 detainees in Guantánamo Bay, Cuba.

The Administration confirmed the identities of at least 10 of these suspects to the 9/11 Commission - including Khalid Sheikh Mohammed, a top Al Qaeda operative, and Ramzi bin al-Shibh, an alleged chief planner of the 9/11 attacks - but refused to allow Commission members to interview the men and would not say where they were being held.

The Geneva Conventions of 1949, which established norms on the treatment of soldiers and civilians captured in war, require the prompt registration of detainees, so that their treatment can be monitored, but the Administration argues that Al Qaeda members and supporters, who are not part of a state-sponsored military, are not covered by the Conventions.

By holding detainees indefinitely, without counsel, without charges of wrongdoing, and under circumstances that could, in legal parlance, "shock the conscience" of a court, the Administration has jeopardized its chances of convicting hundreds of suspected terrorists, or even of using them as witnesses in almost any court in the world.

Since 9/11, as the number of renditions has grown, and hundreds of terrorist suspects have been deposited indefinitely in places like Guantánamo Bay, the shortcomings of this approach have become manifest. "Are we going to hold these people forever?" Scheuer asked.

"The policymakers hadn't thought what to do with them, and what would happen when it was found out that we were turning them over to governments that the human-rights world reviled." Once a detainee's rights have been violated, he says, "you absolutely can't" reinstate him into the court system. "You can't kill him, either," he added. "All we've done is create a nightmare."

Dan Coleman, an ex-FBI agent claimed the CIA liked rendition from the start.

"They loved that these guys would just disappear off the books, and never be heard of again," he said. "They were proud of it."

According to **The Times**, a secret memo issued by President George W Bush's Administration lawyers authorized the CIA to use novel interrogation methods.

The Administration's justification of the rough treatment of detainees appears to have passed down the chain of command.

In late 2003, at Abu Ghraib prison, in Iraq, photographs were taken that documented prisoners being subjected to grotesque abuse by US soldiers.

Three of the Guantánamo detainees released by the US to Great Britain for example, had confessed that they had appeared in a blurry video, obtained by American investigators that documented a group of acolytes meeting with bin Laden in Afghanistan.

As reported in **The Observer**, British intelligence officials arrived at Guantánamo with evidence that the accused men had been living in England at the time the video was made. The detainees told British authorities that they had been coerced into making false confessions.

In February 2020, the oldest prisoner in Guantánamo Bay wrote to Scottish First Minister Nicola Sturgeon to demand she help *"uncover the truth"* of the CIA's use of Scottish airports for extraordinary rendition flights.

Saifullah Paracha, who has been detained at the prison facility in Cuba since September 2004, said he was *"shocked"* to learn that a plane he was transported on had refuelled in Scotland. The 72-year-old has never been charged with a crime during his time in custody, let alone stood trial.

Now, with his health failing after suffering two heart attacks, he called on the First Minister to press the UK government to ensure Police Scotland and the Crown Office gain access to a classified US report into his rendition. Paracha said it was vital to establish the *"full truth"* of what happened to him.

As a postscript, also in February 2020, the **Daily Maverick** reported in its Declassified UK file: *"For more than 15 years successive British governments have covered up the role that the UK's foreign intelligence service, MI6, and its security service, MI5, played in the abduction and subsequent torture of people they regarded as potential terrorists."*

It went on to report: *"Britain's role in the torture of Abdul-Hakim Belhaj and Sami Al-Saadi, senior members of the Libyan Islamic Fighting Group, an anti-Gaddafi body well known to British intelligence, came to light because of documents found among the ruins of the office of Moussa Koussa, Gaddafi's intelligence chief. It was destroyed by bombs, perhaps even British ones, during NATO air strikes on the Libyan capital in 2011.*

"Among the documents discovered was an ingratiating letter from Mark Allen, MI6's counter-terrorism chief, to Moussa Koussa dated 18th March 2004. Allen congratulated Gaddafi's intelligence chief on Belhaj's "safe arrival" in Tripoli, making it clear his capture was the result of British intelligence."

He added: *"This was the least we could do for you and for Libya to demonstrate the remarkable relationship we have built over the years."*

Allen and his new Libyan friend were preparing for what became known as the *"Deal in the Desert"* involving lucrative deals for British companies, in particular oil giant BP.

After offering compensation to his victims and giving up his chemical and nuclear weapons projects, the villain of Lockerbie, the murderer of the British policewoman Yvonne Fletcher, the supplier of weapons and Semtex explosives to the IRA, had become a feted friend.

Urged on by their political masters, MI6 and MI5 ignored evidence reported by Amnesty International, Human Rights Watch, the US State Department and Britain's own Home Office that torture remained endemic in Gaddafi's Libya, meted out especially to those perceived to be opponents of his regime.

The relationship had become so cosy that in June 2007, Tony Blair wrote a personal letter to Gaddafi praising him for leading: *"A genuine transformation in relations between our two countries... from which both our peoples stand to benefit"*.

As British Prime Minister Lloyd George said in 1916: *"If the people really knew the truth, the war would be stopped tomorrow. But of course they don't know and can't know."*

- **Appendix E**

Chapter Four
Foot and Myth

Animal carcases burn in Cumbria during the 2001 Foot and Mouth crisis

DURING a recent dinner party, a long-time friend asked why I always blame the Establishment for so many of our country's problems.

"Surely, if the BBC report it as fact, we can believe the BBC," he said.

As a journalist I have witnessed far too often the lies and dirty tricks that the Establishment will stoop to, to get their own way. Murder, war and disease are the forerunners.

And as a journalist, I also know the deadly propaganda that our mainstream media – including the BBC and Sky TV – will feed the population to give credence to those lies.

One of the biggest lies told to the public happened in 2001 when Foot and Mouth Disease wrecked UK agriculture and set new price thresholds for British meat and dairy products.

Yet the British, Canadian, US and Mexican governments were preparing for an outbreak of Foot and Mouth Disease before it *"officially"* emerged on a Tyneside farm in February that year.

Bizarrely all four countries were staging a co-ordinated Foot and Mouth simulation exercise four months before the outbreak despite the fact that Britain had not been struck by the disease for 34 years and the USA and Canada had not been affected since 1929. And to add smoke to the conspiracy gun, English timber merchants confirmed that they were approached for urgent supplies to tackle the disease by Ministry of Agriculture officials as early as December 2000.

A series of no fewer than three unconnected Deep Throat phone calls over five days began to expose the truth.

Foot and Mouth Disease was actually present in the UK long before it was officially pinpointed at Bobby Waugh's Heddon-on-the-Wall pig farm – nine miles west of Newcastle upon Tyne - on 23rd February 2001. Yet the government's Ministry of Agriculture Fisheries and Food (MAFF) consistently blamed his farm as *"the likely source of the outbreak"*. They had found their scapegoat in a dirty pig farmer.

Within three days of the government identifying the pig farm as the source of the Foot and Mouth Disease outbreak, I independently discovered, via my scientific contacts, that in October 2000, the United States and Mexico had begun preparing for *"a simulated outbreak of Foot-and-Mouth disease"* in all three countries. According to papers leaked to me at the Newcastle Evening Chronicle from a contact at the Canadian Food Inspection Agency, the exercise - which took place between 6th and 9th November 2000 - was *"for the purpose of emergency planning"*.

It took place in Ontario, Alberta, Texas, USA, and Tamaulipas, Mexico. The papers stated: *"This exercise is the first of its kind and provides all three countries with a unique opportunity to apply their emergency response plans in the event of a real disease outbreak"*.

And the exercise - which is estimated to have cost over $1 million - was the first US *"Foreign Animal Disease Response Simulation"* of any kind since 1993. At the same time the UK government was preparing its own contingency plans for a Foot and Mouth outbreak. Yet the last British Foot and Mouth Disease outbreak was in 1967.

I then discovered that MAFF officials had begun telephoning timber merchants as early as December asking if they could supply wood for pyres, should Foot and Mouth strike.

Mike Littlehales, who ran a timber yard in Staffordshire said he received a phone call *"out of the blue"*. He told me: *"I got this call from a lady who said 'This is the Ministry of Agriculture. Would you be interested in supplying timber in case of foot-and-mouth?' because she wanted to update her records.*

"It surprised me, and I thought it was doubly strange when three weeks later the government tell us we have an outbreak of the disease."

Mr Littlehales said the last time his timber business had received a similar call was during the Foot and Mouth outbreak in 1967.

Fran Talbot, a fellow timber merchant at Eccleshall, said she was approached in the first week of February 2001 and was asked about the availability of railway sleepers in the event of a FMD outbreak.

"The woman said 'are you still in a position to supply timber for burning animals in case of an outbreak of Foot and Mouth'? It was a very odd thing to happen just three weeks before an outbreak," she said.

Mrs Talbot's firm had supplied sleepers during the 1967 outbreak but had not heard from MAFF since then.

Tommy Norman, who ran a timber yard at Longtown, Cumbria - the centre of scores of cases of Foot and Mouth Disease - confirmed he had received a similar call from MAFF in January.

"It's difficult for me to say any more," he added. *"I have provided masses of wood for MAFF pyres, but they still owe me a large amount of money."*

US scientist Dr Patricia Doyle, who led a stateside campaign to discover the truth about the UK Foot and Mouth outbreak, said: *"I am convinced that MAFF knew about the virus was on the loose long before February 2001.*

"And the US government was protecting its back because they weren't sure how far the virus had leaked."

Amble-based, animal geneticist Bruce Jobson, added: *"This confirms what we knew all along, that the government was aware Foot and Mouth was on the loose long before they identified it at Bobby Waugh's pig farm.*

"The new Department of the Environment Food and Rural Affairs (DEFRA) must now admit that MAFF had covered up the real cause of this outbreak."

Newcastle-based microbiologist Dr Harash Narang told me: *"I firmly believe that the virus escaped from a MAFF experiment and had infected sheep as long ago as October 2000. This evidence now supports that belief."*

Mr Waugh said he felt vindicated that he was not responsible for the Foot and Mouth outbreak.

In April 2001 he said: *"Again, again and again I have been blamed for this disease, when I knew all along it wasn't me.*

"I want the government to admit they got it wrong and tell us all how this thing really started."

Stuart Renton, a vet for almost 30 years, who worked out of the Newcastle Foot and Mouth Disease centre in Kenton Bar, Newcastle, launched a scathing attack on his MAFF employers.

He said he and many other vets working for MAFF believed Mr Waugh was innocent. He said he had seen enough evidence of old Foot and Mouth sores on infected sheep to convince him the disease was present in the UK long before 15th February 2001.

And he blasted the government for adopting the wrong policies to deal with the outbreak. *"They made our work extremely harrowing,"* he said. The 50-year-old vet's contract with the MAFF was put on the line for daring to tell what he believed was the truth.

Throughout the entire Foot and Mouth epidemic MAFF vets had not been allowed to speak about the crisis.

Instead, any official comment only came from the MAFF press office in London, its chief scientist Professor David King or Agriculture Minister Nick Brown.

Dr Renton said: *"Long standing Foot and Mouth lesions are being found in sheep nationally, indicating the disease was probably present long before the so-called initial outbreak in Heddon. We are still getting pockets of infection in sheep which we cannot trace back to Heddon."*

Dr Renton had been part of the MAFF team diagnosing and overseeing the destruction of animals since taking on a case at Black Callerton, Westerhope near to Heddon-on-the-Wall on 26th February 2001.

He said: *"Along with a number of the veterinary surgeons involved, I have serious doubts over the culling policies being adopted by the government, which makes our work in this outbreak extremely harrowing,"* he said.

MAFF said it was *"unfortunate"* that one of its vets should choose to speak to the press. Although Dr Renton's contract with MAFF could have been terminated by his decision to speak out, he stayed in post because of a dire shortage of replacement vets.

A spokesman for the Canadian government said he was unable to comment on its Foot and Mouth simulation exercise due to agreements it had made with the British government.

A DEFRA spokesman denied that MAFF had tried to cover-up the outbreak.

He said: *"We did not know of Foot and Mouth in this country at a time earlier than 21st February, when it was identified at the abattoir in Essex and then traced to Mr Waugh's farm in Northumberland.*

"There has never been any deliberate concealment. From time to time we do emergency planning exercises and the inquiries about wood may well have been of this nature," he said.

According to official records the last official UK Foot and Mouth contingency plan was in 1993.

More sinister was that UK government officials then tried to gag Bobby Waugh with the Official Secrets Act. The controversial move came after he accused them of making him the scapegoat for the Foot and Mouth Disease epidemic.

But Mr Waugh said he would not be silenced and claimed the government was using Big Brother tactics to cover up the real cause of the outbreak.

Mr Waugh revealed that for 100 days since the disease was linked to his pig farm at Heddon-on-the-Wall, the Ministry of Agriculture refused to allow him to clean up the premises.

He claimed their blanket refusal had cost him £24,500 in wages, rent and lost income. Mr Waugh also damned 10 animal welfare charges brought against him by Northumberland Trading Standards Offices as *"wildly inaccurate"*.

Bobby Waugh was made the scape goat for the whole crisis

Then bosses at MAFF (renamed DEFRA - Department of Environment, Food and Rural Affairs - following the 2001 General Election) said Mr Waugh could only clean up his farm if he signed the Official Secrets Act. A 12-page Ministry of Agriculture contract, dated 4th June 2001 detailed the agreement, which could pay Mr Waugh £10,000 in clean-up compensation.

But to begin the clean-up procedure - which almost every other foot and mouth infected farm has been allowed within days of its animals being culled - Mr Waugh had to abide by Clause 17 of the contract. This states: *"The supplier undertakes to abide and procure that his employees abide by the provisions of the Official Secrets Act 1911 to 1989.*

"The supplier shall keep secret and not disclose any information of a confidential nature obtained by him by reason of the contract, except information which is in the public domain otherwise than by breach of this provision."

The contract was a lifetime gag on Mr Waugh as it also stated: *"The provision of this Condition 17 shall apply during the continuance of this Contract and AFTER its termination howsoever arising."*

Although this may still have allowed Mr Waugh to speak about some aspects of his farm and the Foot and Mouth crisis, experience has shown that the government can take a very wide view as what is a breach of the Official Secrets Act. The contract could even prevent him publicly defending the 10 animal welfare charges made by Northumberland Trading Standards.

But while gagging Mr Waugh the OSA clause allowed the government to say what it likes: *"The Minister shall be free to disclose the terms of this Contract and particulars of the Services as he thinks fit."*

Mr Waugh was now stuck in a Catch 22 situation. If he signed the contract and then spoke out about what he claimed was a government plot to discredit him, he could be imprisoned like a spy or traitor under the Official Secrets Act. But if he refused to sign it he would lose the valuable clean up compensation and could not operate his farm.

"None of this makes sense," said Mr Waugh at the time. *"I have been on the phone to MAFF almost every day since the beginning of March asking when I can clean out my farm. Each time I have either been fobbed off or told permission cannot be granted for legal reasons. Yet within days of me speaking out in the press this contract is sent to me. They are trying to gag me, but they will not stop me saying what I believe is the truth."*

Dr Patricia Doyle said: *"The disease almost certainly started with an accidental release of FMD virus from vaccine trials, possibly as early as October 2000.*

"Mr Waugh was not the best farmer in the world and FMD conveniently found its way to his farm.

"It all stinks of a government cover-up."

A DEFRA spokesman said the delay in cleaning out Burnside Farm was due to problems in disposing of 60,000 gallons of pig slurry and wash water. *"We had a significant problem of waste disposal,"* he said. The spokesman admitted that use of the Official Secrets Act on Mr Waugh may be viewed as heavy handed.

He said: *"We accept that this is an extensive caution, but it is a standard condition which exists in all our contracts. But the farmers are not being gagged."*

But five other farmers I contacted had not received similar contracts. A spokesman for the National Pig Association, the union representing Mr Waugh, said they were outraged by the contract and the inclusion of the Official Secrets Act.

"We have told Mr Waugh not to sign it and we are going to fight his case for him," he added. A National Farmers' Union (NFU) spokesman said they were not aware of other farmers being forced to sign similar contracts and said they would investigate the matter further. Hexham Tory MP Peter Atkinson said the attempted gagging of Mr Waugh by use of the Official Secrets Act was *"sinister"*.

"It is also bizarre as the Official Secrets Act covers very serious stuff so what are the government afraid of here?" he added. *"It reinforces the feeling that they have something to hide."*

What they were hiding was indeed huge!

As my investigations continued there were reports linking the outbreak of Foot and Mouth Disease to Ministry of Defence sponsored experiments both at an MoD base in Northumberland and another close to the SAS base in Hereford.

Then the truth behind the Foot and Mouth Disease outbreak began to slowly emerge. Suddenly it was revealed that a test tube containing the Foot and Mouth virus had gone missing from a top-secret laboratory two months before the outbreak was first reported.

MAFF was alerted when a sample of live virus was reported missing from the biological and chemical weapons laboratory at Porton Down, Wiltshire, following a routine audit. The test tube was stored in a highly sensitive laboratory where scientists also hold other diseases, including Smallpox, TB, Ebola and Anthrax.

The missing phial supported what we already knew that sheep in parts of the UK were carrying the virus long before the outbreak was confirmed in February 2001. According to a report by a French vet, it was detected in a Welsh flock in the Brecon Beacons – close to Hereford as early as January.

Tory MP for North Shropshire Owen Paterson said: *"There are very persistent rumours over missing phials from Porton Down linked to animal rights activists. What I do know is that there is evidence this disease has been round a lot longer than the government was willing to admit."*

A senior military source close to Porton Down said: *"A phial appears to have gone missing from one of the labs following a routine audit last year. Ministry officials were informed immediately and an investigation was launched initially by Special Branch and then by MI5, who are interested in the activities of animal rights protesters."*

Some scientists, including ex-government employees, claimed that the disease had spread due to research on a vaccine and the virus could only have come from a UK laboratory.

Not surprisingly, many people felt that Tony Blair's New Labour administration had something to hide. Included in a letter to the **Western Morning News**, published on 1st September 2001, was the following:

"We know there is an EU wish to rationalise farming, and this would include a Britain which is arable rather than livestock producing.

"We also know Prime Minister Tony Blair wishes to rationalise British farming. So is Foot and Mouth a chance opportunity or an opportunity created?

"Again, there is circumstantial evidence but no smoking gun. Foot and mouth notices were printed ahead of the outbreak. Inquiries about materials to furnish funeral pyres were going ahead weeks before the outbreak. A phial of foot and mouth virus went missing, not an obvious target for a petty thief. Could these things be pure coincidence?"

So, during March and early April, the notion of either environmental terrorists or rogue ministry officials being responsible for the epidemic was being discussed in earnest. Add to that questions concerning the FMD raison d'etre, and there would be sufficient material for any budding thriller writer.

With a pathogen like FMD, the specimen at Porton Down would have been kept under the same security levels which exist at, for example, a nuclear ordnance silo. Any loss of such an item would have resulted in a massive clandestine recovery operation with full reporting restrictions under Official Secrets Act procedures enforced.

As soon as it became clear that the test tube could not be accounted for, a national bio-hazard alert, akin to enacting a state of emergency, would have been declared immediately.

64

**The FMD outbreak was due to an escape of
the virus from a government laboratory**

Mobilisation of the reserve armed forces, to be deployed at full battalion strength once an infection zone was identified, should have been central to the strategy.

And all this could account for the Foot and Mouth Disease simulation exercises being carried out in four countries in October 2000… they were ready for the worst case scenario.

Of course, that scenario was not the one portrayed by the UK government.

The matters of vaccination, animal disease contingency planning and the role of Porton Down were examples of criminal negligence on a scale hitherto never experienced. Worse still, rural communities were subjected to actions involving gross professional misconduct and wholesale abuses of Official Secrets Act procedures.

The New Labour government's saviour from total humiliation on the issue of the Foot and Mouth Disease outbreak came bizarrely on Tuesday 11th September 2001 with the World Trade Centre terrorist attack which was to dominate world news for the next two years. *"Now would be a good time to bury bad news"* was the most honest statement to have emerged from a government apparatchik since 1997.

So, the carnival of blood, mud and fire which characterised the UK in 2001 was avoidable. Whether the government was guilty of either gross incompetence or reckless adventurism and opportunism is debateable. Compelling reasons for the latter are not hard to find.

Firstly, it would force rationalisation of the farming industry, thereby strengthening demands to reform the unwieldy European Union Common Agricultural Policy. Secondly, grazing lands of animals due for extermination could be used for a variety of new schemes, examples being GM crops, forestry and wind-turbine installations. The residue of Britain's livestock would be strictly regulated and eventually absorbed by the multi-national food processing corporations, whose philosophies are not based on green and pleasant lands.

But there is more to the story of cover-up and conspiracy.

During the last nine days of February 2001, severe wintry weather affected Southern Scotland. Heavy snowfall struck on Tuesday 20th February, resulting in many road closures. It was on that day when a highways clearance team from Dumfries and Galloway Council arrived to remove snow from an unclassified road connecting the A7 from Grid Ref. NY388963 to the B6399 at Grid

Ref. NY507953, the latter situated within the Scottish Borders District.

This was unprecedented. Normally, this road was not considered a priority and very rarely received attention from a snowplough. Situated in remote hill-farming country, it was anything but a major thoroughfare. A farmer approached the crew and, after a polite exchange, they departed. According to the workmen, instructions were being merely followed.

As it transpired, the farmer's premises escaped contamination and no livestock were culled.

Shortly after the official declaration of the Foot and Mouth Disease outbreak, a cyclist, who travelled regularly along the roads and byways of South Dumfriesshire/Roxburghshire and Cumbria, was struck by a profusion of Day-Glo orange ribbons tied into neat bows and attached to gate posts, fences, telegraph poles, hedges and trees.

At the time he first noticed them, Foot and Mouth Disease had yet to make its presence felt in southern Scotland. He became suspicious when, within weeks, the disease arrived in areas marked by the ribbons.

He said: *"This seemed to coincide that anyone that got a tape got foot-and-mouth. As if somebody had deliberately done something."*

Meanwhile 420 miles away, the Sage family had lived and worked on West End Farm near Inwardleigh, Devon, for generations. One afternoon towards the end of April 2001, Mrs Sage encountered two men in white overalls outside the cattle shed. Upon asking them to explain their presence on the farm, she was curtly informed that they were MAFF officials who had every right to inspect agricultural premises. One of the men peremptorily requested Mrs Sage to go back indoors.

As she was returning to the house, Mrs Sage took a look inside the Ministry van, its rear door having been left open. There, she saw a severed animal tongue and her main concern was the possibility of contamination: Foot and Mouth Disease was rife in Central and North Devon.

Mrs Sage telephoned the local police station, informing the duty constable of these events, and was told that her call would be returned. The following day, having received no such communication. Mrs Sage contacted the police station again and learned that there was no record of her initial telephone call.

The farm's livestock was subsequently culled.

The outbreak of Foot and Mouth Disease in the United Kingdom in 2001 caused a crisis in British agriculture and tourism. Over six million cows and sheep were killed in an eventually successful attempt to halt the disease. Cumbria was the worst affected area of the country, with 893 cases.

Officially, there were 2,000 cases of Foot and Mouth in the 2001 UK outbreak. But that doesn't do justice to the horrendous toll of the disease.

Each of those cases meant a farm having all of its livestock killed and burned.

The culling policy saw not just the animals on the affected farm killed, but also all the animals in the surrounding area. Exclusion zones made travel in some areas almost impossible and tourism nose-dived. Despite these measures the epidemic continued.

Farmer Philip Heard lost 3,000 cows, ewes and lambs.

"We were all preparing to put our livestock out to grass but with foot-and-mouth we suddenly weren't allowed to move them and we couldn't get extra feed without a special licence," he said.

"It was a horrible thing to see our animals culled. We worked so hard to bring these animals into the world, it went against everything we worked for to see them killed."

It took nine months to bring Foot and Mouth Disease under control, costing the UK's public sector £3 billion and the private sector £5 billion.

Amid the great public outcry the government promised lessons would be learned.

In 2016, Dr Alex Donaldson who was head of the Pirbright laboratory from 1989 until his retirement in 2002 wrote an enlightening article for the **Veterinary Times**:

Pirbright was at the fore at the start of the UK 2001 Foot and Mouth Disease outbreak, making the confirmatory diagnosis and, at the first five reported outbreaks, performing clinical examinations, determining the age of lesions, taking samples, collecting and analysing epidemiological data.

Meanwhile, vaccine matching tests and nucleotide sequencing analysis were being performed to characterise the causal virus – all during the first six days.

It was apparent assistance was needed in the lab with diagnostic, serological and veterinary advisory activities. The speed of the response was magnificent.

Many people volunteered, including former veterinary staff and PhD students; veterinarians from the UK, Australia, Ireland and Italy; staff from the Veterinary Laboratories Agency; staff at Pirbright who transferred from other departments; and wives of staff members.

Dr Donaldson wrote: *"Two FMD events attracted my attention after I retired from Pirbright in June 2002: a series of outbreaks in Surrey and proposals for a radical change in FMD control policy.*

The outbreaks in Surrey occurred in August and September 2007, in two clusters. The first in Normandy, about 5km from the Pirbright site, and the second around Egham, about 18km from Normandy.

Investigations discovered the primary outbreak in Normandy was initiated by the escape of the O1 1860 vaccine strain from a pharmaceutical firm on the Pirbright site.

Drainpipes were damaged by the ingress of roots and it was concluded this allowed the virus to escape and contaminate nearby soil, which was then carried on the wheels of lorries moving off the site. The lorries then travelled along a lane in Normandy and, from there, the virus was transported by unknown means to cattle grazing at the first IP10.

The UK 2001 Foot and Mouth Disease outbreak resulted in the slaughter of around 6.5 million animals and cost an estimated £10 billion. People concerned about Foot and Mouth Disease, in particular policy makers and research leaders, would be well advised to look again so the mistakes of 2001 will not be repeated in the future".

At the time of writing, I discovered that in 2015, the Pirbright Institute applied to patent a live attenuated Coronavirus vaccine in order to combat Avian infectious bronchitis virus (IBV), the aetiological agent of infectious bronchitis (IB).

Five years later in 2020 the world watched as a Coronavirus Covid-19 pandemic began spreading from China – supposedly from dirty open meat markets.

But Larry Romanoff of the Global Research organisation wrote that the virus – like the Foot and Mouth variant – might well have been created *"in a lab"*.

He wrote: *"I refer to a thesis on Biological Weapons by Leonard Horowitz and Zygmunt Dembek who stated that clear signs of a genetically engineered bio-warfare agent were (a) a disease caused by an uncommon, unusual, rare, or unique agent, with (b) lack of an epidemiological explanation - no clear idea of source (c) An "unusual manifestation and/or geographic distribution" and (d) multiple sources of infection.*

"China's coronavirus appears to satisfy all four criteria," he added.

- **Appendix F**

Chapter Five
Big Brother is Watching You

Barnhill on Jura, where George Orwell wrote *Nineteen Eighty-Four*

THE far-reaching eyes and ears of government and its agencies are watching and listening to us every minute of every day.

Whether you are sitting in a wooden lodge high in the Himalayas, lying quietly on a sandy beach in South America or a watching TV in a city apartment in London, Big Brother is watching you... and you'll never know from where or when.

Information is knowledge and knowledge is power, and with power comes control. We live in a world of surveillance.

I cough and allow my mind to drift to a peaceful place sitting in the summer sunshine on the north side of the Isle of Jura watching the sea wash white horses on the rocks below me. Less than 300 yards to the south of where I am sitting while writing this chapter is the isolated cottage known as Barnhill... this was the rented home of writer George Orwell, who lived there intermittently from 1946 until his death in 1950. Orwell completed his novel *Nineteen Eighty-Four* while living there.

It was a place I visited often during my two years living and working as a newspaper editor in the wilds of Argyll, in western Scotland.

Barnhill always held a fascination for me, because *Nineteen Eighty-Four* had remained my favourite novel ever since as a raw 14-year-old I was first mesmerised and frightened by Orwell's vision of a future dystopian world. And I loved to imagine the views he must have taken in while writing that classic of English literature.

First published in 1948, yet set 36 years later, *Nineteen Eighty-Four* tells the story of Winston Smith, a citizen and an ordinary member of the Outer Party:

Winston works in the Records Department in the Ministry of Truth, rewriting and distorting history, under the dictator Big Brother.

But Winston is determined to remain human under inhuman circumstances and begins a diary. Yet telescreens are placed everywhere - in his home, in his cubicle at work, in the cafeteria where he eats, even in the bathroom stalls. His every move is watched. No place is safe.

One day, while at the mandatory Two Minutes Hate, Winston catches the eye of an Inner Party Member, O'Brien, whom he believes to be an ally. He also catches the eye of a dark-haired girl named Julia from the Fiction Department.

A few days later Julia secretly hands him a note that reads: *"I love you."* Winston takes pains to meet her, and when they finally do, Julia draws up a plan whereby they can be alone.

Once alone in the countryside, Winston and Julia make love and begin their allegiance against the Party and Big Brother. They fall in love, and, while they know that they will someday be caught, they believe that the love and loyalty they feel for each other can never be taken from them.

Eventually, Winston and Julia confess to O'Brien, whom they believe to be a member of the Brotherhood (an underground organization aimed at bringing down the Party), their hatred of the Party.

O'Brien welcomes them into the Brotherhood with an array of questions and arranges for Winston to be given a copy of *the Book*, the underground's treasonous volume written by their leader, Emmanuel Goldstein.

Winston gets the book and takes it to the secure room where he reads it with Julia napping by his side. The two are disturbed by a noise behind a painting in the room and discover a telescreen. They are quickly dragged away and separated.

Winston finds himself deep inside the Ministry of Love, a prison with no windows, where he sits for days alone. Finally, O'Brien comes. Initially Winston believes that O'Brien has also been caught, but he soon realizes that he is there to torture him and break his spirit.

O'Brien spends the next few months torturing Winston in order to change his way of thinking - to employ the concept of doublethink, or the ability to simultaneously hold two opposing ideas in one's mind and believe in them both.

Finally, O'Brien takes Winston to Room 101, the most dreaded room of all in the Ministry of Love, the place where prisoners meet their greatest fear. Winston's greatest fear is rats. O'Brien places over Winston's head a mask made of wire mesh and threatens to open the door to release rats on Winston's face.

When Winston screams, *"Do it to Julia!"* he relinquishes his last vestige of humanity.

Big Brother was watching all the time.

Today, the year 1984 has long passed, but Orwell's futuristic vision of hell on Earth remains.

Big Brother is now everywhere. Mainstream newspapers and TV channels feed us daily propaganda – the *facts* which the Establishment wish us to believe. CCTV cameras are on every street corner and inside every store – yet we never know who is monitoring them. Number Plate Recognition cameras are installed at almost every filling station and car park.

Sat Nav satellites pick up every move of our car, van or truck, and if we are on foot our smart phones do the same.

Cookies and spyware follow every finger click we make on our PC or tablet.

Police DNA and fingerprint databases have more than 35% of adults logged on their files.

MSN and Facebook Messenger text messages and private phone calls are harvested by government snoopers at GCHQ.

Our employment, financial and residential history is catalogued in the finest detail by so-called credit reference agencies such as Equifax and Experian.

We, the general population, are being monitored at every step.

As a journalist I have twice had my telephone tapped and private conversations listened to by either the police, government or MI5… and all these years later I am still not sure exactly who it was.

The first occasion was in 1991 while I was living in Argyll and investigating the masonic machinations inside the Scottish Conservative Party – as described in **Chapter Two.**

The second time was in 1996 while similarly investigating the truth behind the Dunblane massacre – also explained in **Chapter Two**.

But these instances are only the tip of the surveillance iceberg. The real conspiracy lies under the surface.

Mass surveillance is the intricate surveillance of an entire or a substantial fraction of a population in order to monitor that group of citizens. The surveillance is often carried out by governments or secret service organizations like the MI5 and the FBI, but it may also be carried out by corporations (either on behalf of governments or at their own initiative).

Depending on each nation's laws and judicial systems, the legality of, and the permission required, to engage in mass surveillance varies. It is the single most indicative distinguishing trait of totalitarian regimes. It is also often distinguished from targeted surveillance.

Surveillance has often been cited as necessary to fight terrorism, prevent crime and social unrest, protect national security, and control the population.

Conversely, mass surveillance has equally often been criticised for violating privacy rights, limiting civil and political rights and freedoms, and being illegal under some legal or constitutional systems.

The government's giant listening station GCHQ in Cheltenham

Another criticism is that increasing mass surveillance could lead to the development of a surveillance state or an electronic police state where civil liberties are infringed or political dissent is undermined by COINTELPRO-like programs.

In 2013, the practice of mass surveillance by world governments was called into question after Edward Snowden's global surveillance disclosure – Edward was an American whistle-blower who leaked highly classified surveillance information from the National Security Agency (NSA) in 2013 when he was a Central Intelligence Agency (CIA) subcontractor.

Reporting based on the documents Snowden leaked to various media outlets triggered a debate about civil liberties and the right to privacy in the Digital Age.

State surveillance in the United Kingdom has formed part of the public consciousness since the 19th century. The postal espionage crisis of 1844 sparked the first panic over the privacy of citizens.

However, in the 20th century, electronic surveillance capabilities grew out of wartime signal intelligence and pioneering code breaking.

In 1946, the Government Communications Headquarters (GCHQ) was formed. It was at first based in Eastcote, but in 1951 moved to the outskirts of Cheltenham, setting up two sites at Oakley and Benhall.

In 1948 the United Kingdom and the United States signed the bilateral UKUSA Agreement. It was later broadened to include Canada, Australia and New Zealand, as well as cooperation with several third-party nations. This became the cornerstone of Western intelligence gathering and the so-called *Special Relationship* between the UK and the USA.

The Regulation of Investigatory Powers Act 2000 (RIP or RIPA) is a significant piece of legislation that granted and regulated the powers of public bodies to carry out surveillance and investigation. In 2002 the UK government announced plans to extend the Regulation of Investigatory Powers Act so that at least 28 government departments would be given powers to access metadata about citizens' web, e-mail, telephone and fax records, without a warrant and without a subject's knowledge.

According to 2011 Freedom of Information Act requests, the total number of local government operated CCTV cameras was around 52,000 over the entirety of the UK.

The prevalence of video surveillance in the UK is often overstated due to unreliable estimates being requoted. For example, one report in 2002 extrapolated from a very small sample to estimate the number of cameras in the UK at 4.2 million (of which 500,000 in London). More reliable estimates put the number of private and local government operated cameras in the United Kingdom at around 1.87 million in 2012.

After the growth of the Internet and development of the World Wide Web, a series of media reports in 2013 revealed more recent programs and techniques involving GCHQ, such as Tempora. The use of these capabilities is controlled by laws made in the UK parliament. In particular, access to the content of private messages (that is, interception of a communication) must be authorized by a warrant signed by the Secretary of State.

The Protection of Freedoms Act 2012 includes several provisions related to controlling and restricting the collection, storage, retention, and use of information in government databases. Supported by all three major political parties, the UK Parliament passed the Data Retention and Investigatory Powers Act in July 2014 to ensure police and security services retain existing powers to access phone and Internet records.

This was superseded by the Investigatory Powers Act 2016, a comprehensive statute which made public a number of previously secret powers (equipment interference, bulk retention of metadata, intelligence agency use of bulk personal datasets), and enables the government to require Internet service providers and mobile phone companies to maintain records of customers' Internet connections for 12 months.

The Act was informed by two reports by David Anderson QC, the UK's Independent Reviewer of Terrorism Legislation: A Question of Trust (2015) and the report of his Bulk Powers Review (2016), which contains a detailed appraisal (with 60 case studies) of the operational case for the powers often characterised as mass surveillance. It may yet require amendment as a result of legal cases brought before the European Court of Human Rights.

Many advanced nation-states have implemented laws that partially protect citizens from unwarranted intrusion, such as the Human Rights Act 1998 and Data Protection Act 1998 in the United Kingdom, and laws that require a formal warrant before private data may be gathered by a government.

The Investigatory Powers Tribunal, a judicial oversight body for the intelligence agencies, ruled in December 2014 that the legislative framework in the United Kingdom does not breach the European Convention on Human Rights. However, in a ruling in December 2014, the Tribunal found that the legislative framework in the United Kingdom does not permit mass surveillance and that while GCHQ collects and analyses data in bulk, it does not practise mass surveillance.

A report on Privacy and Security published by the Intelligence and Security Committee of Parliament also came to this view, although it found past shortcomings in oversight and said the legal framework should be simplified to improve transparency.

However, notable civil liberties groups continue to express strong views to the contrary and plan to appeal the ruling to the European Court of Human Rights, while others have criticised these viewpoints in turn.

But it is not just governments and their agencies which spy on us.

In 2019 hackers were able to remotely install surveillance software on phones and other devices using a major vulnerability in the messaging app WhatsApp. WhatsApp, which is owned by Facebook, said the attack targeted a select number of users and was orchestrated by *"an advanced cyber-actor"*. Subsequently WhatsApp urged all of its 1.5 billion users to update their apps as an added precaution.

The surveillance software involved was developed by Israeli firm NSO Group.

WhatsApp promotes itself as a secure communications app because messages are end-to-end encrypted, meaning they should only be displayed in a legible form on the sender or recipient's device.

However, the surveillance software would have let an attacker read the messages on the target's device.

"Journalists, lawyers, activists and human rights defenders" are most likely to have been targeted, said Ahmed Zidan from the non-profit Committee to Protect Journalists.

The hack involved attackers using WhatsApp's voice calling function to ring a target's device.

Even if the call was not picked up, the surveillance software could be installed. According to the **Financial Times** report, the call would often disappear from the device's call log.

"The attack has all the hallmarks of a private company reportedly that works with governments to deliver spyware that takes over the functions of mobile phone operating systems," Facebook said in a briefing document note for journalists.

Professor Alan Woodward from the University of Surrey said it was a *"pretty old-fashioned"* method of attack.

"A buffer overflow is where a program runs into memory it should not have access to. It overflows the memory it should have and hence has access to memory in which malicious code can potentially be run," he explained.

"If you are able to pass some code through the app, you can run your own code in that area.

Big Brother is watching at every street corner

"In VOIP there is an initial process that dials up and establishes the call, and the flaw was in that bit. Consequently you did not need to answer the call for the attack to work."

The NSO Group company has been referred to in the past as a *"cyber-arms dealer"*. It is part-owned by the London-based private equity firm Novalpina Capital, which acquired a stake in February 2019.

NSO's flagship software, *Pegasus*, has the ability to collect intimate data from a target device, including capturing data through the microphone and camera, and gathering location data.

In a statement, the group said: *"NSO's technology is licensed to authorised government agencies for the sole purpose of fighting crime and terror.*

"The company does not operate the system, and after a rigorous licensing and vetting process, intelligence and law enforcement determine how to use the technology to support their public safety missions. We investigate any credible allegations of misuse and if necessary, we take action, including shutting down the system.

"NSO would not or could not use its technology in its own right to target any person or organisation."

According to the **New York Times**, one of the people targeted was a London-based lawyer involved in a lawsuit against the NSO Group.

Amnesty International, which said it had been targeted by tools created by the NSO Group in the past, said this attack was one human rights groups had long feared was possible.

"They're able to infect your phone without you actually taking any action," said Danna Ingleton, deputy programme director for Amnesty Tech. She said there was mounting evidence that the tools were being used by regimes to keep prominent activists and journalists under surveillance.

"There needs to be some accountability for this, it can't just continue to be a wild west, secretive industry."

WhatsApp did not say whether the attack could have extended beyond the confines of WhatsApp, reaching further into a device and accessing emails, photos and more

"Using an app as an attack route is limited on iOS as they run apps in very tightly controlled sandboxes," said Professor Woodward. *"We're all assuming that the attack was just a corruption of WhatsApp but analysis is still ongoing.*

"The nightmare scenario would be if you could get something much more capable onto the device without the user having to do anything," he said.

Our lives are no longer secret… Big Brother knows all of us.

Which brings me back to beginning…

I stare again at a news item and in something which can only be described as **Nineteen Eighty-Four** meets **Black Mirror** the headline reads: *Implanting Microchips for Convenience.*

The article explains how plans are already being rolled out to implant a tiny microchip in people's hand which could eventually replace the need for credit cards, car keys and much more.

And this dystopian world is upon us right now.

Micro-chipping is almost routine at the Swedish start-up hub *Epicenter.* The company offers to implant its workers and start-up members with microchips the size of grains of rice that function as swipe cards: to open doors, operate printers, or buy smoothies with a wave of the hand.

The injections have become so popular that workers at *Epicenter* hold parties for those willing to get implanted.

"The biggest benefit I think is convenience," said Patrick Mesterton, co-founder and CEO of *Epicenter*. As a demonstration, he unlocks a door by merely waving near it.

"It basically replaces a lot of things you have, other communication devices, whether it be credit cards or keys," he explains.

The technology is not new. Such chips are used as virtual collar plates for pets. Companies use them to track deliveries. It's just never been used to tag employees on a broad scale before.

Epicenter and a handful of other companies are the first to make chip implants broadly available.

While biologically safe, the data generated by the chips can show how often an employee comes to work or what they buy. Unlike company swipe cards or smartphones, which can generate the same data, a person cannot easily separate themselves from the chip.

"Of course, putting things into your body is quite a big step to do and it was even for me at first," said Mr Mesterton, remembering how he initially had harboured doubts.

"But then on the other hand, I mean, people have been implanting things into their body, like pacemakers and stuff to control your heart," he said. *"That's a way, way more serious thing than having a small chip that can actually communicate with devices."*

Epicenter, which is home to more than 100 companies and some 2,000 workers, began implanting workers in January 2015. Now, about 190 workers have them.

A company based in Belgium also offers its employees such implants. And last year a company in Wisconsin has become the first in the USA to roll out microchip implants for all its employees. The initiative, which is optional for employees at snack stall supplier Three Square Market (*32M*), implants radio-frequency identification (RFID) chips in staff members' hands in between their thumb and forefinger.

Once tagged with the implant *32M* says its employees will be able to perform a range of common office tasks with an effortless wave of their hand.

"We foresee the use of RFID technology to drive everything from making purchases in our office break room market, opening doors, use of copy machines, logging into our office computers, unlocking phones, sharing business cards, storing medical/health information, and used as payment at other RFID terminals," says *32M* CEO, Todd Westby.

In the UK, Steven Northam, the founder and owner of Hampshire-based *BioTeq*, told the **Guardian** that most of its 150 implants have been for individuals, while some financial and engineering firms have also had the chips implanted in their staff. *BioTeq* has also implanted them in employees of a bank testing the technology, and has shipped them to Spain, France, Germany, Japan and China.

They cost between £70 and £260 per person. Northam himself and all the directors at *BioTeq* and one of his other companies, *IncuHive*, have been microchipped.

The chips make use of near-field communication (NFC) and are similar to ones already in use in things like contactless credit cards, mobile payment systems, and animal tag implants.

"It will happen to everybody," says Noelle Chesley, associate professor of sociology at the University of Wisconsin-Milwaukee.

Gene Munster, an analyst at Loup Ventures, thinks having embedded chips in human bodies is less than 50 years away.

"The idea of being chipped has too "much negative connotation today," he says, but by 2067 *"we will have been desensitized by the social stigma."*

In 2018, Britain's biggest employer organisation and main trade union body both sounded the alarm over the prospect of British companies implanting staff with microchips to improve security. The CBI, which represents 190,000 UK businesses, voiced concerns about the prospect.

A CBI spokesperson said: *"While technology is changing the way we work, this makes for distinctly uncomfortable reading. Firms should be concentrating on rather more immediate priorities and focusing on engaging their employees."*

The TUC is worried that staff could be coerced into being microchipped. Its general secretary Frances O'Grady said: *"We know workers are already concerned that some employers are using tech to control and micromanage, whittling away their staff's right to privacy.*

"Microchipping would give bosses even more power and control over their workers. There are obvious risks involved, and employers must not brush them aside, or pressure staff into being chipped."

But in the here and now it is mobile messaging which is Big Brother's catch all.

In 2018, the UK Prime Minister Theresa May signalled her desire to crack down on encrypted messaging apps, arguing that the services provide a safe haven for terrorists and extremists.

Three years earlier in 2015, as Home Secretary, Mrs May called for terrorists to be denied *"safe spaces to communicate"* and said a future Conservative government would legislate to restore the *"declining capabilities"* of the British government to intercept communications.

In March 2017, Number 10 repeated a call by Home Secretary, Amber Rudd, for police and intelligence services to be given access to encrypted messages on services such as WhatsApp.

Each time terrorism was the key the Government used for its demands for easier surveillance.

"We cannot allow this ideology the safe space it needs to breed – yet that is precisely what the internet and the big companies that provide internet-based services provide," claimed Mrs May in 2018.

"These companies simply cannot stand by while their platforms are used to facilitate child abuse, modern slavery or the spreading of terrorist and extremist content."

Yet behind these claims is a desire by government to own every form of surveillance for its own ends.

In 2019, Amnesty International launched the *#UnfollowMe* campaign demanding an end to mass surveillance. And they released the results of a global poll of more than 13,000 people across every continent.

Amnesty found that more than 70% of respondents worldwide are strongly opposed to the government monitoring their internet use. The right to privacy is being systematically violated by governments that are increasingly employing sophisticated new mass surveillance technologies to spy on people's private communications.

Amnesty posed the following questions:

1. I am not doing anything wrong, so why should I care?

Would you care if the government installed voice recorders and cameras in your home, recorded every conversation you have with a friend over a coffee, or followed you wherever you go? Those actions are the physical-world equivalent of online mass surveillance.

If our privacy is taken away without a reasonable suspicion of criminal activity, then the assumption is that everyone is potentially guilty until proven innocent.

2. Corporations already know everything about me, so what's the difference?

There's a big difference, providing your data to corporations is voluntary and optional. You disclose information about yourself when you sign up for a social network, email account, or with a telecom company. The difference is: you decided to do that, you are aware that you're doing it, and you can cancel your account.

3. Isn't this a necessary sacrifice to stop terrorism?

There is no evidence that mass surveillance helps to prevent terrorism. Mass surveillance actually increases the risk that intelligence and law enforcement agencies will miss real, credible threats as they are distracted by false positives. The fact is they are gathering information that they couldn't have dreamed of a decade ago and they will always tell us they need more.

4. It's just metadata, not content, so who cares?

If metadata was not a useful source of information about people, would it be collected? Analysing metadata – where you go and who you talk to – provides an efficient way to gain a lot of information about people's lives.

To make this intrusion into our daily lives more palpable, Edward Snowden says: "The people looking at this data are looking for criminals. You could be the most innocent person in the world, but if somebody programmed to see patterns of criminality looks at your data, they're not going to find you – they're going to find a criminal."

So, the next time your child has to stand in line for an eye recognition device to pay for their school dinner, or you use your fingerprint to log into your iPhone, or send a private message to a friend or relative, remember the Isle of Jura and George Orwell's words of warning: *"Big Brother is watching you."*

Chapter Six
Tunnel Vision

IT was a wet February in 1997 and I was ensconced in a four-star hotel in Islington, tasked with bringing home what could be the biggest newspaper story of the decade.

My remit as Chief Investigative Reporter for the Scottish national daily *The Scotsman* was to gather information from Harrods owner, Mohamed Al Fayed, about a conspiracy involving his business rival Tiny Rowland and an alleged £1million bung paid to a senior Conservative government minister.

The directive came from the paper's Editor in Chief Andrew Neil, who said: *"There's not a smoking gun, but things aren't as they seem and it is well worth talking to Al Fayed and looking at his evidence."*

It was an enjoyable and wholly productive three days of interviews with the gregarious and at times incomprehensible Mr Al Fayed, his PA Michael Cole and head of security John MacNamara – a former Scotland Yard senior detective.

The daily routine was purposeful: breakfast at my Islington hotel, a taxi ride across London to Knightsbridge, an escalator to Mr Al Fayed's office on the fifth floor of the Harrods department store, a coffee and croissant with Michael Cole and up to three hours of talking, tape recording, questioning and sifting through reams of documents and photographs.

On the third day, Wednesday 12th February 1997, I arrived as usual at 10am in the reception area outside the office and boardroom. I was greeted cheerily by Mr Cole. But on this morning, he asked me if I minded waiting in an anteroom for half an hour as his boss was expecting a personal visit from Princess Diana.

I was shown into the room and given the usual coffee and croissant plus copies of the day's national newspapers to browse at my leisure.

After 10 minutes waiting, I needed a quick toilet break so quietly made my way to the now familiar private washroom.

Upon my return to my isolated coffee and partly eaten croissant, I stopped suddenly as the most recognisable woman in the world walked by, accompanied by Mr Cole and an as yet unknown to me young Middle Eastern man.

Diana turned briefly and smiled at me. It was a memorable brief encounter which remained fused in my consciousness.

Later that day, I caught my return train to Edinburgh and *The Scotsman* offices at North Bridge. Upon my arrival I was introduced to our new editor Martin Clarke, who had taken up his position while I was away in London.

My first meeting with him was also memorable, but for very different reasons.

I was brusquely told that our investigation into the conspiracy surrounding Tiny Rowland had been spiked. I was also told I was *"wasting my and the newspaper's time"*, not to ask any more questions and to *"get on with some proper reporting"*. I returned to my office, relayed the news to my colleague Stephen and grumbled into my coffee with a few choice expletives.

The months passed, and on 31st August 1997, two events coincided: it was my final day working for *The Scotsman* and the same day Princess Diana, 36, her lover (Mohamed Al Fayed's son)

Dodi Fayed, 42, and their driver Henri Paul were killed in a car crash in the Pont de l'Alma road tunnel in Paris.

My reaction to the deaths at the time was immediate, and the same as it is today: they were murdered.

And it wasn't long after the tragic crash that rumours began to surface around the world that dark intentions were behind the couple's fatal car crash.

French officials concluded that the couple's driver, Henri Paul, was at fault for the crash. According to reports, Paul was impaired by drugs and alcohol and was driving at nearly twice the speed limit when he lost control of the Mercedes car in the tunnel.

But others, most notably Mohamed Al Fayed, believed that Diana was murdered. Rumours persisted that she was killed for being an embarrassment to the Royal family and Al Fayed famously claimed that the death was a conspiracy involving British secret services and the CIA.

And to add oil to the fire, well before her death Diana believed she was going to be killed by the British Establishment. Chief among the evidence to support this claim is a private letter that was disclosed by Paul Burrell, Diana's one time butler, who said he had been given it for safekeeping.

Part of the letter read: *"I am sitting here at my desk today in October, longing for someone to hug me and encourage me to keep strong and hold my head high. This particular phase in my life is the most dangerous. [...] is planning 'an accident' in my car, brake failure and serious head injury in order to make the path clear for Charles to marry."*

The letter appears eerily prescient. And, indeed, it had history: when Diana wrote the letter, she had experienced mechanical problems with her car, had voiced fears about them. An earlier bodyguard had died in an accident that she believed had been a conspiracy.

Diana clearly had concerns about her safety, but there appears to be no official suggestion that she would actually be killed.

Mohamed Al Fayed later claimed that a plot to kill Diana was kicked into high gear as soon as British authorities found out from the CIA that Dodi had picked out a £173,000 star-shaped diamond ring for his future bride.

"The only reason my son and Diana were in Paris that night was so that he could personally collect the ring and he propose to her," he said.

"I spoke to Dodi and he was so excited and happy. Diana was too. They deserved a lifetime's love together, and this beautiful ring was to put a seal on that," he added.

"Diana believed all her married life that she was under surveillance by British and foreign intelligence agencies who reported back to her husband Prince Charles and the British Establishment," said Laurie Mayer, Mr Al Fayed's press spokesman.

"She had every reason to think they intercepted her phone calls. The call she made to Lucia on the afternoon of her death could have alerted them she really was going to marry Dodi and that he, a practising Muslim and the son of a man who helped bring down the British government, would be stepfather to Prince William and Prince Harry."

And at a time when Roman Catholics, let alone Muslims, were barred from the top echelons of the British monarchy, this type of relationship which would permanently link an Islamic family to the future King of England may have been a step too far.

Plus, if they married any children they might have (the step siblings of the future king) would be Muslim, which would create an unprecedented constitutional scandal.

As well as this, Mohamed Al Fayed had been engaged in a long battle with successive British governments over their refusal to grant him a British passport. Seeing his son married to the mother of the future King would have been a remarkable personal triumph and a corresponding slap in the face for the Royals.

It was a game of Royal Roulette that the Establishment was not prepared to play.

Mr Al Fayed meanwhile wanted - and got - files on two photographers, a Frenchman and a Dutchman who were present on the night of the fatal crash.

"These men know what went on that evening," said John MacNamara.

"They filmed the motorbike we know was blocking the exit road, forcing the Mercedes to take the tunnel. That could show the license plate of that bike and another one we believe shot into the tunnel behind the white Fiat Uno.

"The Fiat Uno was waiting at the mouth of the tunnel. There was a collision and since then the bikes and the Fiat have vanished.

"Immediately after the crash, the photographers sent their pictures round the world. Some of those wired to an agency in North London had vital frames showing the vehicles we cannot now trace.

"The agency was broken into just hours after the crash and neither we, nor the police, believe it was an ordinary burglary.

"Many photographs, which show Diana lying in the rear seat of the Mercedes, one arm flung across Dodi and her legs buckled up under, have been seen across the world. But none has shown the bikes or the car."

It was one of far too many unanswered questions over the death of the People's Princess.

But it was only 10 years later at a judicial inquest, following a three-year inquiry into their deaths and possible murder, that my own brief encounter in February 1997 came back to haunt me.

The inquest, under Lord Justice Scott Baker, heard on at least six occasions that at the time of his romance with Diana in the summer of 1997, Dodi Fayed was engaged to an American model, Kelly Fisher.

The inquiry also heard heart surgeon Hasnat Khan give his first detailed account of his two-year relationship with Diana, during which he says he often stayed at Kensington Palace and met the princess's sons. He described how Diana broke up with him after she got back from a holiday with Mohammed Al Fayed and his family in August that year.

It was a line followed by all UK national newspapers who repeated without question the claim that Diana and Dodi hadn't started any sort of relationship until a month before the crash.

The **Daily Mirror** reported on 31st August 1998: *"It wasn't until July 1997 that Diana and Dodi started a relationship during a luxury summer break in the south of France."*

And it went on to say: *"Princess Diana and Dodi Fayed are only believed to have become an item just weeks before they died in a horror crash on August 31, 1997.*

"The princess had endured a turbulent personal life which saw her clash with the royal family and battle bouts of severe depression.

"But, in the weeks leading up to her death, it seemed Diana had found true happiness with Dodi, the millionaire son of Harrods tycoon Mohammed Al-Fayed.

"The pair moved in similar circles and had seen each other at polo events and film premieres in London's West End.

"Diana was still reeling from her split from the surgeon Hasnat Khan when she accepted Mohamed Al-Fayed's invitation to stay at his palatial villa in St Tropez with William, 15, and Harry, 12.

"Throughout the late summer, a care-free Diana was pictured relaxing with then 42-year-old Dodi, who had reportedly broke off his engagement with an American model to be with her.

"That summer he showered her with gifts and soon the pair had embarked on a whirlwind romance.

"She was pictured lounging on the deck of the yacht with Dodi, kissing him, and cuddling in the warm sea and sprawled in the sun."

The inquest dismissed reports that Dodi and Diana were in a relationship prior to that summer and therefore any talk of an impending engagement in August 1997 – and possible motive for their murder - were subsequently rubbished.

The Inquest jury returned a majority verdict that Princess Diana and Dodi Al Fayed were unlawfully killed due to the gross negligence of their driver, Henri Paul, and the paparazzi.

If that is true, I am still left with the haunting question: what were Diana and Dodi doing making a close personal visit together to Mohamed Al Fayed on 12th February 1997 – a full five months before they were supposed to be *"an item"*?

Where are the missing bits? And why did the Establishment go to such lengths to paint a different narrative of the months leading up to Diana and Dodie's death?

A fellow investigative journalist may have provided a few answers.

John Morgan was a New Zealand born journalist and author and has delved deeper than anyone else into the truth about the death of Princess Diana. He wrote a series of books on the definitive in-depth research and analysis of over 10,000 files taken from the Princess Diana death inquest and the findings of *the Paget Report* – an official investigation into a possible conspiracy to murder her.

Morgan concludes that the fatal 1997 Paris crash was orchestrated by agents of the British state.

In 2005, Morgan began full-time research into the events surrounding the deaths of Diana and Dodi Al Fayed. After studying *the Paget Report* on its publication in December 2006, he was shocked by its content. He realised that the £4 million report which took three years to produce was littered with inaccuracies and poorly drawn conclusions.

His 2007 book, ***Cover-up of a Royal Murder***, was the result of his subsequent investigation into *the Paget Report*.

The Diana Inquest series of books was the result of his thorough research and investigations.

Based on the evidence heard during the inquest, his book ***The Untold Story*** revealed the minute-by-minute events that were occurring both inside and outside Diana's ambulance. It establishes precisely what led to Diana being almost dead when she finally arrived at the hospital at 2.06 am - 1 hour and 43 minutes after the crash.

He claimed there were inconsistencies in the blood samples taken, errors in identifying the body and he further said key witnesses were not allowed to give evidence at the inquest.

He alleged that tests revealed traces of prescription drugs which Mr Paul was not taking, while finding no evidence of other medication he was known to be using.

Mr Morgan told the ***Daily Express***: *"When you carefully put all the pieces of this huge complex evidential jigsaw together, you can see this is a dead person who has been framed. Were it not so serious, I would say the inquest carried out at the Royal Courts of Justice in London was a joke."*

He asked whether there were two bodies in the room at the time of the post-mortem examination.

Some photographs showed the only body tag on a wrist, other images showed the only tag on an ankle.

A conspiracy to cover up the events was in full swing.

One of the paparazzi involved, James Andanson, was found dead in a burned-out BMW with a hole in his head, in May 2000. He died after boasting to friends of having secretly taken *explosive* photos of the Paris crash scene. He had previously owned a white Fiat Uno.

Not long after his death, his photo agency, Sipa, was raided by armed masked men.

Former British intelligence officer Richard Tomlinson claims that MI6 planned and executed the *accident,* causing Henri Paul to crash by blinding him with a strobe flash gun. It replicated a version of an operation that had been originally planned for the assassination of former Serbian president Slobodan Milosevic. CCTV cameras covering the route were inexplicably turned off.

It also emerged that Paul had received a series of mysterious payments – Tomlinson suggested he was an MI6 informant and that that MI6 was monitoring Diana and Paul in the months before the *accident.*

Tomlinson had joined MI6 in 1991. He completed his training with MI6 as the best recruit on his course, being awarded the rarely given *Box 1* attribute by his instructing officers.

He then served in the SOV/OPS department, working during the closing phases of the Cold War against the Soviet Union, before being posted to Sarajevo as the MI6 representative in Bosnia during the break-up of the former Yugoslavia. His next posting was to work as an undercover officer against Iran, where he succeeded in penetrating the Iranian Intelligence Service.

But he was sacked without warning for undisclosed reasons in 1995. MI6 failed to follow British legal procedures intended to protect employees from abusive employers - giving him no written warning or reasons for the dismissal and refusing to allow him access to a Union representative.

Tomlinson disputed the reasons for, and legality of, his dismissal and attempted to take MI6 before an employment tribunal, but this was blocked by MI6 using a Public Interest Immunity Certificate.

Lacking further legal recourse, Tomlinson left the United Kingdom and pursued his arguments against MI6 publicly, publishing articles in the international press about his treatment, and began work on a book (which later became **The Big Breach**).

On returning to the UK in 1997, Tomlinson was arrested on suspicion of breaking the Official Secrets Act by giving a four-page synopsis of his proposed book to an Australian publisher. Unusually, for someone with no prior criminal record, and for a non-violent offence, Tomlinson was remanded in custody at HMP Belmarsh as a Category A prisoner - normally reserved only for dangerous offenders.

When it was announced that the trial would be held in a High Court, meaning that Tomlinson would be held on remand for up to two years, longer than any likely sentence, he pleaded guilty to breaking the Official Secrets Act.

Tomlinson, who was not allowed to call any witnesses in his defence, was given a 12-month custodial sentence. He served six months in Belmarsh before being released early for good behaviour on 1st May 1998.

Since 1998, foreign police services, including those of Switzerland, Germany, Italy, France and Monaco have all arrested and detained him at the request of MI6, but he has not been subsequently charged with any offence. It was clear as daylight that this brilliant former intelligence agent had become a thorn in the side of the British Establishment, who would discredit anything he might say.

On completion of his three months probationary licence on 31st August 1998, Tomlinson left the UK to live in exile. He set about completing *The Big Breach*, which was published in 2001 in Russia.

Tomlinson has since alleged that there exists a secret paramilitary unit called *The Increment* which carries out covert operations on behalf of the British government. He claims that operators are selected from the *"cream of the crop"* of the SAS and SBS, and work on Security Service and Secret Intelligence Service supervised missions. The author Chris Ryan used the term in the title of his 2004 novel *The Increment.*

Recent revelations have shown that there are rogue elements in the British Secret Service who act as more or less autonomous cells. Former Labour Home Secretary Jack Straw claimed they once tried to destabilise the 1970s Labour government. It is not inconceivable that the same agents who believed John Lennon was capable of leading revolution also believed Diana was capable of fomenting popular unrest.

Many also believe that MI5 was behind the leaking of the so-called *Squidgygate* phone tapping tapes of Diana's private conversations which were designed to damage her public image during the marital break-up with Prince Charles.

A couple who witnessed the aftermath of the Paris crash say it was *"no accident"*. Robin and Jack Firestone told a UK newspaper that they were on their way to their hotel in the back of a taxi when they drove into the Pont de L'Alma tunnel just minutes after the collision.

They claim they still live in fear for their lives after reporting seeing two dark and mysterious cars which had stopped at the front of the Princess's Mercedes S280. But it was only the next morning they realised the woman inside the Mercedes was Diana.

The property owners found a French police officer to report the mysterious cars they'd spotted. Robin said: *"We went up to him and I said "listen we were in the tunnel last night and we need to talk to the police because there are things that we saw.*

"Without hesitation, he said they have enough witnesses. Don't worry about it.

"We were dumbfounded. One of the most famous women in the world is killed and they don't want to speak to witnesses."

Despite being eyewitnesses, they claim they were stopped from giving evidence by French authorities and then the British, because their testimony was so controversial. They were not even called to the first inquest which took place in London in January 2007.

In September 1999, French Judge Herve Stephan had thrown out charges of manslaughter against nine photographers and a press motorcyclist, saying that drugs and alcohol taken by driver Henri Paul, as well as excessive speed, caused the deaths.

The couple met with Fayed's legal team in New York, who then presented their statement to Lord Justice Scott Baker, who was chairing the inquest.

However, Robin claims it was clear neither the English nor the French wanted to listen to her testimony.

Robin said: *"We still live in fear today because of what we saw and what we were told.*

"I do not think Diana's death was an accident, and the action of the authorities makes me believe that to this day more than ever.

"The whole crash was an Establishment thing," she added.

Robin and Jack say they believe *"something bad"* could happen to them in a bid to silence their testimony.

Meanwhile, Mohamed Al Fayed said of John Morgan's investigations: *"I believe that John Morgan has done more to expose the facts of this case than the police in France and Britain.*

"He has shown how vital evidence was suppressed or simply hidden from the jury, how witnesses were either not heard at all or not asked the right questions and how the so-called investigators were more interested in covering up what really happened than honestly delving for the truth.

"The fact that he carried out his epic work at a time when he is in very poor health is nothing less than heroic. I salute John Morgan and I thank him. He has performed a service to anyone in the world who cared and continues to care about Princess Diana and my son."

Highly respected British lawyer Michael Mansfield, QC, who served as the main barrister for Mohamed al Fayed throughout the six months of the Diana inquest in 2007-08 said of Morgan: *"I have read all of the books that John Morgan has produced.*

"During the inquests ... I referred to the books that he had then published. Others have come out since. All of John's books are packed with the most incredible detail and the most careful analysis. He picks up the points that other authors have missed. He reaches compelling conclusions and offers telling comments.

"I have no doubt that the volumes written by John Morgan will come to be regarded as the 'Magnum Opus' on the crash in the tunnel that resulted in the unlawful killing of Diana, Princess of Wales and Dodi Al Fayed and the cover-up that followed."

And Sue Reid, Investigations Editor at the **Daily Mail** stated: *"John Morgan's books lift the lid on the biggest scandal of our age. His perceptive forensic analysis of Princess Diana's death reveal an orchestrated cover up by the British Establishment, including powerful members of the judiciary, police, Labour government politicians and intelligence services.*

"He shows that it was not a car accident caused by a drunken chauffeur that killed the Royal icon: Diana was murdered in a clever plot to stop her marrying the playboy son of a Muslim shopkeeper.

"As mother of William, the future King and head of the Church of England, she had to be stopped. And Morgan shows us how they did it, and then tried to hide the truth from the world - until he came along."

John Morgan died in 2015. His work is a true cornerstone of investigative journalism, and full acknowledgement must also be made to the testimonies of Richard Tomlinson.

But we still have far too many unanswered questions over the death of the *People's Princess* to accept that it was just an *accident*.

Chapter Seven
Inside the Fourth Estate

The treachery of the Fourth Estate

THE Sun's infamous claim following the 1992 General Election that *"It's the Sun Wot Won it"* is widely known.

After all, in almost half of all General Elections since 1918, one newspaper or another has claimed to have swung the result. So, is each General Election already decided by the opinion formers within our national newspapers? And if so, who has made these decisions?

Former newspaper editor Roy Greenslade says: *"Sadly, one key question not asked of people interviewed by the opinion pollsters, is: who are their prime news providers It would be fascinating to know whether they read a daily national newspaper and, if so, which title."*

It is easy to see without looking too far that most of our press supports the Tory government, whether it is led by David Cameron, Theresa May or Boris Johnson and they also backed Brexit.

The big sellers, for example, all backed the Leave campaign and in doing so defined the future of politics in the UK for the foreseeable future.

The Daily Mail (2019 circulation: 1,136,247) has been a rabid right-wing rag since it supported Hitler and Oswald Moseley's Black Shirts back in the 1930s.

Since the EU sceptic argument began to surface in the late 1980s, it consistently urged Britons to *"Believe in Britain"* and vote to leave the EU.

In 2016, **The Sun** (2019 circulation: 1,223,771) told readers to *"Beleave in Britain"* and back Brexit, arguing that a vote to Leave would allow voters to *"reclaim our country"*.

Its stablemate **The Sunday Times** (2019 circulation: 665,618) also wanted Britain to leave, and in 2019, along with its daily sister title **The Times** *(circulation 376,975)* backed the Conservatives in the General Election campaign.

Similar right-wing newspapers: **The Daily Express** (2019 circulation: 302,690), **The Daily Telegraph** (2019 circulation: 308,015), and **The Sunday Telegraph** (2019 circulation: 246,797), all supported a long-standing crusade to *"Get Britain out of Europe"*. And supported a right-wing Hard Brexit agenda to boot.

Only the more left-wing British press backed the Remain campaign - **The Guardian** (2019 circulation: 128,492), **The Observer** (2019 circulation 160,068) and **The Daily Mirror** (2019 circulation: 463,256).

They also back Labour in most General Elections but were lukewarm to then leader Jeremy Corbyn and sometimes hostile to his alternative policies.

So, who is making these General Election opinion-forming decisions, and why?

Almost 80% of our press is owned by a handful of mostly foreign-based billionaires. And the political position of a paper is set by its owner. Our press barons wield far more power and influence than all but a very few MPs and have, unsurprisingly, used it to further their own interests.

The Sun, Sun on Sunday, The Times and **Sunday Times** are all owned by Rupert Murdoch, a US-based billionaire who owns 24.9% of the British press and has supported the Tories since 2010, after a brief cosy-toes with Tony Blair and his New Labour/Tory brand.

Journalist Anthony Hilton once asked Murdoch why he opposed the European Union. He replied: *"That's easy, when I go into Downing Street they do what I say; when I go to Brussels they take no notice."*

Small wonder that David Cameron, George Osborne and latterly Theresa May and Boris Johnson are the first invitees to his Park Lane cocktail parties.

The Daily Express, **Sunday Express** and **Star** newspapers are owned by billionaire pornographer Richard Desmond who has also supported the Tories since 2010.

"Richard Desmond was furious when, after a decade of greasing palms in Labour and the Tories, both decided not to grant him either a knighthood or a peerage," says media pundit Gavin Haynes.

The fallout from that colossal sulk was partly why he ended up giving a million pounds to UKIP just before the 2015 General Election. But with May, followed by Johnson in charge, he reverted back to the Conservatives.

The Daily Mail, **Mail on Sunday**, the **i** and **Metro** are all owned by Jonathan Harmsworth Viscount Rothermere (owner of 27.3% of the British press) who lives in France and is non-domiciled for tax reasons.

He too is a strong supporter of the Tories. Lord Rothermere is usually hands-off, preferring to let editor Paul Dacre run things, in his own cavalier way – remember his vicious attack on Ed Miliband's late father, during the 2015 General Election.

The Daily Telegraph and **Sunday Telegraph** are owned by reclusive property billionaires David and Frederick Barclay – former close friends of Margaret Thatcher – who live on a private island near Sark.

The Barclay brothers certainly have enough experience in electoral manipulation. In 2008, the 600 people who live on Sark voted against the Barclays' chosen candidates for the island's governing council. As a result, the Barclays sacked vast numbers of workers at the hotels on Sark they owned.

At the time of writing this chapter, the Barclays, now both aged 87, and who until recently were paying former Conservative Prime Minister Boris Johnson £250,000 a year for producing one article a week, are negotiating to sell their interest in the *Telegraph* stable.

As Bob Dylan once wrote: *"Money doesn't talk, it swears"* and it is those filthy rich billionaires who own our press who pull the strings of the decision formers in our society.

Now in the third decade of the 21st century, we are witnessing a complete bankruptcy of freedom within our Fourth Estate. And within that bankruptcy comes the manipulation of the electorate.

For the uninitiated, the Fourth Estate commonly refers to the news media, especially print journalism or *"the press"*.

Thomas Carlyle attributed the origin of the term to Edmund Burke, who used it in a parliamentary debate in 1787 on the opening up of press reporting of the House of Commons.

The Fourth Estate was a civil watchdog to keep an eye on those in power, and provided the philosophical argument for defining the public citizenry and the nation-state as two separate entities with differing interests. But this position has now been hijacked by big business ownership of our media and the aforementioned media moguls.

If we accept the premise of the Fourth Estate, we also have to ask ourselves if the *national* and the *public* interest are the same thing.

In today's world, both are divided along class lines.

In this context, the national interest is about state secrecy and keeping things from us. On the other hand, the public interest is about disclosure and our right to know.

For instance, if we look at who trained and funded the ISIS terrorists and which countries now sustain them to carry out attacks such as those on Paris and Beirut, the press has not been forthcoming in its reporting.

Instead, it focuses on Muslims, refugees, border controls and divisions within the Labour Party.

This separation between the people and the state becomes more important when the economic interests of the powerful so frequently dominate society.

Today, the state is the executive branch of the ruling class and its big business paymasters.

Our newspapers like to paint their own role as heroic – they are the brave defenders of democracy who hold our elected representatives to account. But too often, far from protecting our democracy, our papers subvert it.

Editorial independence is a sham. Proprietors choose editors who they know share their views.

Likewise, the mechanisms through which owners can, and do, interfere with or shape content to promote particular viewpoints are not difficult to identify; they range from directly dictating the line a newspaper should follow on particular issues, to appointing senior staff with a shared political outlook, as well as forms of indirect influence over the ethos of the organisation which may prompt journalists to engage in 'self-censorship'.

The Fourth Estate is now more powerful than ever, but it is no longer the once heralded *"civil watchdog to keep an eye on those in power".*

t is now fake news and spin to maintain the status quo and the power of the super-rich.

Trust has broken down threefold, between people and politicians, media and people, journalists and politicians, with the latter two now observing each other with deep distrust and mutual antipathy.

A vicious circle has established itself under the nod of all powerful billionaires

And there are only a few things in life I really hate more than the rest and one of them is **The Daily Mail**. In my opinion it is a poisonous rag which cloaks itself in the clothes of middle-class decency while demeaning everything which is good.

As a journalist, I find its pretense at factual reporting frightening. Its so-called news reeks of innuendo and loaded propaganda. And its agenda is unwavering: preserve Conservative Britain from the rabid threat of Marxism, the Labour Party, Comrade Corbyn, trade unions and working people.

Men of power and influence: the media moguls Lord Rothermere, Rupert Murdoch and Richard Desmond

The Daily Mail has a casual attitude towards the truth which it pretends to be both seeking; such as the way that minorities which don't fit within its own norms and values are ridiculed and made to feel as though they're personally to blame for their lot; how it randomly chooses which causes to back and which to dump; the way in which *outsiders,* such as recent immigrants are demonised and assaulted and how on the biggest issues, which can only be discussed, debated and voted upon in a calm manner, it routinely sensationalises and gives the loudest voice to those who, for one reason or another, are seeking the most extreme response.

None of the above though come close to when the press is at its most intrusive, insensitive and unthinking - when someone in a position of authority or fame suddenly either dies or is seriously injured, especially if it's through their own hand, journalists (although technically it's their editors who should get the blame) at large suddenly decide that it's a wonderful opportunity to delve into their past for either demons or affairs.

My own dealings with the *Mail* as a journalist were rather more obscure.

I take you back to 1997. I was at the pinnacle of my career working as the Chief Investigative Reporter for *The Scotsman*... a Scottish national broadsheet daily, based in Edinburgh. A whole world away from *The Daily Mail.*

In three years, I had broken a series of major exclusive national investigations. Many of these are written up in this book. I had also been honoured with two back-to-back awards as *Scottish Journalist of the Year* and was in line for a third.

I loved my job and the collegiate atmosphere I worked in. I honestly believed I would spend the rest of my working life at North Bridge, with no aspirations other than to continue in my role.

But all that changed when in December 1996, our independently owned newspaper was surprisingly bought out by the aforementioned property billionaires, the Barclay Brothers. With the new owners came a new Editor in Chief, the infamous Andrew Neil. There was a corporate intake of breath as we all wondered for the future of the paper and our jobs.

That intake turned into something approaching apoplectic choking when our much-loved editor, Jim Seaton, was placed on *'gardening leave'* awaiting an enforced early retirement, and a new editor Martin Clarke was announced. We all winced... Clarke was well-known. He had trained under Paul Dacre at *The Daily Mail* and had a reputation as a *"Rottweiler"* in the newsroom.

Clarke's editorial demeanour attracted a range of tributes from former colleagues: *vile, offensive, appalling, obsessive, childlike* and *foul-mouthed* being among the less flattering.

Like Dacre, whose briefings were called *"the vagina monologues"* for their reliance on one particular expletive, Clarke went one better.

"He would start by saying, "You're all a fucking disgrace and one of you is going to be fucking sacked this week," and the terrible thing was, one of us usually was," said Alexandra Blair, *The Times* educational correspondent, who worked for him for a year and a half at *The Scotsman*.

Another reporter who worked under Clarke said: *"He once said to me: "You've got to go and shout at the bastards or they won't respect you."*

My stay under Clarke's editorship was brief... just six months.

I moved on after being told to follow his loaded agenda, which included one weird instruction to prove that wild deer being pursued by hounds are *"no more stressed than a cow in a slaughterhouse"*! This was done in his own mind to *rubbish* a ban on deer coursing proposed by the Labour government.

The final straw came in a bleak week, which began by Clarke blanking me at a press awards lunch after I had been highly commended as *Scottish Reporter of the Year* and finished by him standing over me at 10pm on a fourth rewrite of a story, berating my journalism as *"fucking bollocks"*.

Let me introduce a clipping of a piece written shortly after my departure, by **Guardian** journalist Rob Brown in June 1997:

"Senior writers and sub-editors now find themselves being showered with expletives by their new editor Martin Clarke, whose lexicon of abuse is fairly extensive.

"Several executives have resigned in disgust. They included the picture editor Paul Dodds, who quit after being ordered to get better pictures from his "f***in' monkeys".

"Also out is associate editor Lesley Riddoch, who suddenly found her articles being repeatedly spiked.

"One of the journalists who has quit in disgust said: "I have worked for some brutal editors in my time, but Martin Clarke behaves like a feudal squire and treats his staff like serfs. Change was certainly needed at The Scotsman, but not this. He is running amok, creating a totally demoralised and demotivated staff."

"Clarke, 32, says the complaints are emanating from only a couple of "malcontents". Some people, he says, are driven by "personal pique because they never got a job they wanted". Nic Outterside, head of the paper's investigative unit, left last week. Clarke says the unit was disbanded because it was "a crock of shit".

"Others, according to Clarke, have become "malcontents" simply because they cannot stand the new pace in the newsroom.

"I demand a greater level of working than perhaps some people are used to here and I can be robust at times, like all editors," he says.

"Clarke confirms that he drew up a five-and-a-half page document a few weeks after he took charge recommending that a number of senior Scotsman staffers should be removed from their posts. This operation review leaked from

the editor's office into the newsroom, where it was seen as a sinister hit list. Clarke admits to some regrets about that.

"Of course, it was bloody unfortunate, but you don't expect to work in a place where such illegal activities take place. It was stolen from my computer. I've worked in some pretty rough newspapers, but nowhere where people are that underhand."

Clarke was, for many years, tipped to succeed Paul Dacre as the next editor of **The Daily Mail**.

The art of being underhand is surely what the **Mail** is all about.

But what of the so-called impartial and publicly funded BBC?

Soon after Jeremy Corbyn's election as leader of the Labour Party in September 2015, the BBC was accused of an *'anti Corbyn bias'* and challenged with a 61,000 strong petition demanding that they stop using the prefix *'left-wing'* when reporting on events related to his leadership.

Even before he won a stunning 59.5% of the vote, ensuring the largest democratic mandate of any Labour leader in modern history, Mr Corbyn was subject to what a source from his leadership campaign described as a *'complete hatchet job'*.

Former BBC political editor Nick Robinson even wrote to his colleagues over concerns about the Corporation's bias against Mr Corbyn, and Channel 4's Michael Crick issued a stunning rebuke to broadcasters referring to non-left MPs as *moderates*.

Despite these protestations the BBC's agenda did not change.

In Janaury 2016, Mr Corbyn's so-called *'revenge reshuffle'* led to the revelation that BBC political editor Laura Kuenssberg, **Daily Politics** presenter Andrew Neil and Labour MP Stephen Doughty planned his live resignation from the shadow cabinet on their programme.

Despite the fact that a live on-air resignation could be considered dramatic broadcasting, it beggars belief how it is the job of the BBC's political editor to be of service to an evidently resentful shadow cabinet member intent on weakening the Labour leadership.

Then that evening the producer of the programme bizarrely admitted in a BBC blog – quickly deleted – that Neil, Kuenssberg and himself manipulated the news to negatively impact Mr Corbyn during Prime Minister's Questions (PMQs).

In the blog, the producer – Andrew Alexander – admitted that the BBC team were not just reporting the day's news but trying to influence it:

"This was a story where we could make an impact," he wrote.

"We knew his resignation just before PMQs would be a dramatic moment with big political impact. We took a moment to watch the story ripple out across news outlets and social media. Within minutes we heard David Cameron refer to the resignation during his exchanges with Jeremy Corbyn."

As a fellow journalist I find this admission shocking, but also symptomatic of degraded and politically biased journalism.

BBC News forms a major department of the Corporation, and for years has received complaints of bias in favour of the conservative Establishment.

The commentator Mehdi Hasan in the **New Statesman** pointed out the right-wing backgrounds of many BBC presenters and journalists.

Guardian columnist Owen Jones is also of the opinion that the BBC is biased towards the right, owing to numerous key posts being filled by Conservatives.

A study by Cardiff University academics, funded by the BBC Trust, and published in August 2013, examined the BBC's coverage of a broad range of issues. One of the findings was the dominance of party-political sources. In coverage of immigration, the EU and religion, these accounted for 49.4% of all source appearances in 2007 and 54.8% in 2012.

The data also showed that the Conservative Party received significantly more airtime than the Labour Party.

In 2012, Conservative leader David Cameron outnumbered Labour leader Ed Miliband in appearances by a factor of nearly four to one (53 to 15), while Conservative cabinet members and ministers outnumbered their Labour counterparts also by more than four to one (67 to 15).

Former Director General of the BBC, Greg Dyke, has criticised the BBC as part of a *"Westminster conspiracy"* to maintain the British political system.

The intellectuals of the 18th and 19th centuries who gave us the conception of the *Fourth Estate* as a civil watchdog to keep an eye on those in power, also provided the philosophical argument for defining the public citizenry and the nation-state as two separate entities with differing interests.

The *Fourth Estate* must be called to account when overstepping the bounds of what citizens will support, or when taking actions that are clearly not in our interests.

In his inquiry into press intrusion, Lord Leveson quoted some lines from Tom Stoppard's *Night and Day:*

Milne: "No matter how imperfect things are, if you've got a free press everything is correctable, and without it everything is concealable."

Ruth: "I'm with you on the free press. It's the newspapers I can't stand."

In a free press, the nature of the newspapers matters very much.

Newspapers exercise power and influence in many ways. And one of their most powerful forms of influence is the ability to effectively set the political agenda for the other media and more widely, in parliament, the workplace, the home and the pub.

Newspapers put great store by the concept of editorial independence. Sometimes, it is a reality. The Lebedevs, for example, own papers – **The Independent** and the **Evening Standard** – which take markedly different political stances.

Too often, however, editorial independence is a sham.

Proprietors choose editors who they know share their views.

Rupert Murdoch's candour at the Leveson Inquiry was revealing. He said that if someone wanted to know his opinion on a subject they should just read the leader in the **Sun**.

That most newspaper owners should seek to define the political stance taken by their publications is not especially surprising. Newspapers are rarely profitable and it is therefore difficult to avoid the conclusion that the press barons are in newspapers for power, influence and easy access to the establishment.

Likewise, the mechanisms through which owners can, and do, interfere with or shape content to promote particular viewpoints are not difficult to identify; they range from directly dictating the line a newspaper should follow on particular issues, to appointing senior staff with a shared political outlook, as well as forms of indirect influence over the ethos of the organisation which may prompt journalists to engage in 'self-censorship'.

The Fourth Estate is now more powerful than ever and is shaped by two dominating principles - sensationalism and oversimplification, the consequences of hyper commercialisation. It has led to ever fiercer ratings and circulation wars, which inevitably leads to what is called *"dumbing down"*. To succeed, the media industry tries to appeal to the lower instincts of people.

One has to face an unpalatable reality: Rupert Murdoch's media outlets are giving the people what they want - fun, games and entertainment – which in some ways is more democratic than the cultural elites, who tried imposing their values and standards on the masses.

In the democratic age news and information have been transformed. The way politics is covered has changed radically.

Papers don't report news, they present it according to their preferences and prejudices. The growth of columnists has led to the birth of a commentariat.

This contains a few excellent and analytical minds, but all too often, reasonable, balanced voices are drowned out by journalists who seem untainted by facts or deeper knowledge but replace this with gleefully presented prejudices.

A lot of modern political journalism ignores context and complexity, presenting everything in black and white, while the nature of politics most of the time is a balancing act between contradictory interests and demands.

News has thus become more superficial and sensational. The need for images and pictures is greater than ever. Note how the single photograph of a dead Syrian child on a Mediterranean beach in 2017 shaped the Western view. For a short time our newspapers referred to the hapless refugees by the correct terms rather than the *"swarms of migrants"* favoured by David Cameron and Nigel Farage.

Sensationalism and oversimplification are affecting the output of all media. There is less room for a balanced approach, for analysis, instead of going for the crass headline or extraordinary story.

The merciless hunt for weaknesses and inconsistencies of politicians and other public figures has become prevalent.

All this has contributed to changing democratic politics for the worse. The electorate has become hostile and distrustful of the media and politicians alike. The chances of the public receiving the information they need to participate in democracy is declining even more.

Democracy and civil society need informed citizens, otherwise they will have difficulties in surviving. Without a free Fourth Estate, aware of its own power and responsibility, an informed citizenship cannot be sustained.

What our democracies have got today is an electorate which is highly informed about entertainment, consumer goods and celebrities, while being uninterested in and deeply cynical about politics, equipped with short attention spans and a growing tendency to demand instant gratification.

The Fourth Estate is now more powerful than ever, but it is no longer the once heralded *"civil watchdog to keep an eye on those in power"*.

A vicious circle has established itself as the deepest and most sinister conspiracy in Western society.

- **Appendix G**

Chapter Eight
Depleted Lives

A Depleted Uranium artillery shell being test fired at Dundrennan

MY biggest investigation all began in September 1992, when as a newly ensconced chief reporter at the *Galloway Gazette* – a weekly newspaper in South West Scotland - I began investigating a report into high levels of radiation in the local waters of the Solway Firth.

At the time, the worrying measurements of Caesium 137 and Americium 241 – a decay product of Plutonium – were ascribed to radioactive waste from the Sellafield Nuclear Reprocessing Plant across the Solway Firth in Cumbria.

Over the winter of 1992-1993 I ran a small campaign in our newspaper to investigate these high levels of radioactivity in the sea water.

Then in February 1993, I suddenly stumbled across a report to Dumfries and Galloway Regional Council which claimed that the radiation from Sellafield could be responsible for *excess* incidences of leukaemia in our local area.

The report by medical consultant Dr James Chalmers said radiation exposure was of *"particular concern"* to people in the region, because of the proximity of Sellafield and a nuclear power station at Chapelcross, near Dumfries.

"The main conclusion is that there appears to be a higher-than-expected incidence of acute leukaemia in Dumfries and Galloway," he said.

"And some areas have markedly higher than expected incidences. These include areas where there is concern about high exposure to radiation – Kirkcudbright and Chapelcross. In some places recorded incidences are twice the expected level for those areas."

While the local Conservative MP Ian Lang gave public assurances that the *"levels of radiation on the Galloway coast pose no threat to public health",* both the regional council and the four district councils demanded a closer investigation.

Like a terrier with a bone, my journalistic mind kicked in, and I could smell an investigation into what the truth really was.

By the end of the month, nuclear experts and spokespeople for Friends of the Earth and Greenpeace claimed that both BNFL (the operators of Sellafield) and the government were *"covering up"* the true levels of radiation and the risks to public health.

Dr Patrick Green – who had conducted detailed research for Friends of the Earth – said the government testing of critical groups of local fish eaters had underplayed the levels of radiation uptake by more than half.

By April 1993, Alex Smith, the Labour Euro MP for South West Scotland called on Ian Lang (who was also the Secretary of State for Scotland) to speak out about the contamination from Sellafield.

My own campaign into shedding light on the radiation threat to the Galloway coast rumbled throughout the spring and summer of 1993, and by August it was receiving attention from local radio and Scottish national newspapers.

But nothing prepared me for what was to happen next.

Galloway resident Teresa Spurling, who was worried about the radiation levels in the sands at Cumstoun, near Kirkcudbright, was one of many who contacted me, and became a key contact over the following year.

Teresa, who had lost her four-year-old daughter Alix with a rare combination of cancers 16 months earlier, was campaigning vigorously for more attention to be paid to the high levels of radiation in the area where her daughter once played. She pointed accusingly at the contamination from Sellafield but also at the test firing of Depleted Uranium (DU) artillery shells into the sea from the Ministry of Defence (MoD) base at Dundrennan – some eight miles from her home.

"I have come to know so many children who have cancer along this stretch of coast," she said, before showing me a list of local children who had died from cancer within the previous eight years.

The list included an 11-year-old girl from nearby Kirkcudbright, an eight-year-old from the same town, a three-year-old from Newton Stewart and a two-year-old who died from leukaemia.

"When Alix was ill one doctor said she may have ingested a particle of uranium… it can't all be coincidence," added Teresa.

My senses were heightened. I hadn't realised that there was a MoD base at Dundrennan, and what the hell were they doing firing radioactive shells into the local coastal waters?

Quickly my campaign into a link between radioactive contamination of our coastline and cancer clusters took on a new dimension as I gradually managed to expose years of test firing of these DU shells into the Solway Firth and their link to local cancer clusters – particularly childhood leukaemia.

Public anger over what was perceived as a government cover-up of the test firing grew by the week and fuelled dozens of questions in the House of Commons plus reports by the national press and the BBC's Panorama TV programme.

In late October the MoD invited me and other journalists to visit the Dundrennan firing range.

In an effort to placate the feral press we were briefed by smartly uniformed senior ranks that the DU shells posed no threat to health and everything was *"above board"*.

But this sugar-coated PR attempt backfired in the afternoon when at a public briefing by Tory Secretary of State for Defence Jonathan Aitken and his PPS Stephen Milligan, the public concern and blame was wholly turned on the *"local press"* (me). Mr Aitken said we were spinning lies and: *"No-one should believe the reports from this backwoods gutter press"*.

Campaign for inquiry into cancer gains force

HIGH incidences of leuk-
aemia and childhood
cancers are prompting calls
for a full inquiry into a possible link with radioactive
contamination of the Gal-
loway coast.

A two-month long Gazette
investigation has revealed
worrying statistics and a number of bereaved parents who
blame their children's deaths
on the highest levels of coastal
radiation in the country.

With official figures showing
incidences of acute leukaemia
double the expected rate and numerous cases of childhood cancer
near recognised nuclear hotspots
at Kirkcudbright and Wigtown
Bay, the momentum for an independent inquiry is gaining ground.

Grounds for concern are supported by the Scottish Office
Health Journal of May 1987 which
states that the cancer clusters in
Dumfries and Galloway are "not
by chance".

Scottish Office statistics show
the region has one of the highest
rates of leukaemia in Scotland
with a standardised registration
ratio (SRR) of 106 — 17 points
higher than Lanarkshire and a
staggering 21 points higher than
Argyll.

In January this year the chief
medical officer's report for Dumfries and Galloway Health Board
revealed much "higher than
expected" levels of leukaemia
across the region.

The report's author, Dr James
Chalmers, charted a 15-year period
between 1975 and 1990 and studied 13 cases of leukaemia in the
Newton Stewart postcode area, set
against an expected rate of 8.28,
and a further 12 in the Gatehouse/
Castle Douglas area against 7.59
expected cases.

Incidents in Thornhill and postcode areas close to Chapelcross
were double the expected number.

This week Dr Angela Thomas
of the United Kingdom Children's
Cancer Support Group (UKCCSG)
in Edinburgh said the figures concerned her.

She was particularly worried by
the generally high trend of leukaemia cases throughout the whole
region.

"These are very high," she
stated.

"Averaging the rates of observed
cases against expected cases you
would expect an average of one"

By NIC OUTTERSIDE

Dr Chalmers' average ratio for the
15 postcode areas is 1.6.

"You have to question that the
expectation rate was too low, or
there is another factor at work"
she added.

Local anti-nuke campaigner
Dan Kenny claims the statistics
mask an even greater incidence of
leukaemia than is admitted.

As official breakdowns of leukaemia registrations for the 0-24 age
group in postcode area DG7.3
showed four cases between 1968
and 1984 but no cases between
1985 and 1990.

"Just from local knowledge I
know there are more than six cases
in those years," he says.

"Are they not even aware of the
tragic case of Jennifer Hamilton,
born 1987 and died of leukaemia
1989?"

The Gazette also discovered
another 13-year-old victim from
Bridge of Dee who died during the
same period of time.

Last week the region's health
council discussed Dr Chalmers'
report and concurred that "further
work ought to be undertaken" to
establish the cause of the "incidents".

In 1984 the Black Report, which
looked at leukaemia clusters
around Sellafield, concluded,
"Radiation is the only environmental cause of leukaemia, within
the limits of present knowledge".

Nuclear expert Jack Cade
added, "Children are most vulner-
able to radiation so are good
indicators of the effects of
radiation in the community".

Ruth Hiddlestone of Princes
Street, Kirkcudbright, is convinced
that the lymphoma which killed
her six-year-old son Brian in 1985
was caused by "something in the
atmosphere or water".

"I feel strongly that something
is being hidden and I will not rest
until I find out," she said. "We
need some sort of inquiry."

Stewartry housewife Kerry Hut-
chinson, whose son Fraser (8) died
in April this year of Neuroblas-
toma, questioned his doctor on the
likely cause of the cancer.

"He was diagnosed four years
earlier, shortly after Chernobyl,
and I asked if it was to blame," she
said.

"But the doctor just said
nothing . . . I would still like to

find out what caused it and the
radiation worries me."

Teresa Sparling, who lost her
daughter Alix with a rare combination of cancers just 16 months
ago, has campaigned vigorously
for more attention to be paid to
the high level of radiation in the
sands at Commoire where her
daughter used to play.

Teresa is now engaged full-time
in raising money for a children's
hospice for the region, but she is
also determined that her daughter's death and those of many
other children should not pass
unnoticed.

She points accusingly at the
local area poisoned by radioactive
contamination from Sellafield,
Chernobyl, and the firing of depleted uranium shells at the MoD
base at Dundrennan.

"I have come to know so many
children who have cancer along
this stretch of coast," she said.

"When Alix was ill one doctor
said she may have ingested a particle of plutonium or uranium —
it all can't be coincidence," she
adds.

Teresa showed the Gazette a list
of local children who have died of
cancers within the last eight years.

The list includes an 11-year-old
girl from Kirkcudbright who died
last month, an eight-year-old from
the same town who died in 1989,
a three-year-old Newton Stewart
boy who died in 1990, a two-year-
old who died of leukaemia in 1989,
and many more.

The Gazette spoke to many
parents — time and again fingers
pointed to the high levels of radioactive contamination caused by
discharges from Sellafield.

But the radiation matrix is con-
fused by the Chernobyl accident of
1986.

One inland area on the Machars
peninsula — between Sorbie and
Whithorn — experienced one of
the highest known levels of Chernobyl contamination in Britain.

Radioactivity shortly after the
accident is estimated to have
reached 95 per cent of the level at
which sales of local milk should be
banned.

In September 1992 the Gazette
revealed that Wigtownshire has the
highest level of radioactive sea
water on the west coast of Scotland.

In November a leaked report of
an independent study by the nuclear industry showed that radioactive pollution in rivers in south-

Continued on page 8

One of my early reports into childhood cancer

Ironically in 1999, the same Jonathan Aitken was jailed for 18
months for perjury and lying about his arms dealing with Saudi
Arabia. Stephen Milligan was found dead in his London flat in 1994,
naked except for a pair of stockings and suspenders, with an

113

electrical flex tied around his neck and a black bin liner over his head, with an orange in his mouth.

Like something out of *Drop the Dead Donkey*, you really couldn't make it up!

My newspaper campaign accelerated in the New Year when a report for the magazine **Red Act** revealed that 10 per cent of US servicemen who served in the Gulf War had qualified for disability compensation after suffering medical symptoms attributed to exposure to Depleted Uranium (DU) tank and artillery shells. More than 1,600 American Gulf veterans had also died from similar symptoms.

The report stated: *"Of 600,000 American soldiers sent to the Middle East to confront Saddam Hussein, more than 54,000 have qualified for disability compensation."*

Their symptoms included chronic fatigue, skin rashes, eye and ear infections, bleeding gums, facial paralysis, headaches, memory loss, muscle and joint pains, liver problems and cancer.

The report also referred to the MoD base at Dundrennan, where it said an estimated 4,000 DU shells had been fired into the Solway Firth.

It concluded: *"The MoD plans to develop and fire new DU shells there, which will increase local toxic and radioactive contamination."*

The report *Depleted Uranium, Sick Soldiers and Dead Children* came just two weeks after a parliamentary statement by Defence Minister Jeremy Hanley confirmed that sizeable stocks of DU shells were held at the Dundrennan firing range.

"On 15th December 1993, 111 DU rounds were held at the Dundrennan range in anticipation of a number of trials," he said. His statement completely contradicted an earlier parliamentary answer by Mr Aitken, who in June 1993 had said there were no stocks of Depleted Uranium shells at Dundrennan, *"nor any future arisings expected"*.

But I was in for another shock… but this time a pleasant one!

Suddenly, and without any warning, I was given two national press awards for my work into the DU shell firings – the first was a *Judges' Special Award for Investigative Journalism* – the first time this award had ever been given.

Then a few days later I was informed that 53 MPs had signed an Early Day Motion (EDM) in the House of Commons praising my investigation (and that of Angus McLeod, a dear and late colleague at the **Sunday Mail**) into the link between DU shell firing and the serious risks to health – including cancer.

The EDM read: *"That this House congratulates Nic Outterside, chief reporter of the Galloway Gazette, for his special award of the year 'for his investigative journalism and individual tenacity', and Angus Macleod of the Sunday Mail, for his 'talent for disclosing stories in an aggressive and attacking writing style' in winning the journalist and reporter of the year award in the Scottish Press Awards made on 26th April; notes that both reporters revealed the hidden dangers of Depleted Uranium shell tests at Ministry of Defence test ranges, and unveiled the links between vapourised Depleted Uranium dust and the Gulf War or Desert Storm syndrome; believes these Scottish reporters have properly publicised a problem of national and international importance as recognised by investigations in the United States Congress and the United Nations Compensation Committee; and reiterates its call for an urgent public inquiry."*

It was like a personal shield of honour, and a vindication of 18 months of time-consuming investigations.

In June 1994, I moved to **The Scotsman** in Edinburgh for career advancement and thought I had left my investigations into the Dundrennan cover-up behind.

But the story did not die, and at the time of writing this book in 2022, it is still ongoing.

Scientific studies since 1994 showed that exposure to Depleted Uranium definitely leads to cancers, birth defects, memory loss, damage to the immune system and some neuro-psychotic disorders.

Yet, the MoD still steadfastly claimed since the first Gulf War that: *"DU does not pose a risk to health or the environment"*.

But this claim was undone when in 2004 it was revealed that the British Army told soldiers in Iraq that exposure to depleted uranium CAN cause ill-health. An MoD card handed to troops on active service in the second Gulf War, in 2003-2005, read: *"You have been deployed to a theatre where Depleted Uranium (DU) munitions have been used. DU is a weakly radioactive heavy metal which has the potential to cause ill-*

health. You may have been exposed to dust containing DU during your deployment.

"You are eligible for a urine test to measure uranium. If you wish to know more about having this test, you should consult your unit medical officer on return to your home base. Your medical officer can provide information about the health effects of DU."

Meanwhile, a UN sub-commission ruled that the use of Depleted Uranium ammunition breaches the Geneva Convention and the Genocide Convention.

Depleted Uranium has also been blamed for the effects of Gulf War Syndrome among some 200,000 US troops. It has led to birth defects in the children of veterans and Iraqis and is believed to be the cause of the *"worrying number"* of anophthalmos cases – babies born without eyes – in Iraq. A study of veterans showed 67% had children with severe illnesses, missing eyes, blood infections, respiratory problems and fused fingers.

Professor Doug Rokke, the ex-director of the Pentagon's DU project and a former US Army colonel who was tasked by the US defence department to deal with DU after the first Gulf War, said: *"The MoD card acknowledges the risks. It contradicts the position it has taken publicly – that there was no risk – in order to sustain the use of DU rounds and avoid liability."*

Dr Rokke attacked the US and UK for *"contaminating the world"* with Depleted Uranium munitions and said the issuing of the card meant that they had *"a moral obligation to provide care for all those affected"* and to clean up the environment in Iraq.

"DU is in residential areas in Iraq, troops are going by sites contaminated with it with no protective clothing or respiratory protection, and kids are playing in the same areas."

Dr Rokke said that the use of DU in Iraq should be deemed a war crime: *"This war was about weapons of mass destruction, but the US and UK were the only people using WMD – in the form of DU shells."*

Ray Bristow, trustee of the UK's National Gulf Veterans and Families Association, said the MoD card *"confirms what independent scientists have said for years"*. Mr Bristow suffered from chromosomal abnormalities and conditions similar to those who survived the nuclear bomb in Hiroshima.

Receiving the Judges' Award for Investigative Journalism in 1994

A former warrant officer in the medical corps in the first Gulf War, he was only able to walk short distances with a walking frame and often has to use a wheelchair.

"While the card may have been issued to British troops we have to ask, 'what about the Iraqi people?' They are living among DU contamination. And what about the people in Dundrennan?" he said.

"The MoD line has always been that DU is safe – it has been caught out in a lie."

Mr Bristow said some 29,000 British troops could be contaminated. He was found to have uranium in his system more than 100 times the safe limit. *"I put on a uniform because I believe in democracy and freedom,"* he said. *"Now I can't believe a word my government says."*

Chris Ballance, the Green MSP for the south of Scotland added: *"DU is a weapon of mass destruction that must be banned."* He said the MoD must remove the shells that had been fired into the Solway Firth and tell the people of Dundrennan about the risks.

Malcolm Hooper, emeritus professor of medicinal chemistry at Sunderland University and an expert on Depleted Uranium, said it was *"administrative deception"* for the MoD to claim DU was not a risk to health while issuing warnings to troops.

Dr Hooper described the government's behaviour as *"a dreadful experiment ... an obscenity ... and a war crime against our own troops".*

A dear friend and fellow investigative journalist Felicity Arbuthnot took the investigations into the effects of the firing of DU shells even further. She persevered with her enquiries for more than 25 years.

In 1999 she reported: *"More ordnance was rained down on Iraq during the six weeks of the Gulf War than was dropped in the whole of World War 2. Unknown to the public or the Allied troops at the time, much of it was coated with Depleted Uranium.*

"This nuclear waste has replaced titanium as a cheap coating for weapons which can pierce armour. It burns on contact, producing a fine dust which can be ingested and inhaled and which enters the food chain via water and soil.

Such radioactivity only begins to diminish after 4,500 million years.

"In 1990 the UK's Atomic Energy Authority sent a report to the British government, estimating that if 50 tonnes were left in the Gulf area should there be a war, then these would lead to an estimated 50,000 extra cancer deaths in a decade. Experts now estimate that there may be 900 tonnes remaining, travelling where the wind blows.

"By early 1992, doctors in Iraq were bewildered by the rise in birth deformities -- some so grotesque and unusual that they expected to see them only in textbooks and perhaps once or twice in a lifetime. They compared them to those recorded in the Pacific islands after the nuclear testing in the 1950s. Cancers too were rising, especially amongst the young; the most susceptible to radiation.

"It was not until 1993 that the fact that DU had been used in the Gulf War began to emerge.

"In Iraq, children were (and are) collecting fragments of bullets or missiles as a way of coming to terms with the war. They bring them home or take them to school for display.

"Professor Seigwart Horst Guenther, scientist, founder of the American Yellow Cross and Director of the Albert Schweitzer Institute, collected one such bullet from Basra in southern Iraq for analysis and transported it to Germany -- correctly encased in a radiation-proof lead box. On arrival at Berlin airport he was promptly arrested for transporting radioactive material -- it had activated all the radiation sensors.

Among those soldiers returning from the Gulf War alarming symptoms appeared almost immediately. Eddie Blanche, from Newcastle upon Tyne, had been an army fitness instructor, passed *A1-fit* immediately prior to action in the Gulf.

"I ran 30 kilometres with a 15-kilo pack on my back. I went there a physical specialist and came back a physical wreck," he said wryly. He has lost the sight of one eye, can walk only for short distances - with the shortest of breath - and suffered agonising joint pains.

Felicity continued: *"In the US over one-third of the 600,000 veterans deployed in the Gulf have sought help from Veterans' Administration hospitals; in Britain 8,000 of the 29,000 troops are ill and over 400 have died.*

"A study of cancers and leukaemias among 1,400 Iraqi soldiers who had been in the heavily bombarded area around the southern town of Basra showed chilling increases; for example, ten cases of lymphomas in 1991 and 106 in 1996. Brain cancer too showed a startling rise; one case in 1991 and 40 in 1996."

Felicity kept investigating and in 2007 she reported: *"The term Gulf War Syndrome is now known world-wide – but - after the 1991 Iraq war, as formerly A1 fit soldiers fell ill with debilitating symptoms, in their thousands, the cause was, for two years, a 'mystery'.*

"It was in 1993, when a group of 24 affected soldiers approached Professor Asav Durakovic, one of the world's leading experts in the effects of radiation that a true cause came to light.

"They had many times the recognised safe level of chemically toxic and radioactive Depleted Uranium (DU) in their bodies. Duracovic, although a senior officer in the US army during the first Gulf war, had been unaware that the weapons used had contained Depleted Uranium."

Durakovic, who is also medical consultant for the Children of Chernobyl project at Hadassah University, Jerusalem, lost his job as Chief of Nuclear Medicine at the Veteran's Administration Medical Facility at Wilmington, Delaware, as a direct result of his work with Gulf war veterans contaminated with radiation.

"Two other physicians, Dr Burroughs and Dr Slingerland of Boston VA also lost their jobs when they asked for more sensitive equipment to better diagnose the soldiers referred to them by Professor Durakovic," reported Felicity.

"Oddly, all the records pertaining to the sick soldiers at the Delaware VA went missing.

"Two years before Durakovic's discovery, the United Kingdom Atomic Energy Authority (UKAEA) self-initiated a report warning the government that if 50 tonnes of the residual dust, from the explosions of the weapons on impact, was left in the region, they estimated it would generate half a million extra cancer deaths by the end of the century (2000)

"Further, the term depleted is a misnomer. These weapons are made from waste from the nuclear fuel cycle and thus contain the whole lethal nuclear cocktail. DU weapons (sold to 17 countries that are known and possibly others) are equivalent to spreading the contents of a nuclear reactor around the globe.

"And far from 50 tonnes and that chilling warning, in Iraq several thousand tonnes now cover this ancient, Biblical land and with the bombs raining daily, the audit rises nearly hour by hour.

"Even European peacekeepers on relatively short tours of duty became ill, developed leukaemias and other cancers and a number died. A five-man film crew from BBC Scotland all tested DU positive after filming for less than a week there.

*"A report in Lebanon's **Daily Star**, that Dr Khobeisi, a scientist, had measured gamma radiation in a bomb crater at Khiam in the south of the country, at 10 to 20 times higher than naturally occurring background radiation, was alarming.*

"The following month, Dai Williams, an independent researcher went to Lebanon on behalf of Green Audit, to investigate and bring back samples to the UK for testing. He also brought back an air filter from an ambulance. Tested at the Harwell UKAEA laboratory: "The results were astonishing."

"Both soil and filter contained enriched uranium with the soil sample containing uranium about nine times higher than the natural background.

120

"The soil sample was also sent to the School of Ocean Sciences, at Bangor University in North Wales for a second test by a different method for certainty. The results were the same.

"Williams returned to Lebanon and brought back soil and water samples from Khiam and other sites. Enriched uranium was found in water samples from two separate craters in Khiam and in one of the soil samples.

"And since it is in the ambulance air filter, it is also in the lungs of the inhabitants ... the Lebanese people have been sacrificed to cancers, leukaemias, birth defects, like the people of the Balkans, Afghanistan and Iraq."

Felicity continued: *"The soaring cancers and birth defects linked to the use of DU in Iraq and wherever else they have been used – mirrored in US servicemen, women and families are chilling proof of the voracity of the warnings. DU has a half-life of 4.5 billion years. Its use condemns and curses the not yet even conceived – until the end of time."*

In 2008 the European Parliament called for a global ban on DU weapons and a moratorium on their use.

In 2013, **Science Daily** reported: *"Ten years after the Iraq war of 2003 a team of scientists based in Mosul, northern Iraq, have detected high levels of uranium contamination in soil samples at three sites in the province of Nineveh which, coupled with dramatically increasing rates of childhood cancers and birth defects at local hospitals, highlight the ongoing legacy of modern warfare to civilians in conflict zones."*

Writing in the journal **Medicine, Conflict and Survival**, scientists Dr RA Fathi link their findings with dramatic increases in cancers reported to the Mosul Cancer Registry and the Iraqi national cancer registry.

Their report *Environmental pollution by Depleted Uranium in Iraq with special reference to Mosul and possible effects on Cancer and Birth Defect Rates* begins with a literature review that collates health-related data from a range of sources, including a report by the World Health Organisation (WHO) in 2003, which states that childhood cancers - particularly leukaemia - are 10 times higher in Iraq than in other industrialised countries.

"Although there is already significant evidence of cancers and related illnesses in adults, the authors emphasise that it is the dramatic rise in the incidence of cancer and birth defects in children under 15 years of age since the second Gulf War that points to the terrible legacy of DU weaponry.

"Childhood cancers are now some five times higher than before the two Gulf Wars (currently around 22 children per 100,000, compared with approximately 4 children per 100,000 in 1990).

"Nevertheless, with the WHO predicting that global cancer levels will rise by 50 per cent between 2003 and 2020, the presence of so much carcinogenic material across Iraq suggests that the public health legacy of the two Gulf Wars is only going to get worse."

And the Depleted Uranium misinformation and cover-up agenda didn't stop there.

In 2017, US officials confirmed that the American military, despite vowing not to use Depleted Uranium weapons on the battlefield in Iraq and Syria, fired thousands of rounds of the munitions during two high-profile raids on oil trucks in Islamic State-controlled Syria in late 2015.

The air assaults marked the first officially confirmed use of this armament since the 2003 Iraq invasion, when it was used hundreds of thousands of times, setting off outrage among local communities, which alleged that its toxic material caused cancer and birth defects.

US Central Command spokesman Major Josh Jacques confirmed that 5,265 armour-piercing 30 mm rounds containing Depleted Uranium were shot from Air Force A-10 fixed-wing aircraft on 16th November and 22nd November 2015, destroying about 350 vehicles in the country's eastern desert.

Earlier in the campaign, both coalition and US officials said the ammunition had not and would not be used in anti-Islamic State operations.

In March 2015, coalition spokesman John Moore said: *"US and coalition aircraft have not been and will not be using Depleted Uranium munitions in Iraq or Syria during Operation Inherent Resolve."*

Later that month, a Pentagon representative told *War is Boring* that A-10s deployed in the region would not have access to armour-piercing ammunition containing DU because the Islamic State didn't possess the tanks it is designed to penetrate.

As the Jonathan Aitken perjury trial might have said: *"There are lies and damned lies."*

Chapter Nine
Death is Not the End

The late and much-loved John Bauldie

I NEVER thought for one minute that a life-long obsession with music legend Bob Dylan would collide head on with my 30-year career as an investigative journalist.
But it did… in the most unexpected way imaginable.

It is a story of a common love, friendship, a sudden and tragic death and an ongoing murder conspiracy; a conspiracy which may touch the highest levels of British society.

My love of Bob Dylan has spanned more than 40 years.

But it was back in 1987-1988, while I was hospitalised in Cardiff with cancer, that a new world of *His Bobness* was unexpectedly opened to me. And with it an equally unexpected friendship.

To while away the hours and weeks of radiotherapy, my mother bought me a copy of Robert Shelton's definitive Dylan biography **No Direction Home**. I consumed the book in a couple of days. And while meandering through the appendices I noted mention of a quarterly Bob Dylan fan magazine, simply titled *The Telegraph*.

With an annual subscription of just £10, including delivery, I wrote off and subscribed to the magazine instantly. And so began the expansion of my world of Bob Dylan and an enduring friendship with the magazine's editor John Bauldie.

John was an ebullient personality, sometimes sounding dour with his native Lancashire drawl, but always enthused by anything to do with Bob Dylan and his hometown football team Bolton Wanderers.

And as a fellow journalist, we automatically had a lot in common and became friends.

John was one of the world's foremost authorities on Dylan's music. He wrote several key books on him as well as since 1981 editing and publishing the superb *The Telegraph*.

Yet there was nobody less like the stereotyped *anorak* than John. A former lecturer in English literature, he was a dapper and cultured man, who brought a well-rounded intelligence to his quest. With his inimitable blend of scholarship and devotion, he elevated the narrow world of music fanzines to a different realm.

A friend and fellow author of books about Bob Dylan, the American journalist Paul Williams, rated John's efforts as: *"Scholarship in the best possible sense. He amassed an extraordinary trove of responsible information. It was of such a high level of intellectual quality, information naturally gravitated to it."*

John's vocation was to amass the data and win for his hero the serious appraisal that is due to an outstanding writer and performer.

He only met Bob Dylan once, and that was by accident. Following the 1986 US tour, he was passing the singer's tour bus when Dylan sauntered out. The two men held a brief and genial conversation, in the course of which John won a much-prized endorsement for his magazine.*The Telegraph*. Bob murmured, *"I seen a few issues of that. It's pretty interesting."*

That was all the recognition that John ever required.

Then in 1987 – coinciding with our first contact - he left his teaching days behind him and joined the small editorial team at the newly-launched **Q** music magazine as its sole sub-editor.

Meanwhile, I quickly became a regular contributor to *The Telegraph* and would often engage in long telephone conversations with John at his home in Romford, swapping his immense knowledge of Dylan with my suggestions for magazine lay-out and typography.

He seemed like a god to me and was always the first person I turned to for tickets to Dylan gigs – usually within an hour after he broke the news of the great man's next tour.

John also loved to travel with his longstanding partner, Penny Garner, and would invariably plan his year around Dylan's interminable tour itineraries.

He always cut a memorable figure at those gigs. You'd spot him, immaculately turned-out in his camel-hair coat as he shared his insights with fellow fans over a glass of wine, his educated Lancashire twang rising above the noise of those who hung on his every word.

And it was wholly due to John that I joined him on a flight to Brussels in the summer of 1989 to follow Bob Dylan around Europe, and witness one of Dylan's greatest gigs at the Statenhal in Den Haag in the Netherlands.

When I moved to Scotland in late 1990 to begin a full-time job as a newspaper editor, our telephone conversations became less frequent, but we still had time to meet for a chat before Dylan's two gigs at Glasgow's SECC in February 1991.

And my quarterly copy of *The Telegraph* still arrived promptly every three months.

So, it was in utter shock and disbelief when I discovered that John, aged just 47, had been killed in a seemingly freak helicopter crash in Cheshire. It was the same crash which took the lives of

Chelsea FC's multi-millionaire vice chairman Matthew Harding and three other people on 22nd October 1996.

Harding had given John a lift in his private helicopter to watch his first love, Bolton Wanderers, defeat Chelsea in a Coca-Cola Cup tie at Burnden Park.

Ironically, it was their mutual love of Bob Dylan which first brought John and Matthew Harding together.

Already a passionate fan of the club, Harding joined the Chelsea board in 1994 and he made available millions of pounds towards the construction of the first new stand at Stamford Bridge in over 20 years. The new North Stand was renamed after Harding immediately after his death and it bears that name to this day. He is still regarded as a Blues' legend.

John Bauldie was also widely loved and hugely respected.

His close friend David Dingle wrote after the crash: *"John's great love of all things was reflected by the friends and colleagues who spoke, and the music that was played at the funeral at Mortlake Crematorium attended by several hundred people.*

"All the speakers in reflecting John's life bought not only tears of sadness to our eyes, but also tears of laughter in recalling the character that he was. On the morning of the 23rd October when the news of the accident reached me, I was preparing to attend another funeral, and when the priest spoke of how one's life is measured by the effect you have on those you leave behind, I couldn't help but think how much we've all been affected by his achievements and his presence."

Respected photographer Andrea Orlandi added: *"John was a sweet and very talented gentleman, to whom so many owe so much in terms of renovating their love for Dylan and his work.*

"His writing was always so good, intense, personal, cute and gave me every time strong feelings and new perspective. I had the honour to know him personally: I enjoyed talking to him as much as reading him, if not more."

Some months later after the crash I wrote to John's widow Penny, expressing my condolences and deep sadness at his death.

Penny replied almost immediately, and I have treasured her hand written letter for the past 25 years.

And there my grief and memory of John Bauldie should have remained.

But in 2016 – exactly 20 years after his death - my investigative senses were stimulated by a chance meeting and conversation with another Dylan fanatic at record fair in my local town. He told me that Penny had died destitute a few years after John's tragic death, and both their deaths were not as they might seem.

My investigative senses raced and we chatted for a further 15 minutes.

I was spurred to know more; after all John was a guy I loved and respected for many years.

On arriving home, I quickly found online a copy of the official report into the helicopter crash which took John's life.

The report said that the pilot of the twin-engined French Aerospatiale AS 355F1 Squirrel had neither the qualifications nor experience to control the aircraft after it got into difficulties.

Michael Goss, 38, had gone off route on the night of the crash and headed for an area of high ground in near Middlewich in Cheshire which a weather forecaster had advised him to avoid.

The report said that upon taking off from Bolton after the match, the flight had to operate below an overcast cloud layer which was beneath the minimum safe en-route altitude.

At the inquest into the crash the jury heard a tape-recording on which Mr Goss, who had drifted off course, asked air traffic control for permission to climb to 3,000 feet before requesting a bearing straight to Manchester Airport.

He was given permission to climb and was then asked what bearings he wanted for an ILS (instrument landing).

The pilot's last words were: *"Yeah, I'm looking for vectors for an ILS ... I think I'm in a descent at the moment ... hold on."* The aircraft is believed to have crashed moments later.

In 1998, Penny issued a writ for negligence against Michael Goss, and Bristol-based Polo Aviation, under whose licence Captain Goss was flying.

Mechanical failure was ruled out as a cause for the accident by air investigators. It was thought that Mr Goss crashed after becoming disorientated in low cloud and fog at night.

However, claims contained in the High Court documents compiled by Penny's solicitors suggested that the passenger door was not shut properly on take-off and slid open during the doomed flight.

Penny also claimed that the pilot was not licensed for commercial flights, he was suffering from fatigue and the helicopter was overloaded. Her action sadly came to nothing.

But my further inquiries uncovered allegations that Matthew Harding and his fellow passengers died, not because of an incompetent helicopter pilot, but because of their knowledge of police and local council corruption in property development schemes within the London Borough of Havering. And it was the friendship between Harding, John Bauldie and his partner Penny which may explain a conspiracy surrounding their deaths.

Penny Garner was a Biology lecturer at Havering College of Further and Higher Education – not far from her and John's home in Romford. She prepared her students for their A-levels and future careers in Medicine, Dentistry, Pharmacy and Industry.

During the mid-1990s, Penny witnessed criminal issues at the college, created in a failed attempt to close the educational institution for property development.

A Deep Throat source emailed me to say: "Penny struggled with these issues not least due to the wayward management of a faculty head who failed to deal with a member of staff who had illegally purchased a machine gun with live ammunition on college premises.

The machine gun was then fired on college grounds with a resulting flood of calls to Havering police.

The college had a large number of students from Irish backgrounds, and with the Northern Ireland troubles still flaring many feared there might be links to IRA terrorism.

But witnesses later swore that a Conservative councillor had encouraged the sale of the machine gun at the college, via a party intermediary resident in Lake Rise, Romford.

The gun was later resold, by a science technician in Penny's faculty who was encouraged by a well-known local Tory involved in the property development plans.

There were further allegations that their friends in the local police had full knowledge of this campaign and were turning a blind eye. Penny made John aware of these events.

THE TELEGRAPH

PO Box 307, Richmond, Surrey TW10 5AQ

Dear Nic,

Thanks for your letter. John and I lived together for over twenty years we had no children but were very happy together

I have enclosed T.54.55. T56 should be available soon I will then post that to you

Best.

Penny

Penny's brief letter to me following John's death

John and his editorship of **The Telegraph** was meanwhile being investigated in an attempt to find *"dirt"* against those opposing the closure of the college for property development.

The conspiracy to silence Penny and John from saying too much was far-reaching.

The corruption involved was such that the attempt to close the college was stopped for fear of official enquiries into the conduct of the Romford, Hornchurch and Upminster Conservative Parties and associates in the local police station.

Shortly before his death, John told Matthew Harding about the events at the college. Matthew took a keen interest to find out more and promised to look into the matter.

Harding also had a political axe to grind as he disliked the Conservative Party and had recently donated funds to Tony Blair and New Labour.

But the conspiracy got even deeper…

In 2014, it came to light that murdered BBC *Crimewatch* host Jill Dando had been probing the death of Matthew Harding and his four friends. As most people reading this will know, Ms Dando was gunned down on her doorstep in Fulham, south-west London, in April 1999.

The killer has yet to be caught, but much evidence points to MI5 and political corruption at the highest level.

A source claimed Harding first told a friend, Irish investigative journalist Veronica Guerin, about his fears about corruption and money laundering over property developments and criminal activity in football. A few weeks later, in June 1996, the 37-year-old Guerin was gunned down while working on a drugs inquiry. She was shot six times whilst stopped at traffic lights in Dublin.

A panicked Harding then repeated his concerns to Ms Dando.

He died just four months later.

My source added: *"Jill told me she had begun investigating Matthew's death and the concerns he had shared with her.*

"Somebody tried to warn her off, but she persisted in her inquiries."

But then I found an article written by a former colleague and award-winning investigative journalist Don Hale… a reporter I know personally and whose judgement I trust.

Don claimed that Jill Dando was investigating the death of Matthew Harding amid allegations of money laundering and match-fixing.

And the helicopter crash which killed the Chelsea millionaire and John Bauldie occurred just months after he raised concerns about crime and corruption in British football.

A source quoted in Don's article, and a close friend of Dando, believes she was the victim of a professional hitman hired to halt the football investigation.

The whistle-blower, a former BBC employee living in the East Midlands, decided to speak out after claims that Serbian assassins targeted Dando because of the TV appeal she fronted for refugees.

It had been suggested that the killing was revenge for the bombing of a television station in Belgrade owned by Serbian commander Slobodan Milosevic's family, in which 16 people died.

But my source said this was absolute rubbish.

"This Serbian claim is a red herring," she said. *"Jill told me she was investigating the death of her friend Matthew Harding and money laundering claims. She was killed after ignoring two warnings to back off."*

Match-fixing is a lucrative business, especially in the Far East where crime cartels influence results.

In 2010, Europol announced that it had found evidence of match-fixing of some top international football games after conducting the biggest-ever investigation into the crime in Europe.

Europol's Soren Kragh Pedersen said: *"When we look around Europe it is practically everywhere and in some of the major leagues but, of course, also the minor divisions. We see it everywhere so it would be a surprise if you did not find it in England also."*

Indeed, in November and December 2013 several individuals were arrested by the National Crime Agency (NCA) on suspicion of fixing English Association football matches.

The arrests occurred as a result of two separate newspaper investigations, by the **Daily Telegraph** and the **Sun on Sunday**, as well as information supplied by the European online gambling watchdog FederBet.

On 17th June 2014, a jury at Birmingham Crown Court found Michael Boateng, Krishna Sanjey Ganeshan and Chann Sankaran guilty of conspiracy to commit bribery, while Hakeem Adelakun was cleared of the offence. Sankaran and Ganeshan were later sentenced to five years in prison, with Boeteng given an 18-month sentence.

Don Hale went on to write:

"Dando was shot dead on her doorstep in Gowan Avenue, Fulham, in April 1999. She was murdered within 20 seconds of leaving her car, killed by a single shot to her head at very close range.

"Police initially believed it had the hallmarks of a professional killing but were later persuaded by a crime analyst that it was probably the work of a local man with obsessive tendencies.

"Barry George, a part-time stuntman who had lived in Walsall in the early 1980s, roughly fitted such a description. He was arrested, quizzed and eventually convicted of Dando's murder in July 2001.

"But he was acquitted in August 2008 after doubt was cast on gunshot residue evidence. He is set to take a million-pound compensation claim to the European Court of Human Rights.

"George's sister Michelle Bates, who campaigned for his release, said: "Obviously we don't know who killed Jill but I am pleased the murder is being looked at again.

"I believe the authorities knew it wasn't Barry all the time. He was just a scapegoat."

"When I visited George in Whitemoor Prison in October 2002 - the first journalist ever allowed to interview him in this high security environment - he told me he believed the murder was an underworld killing.

"Despite being behind bars, he was terrified of being killed. He told me he was very concerned for his own safety. "I never shot Jill," he said. "I keep telling them that somebody in the underworld was responsible but they don't want to know.

"There are whispers through the prison grapevine that she was nosing around in something she shouldn't have been and was taken care of."

John O'Connor, the former head of the Flying Squad is convinced Dando was the victim of a contract killing. *"All my instincts tell me this was a professional hit from a gunman brought in specifically to do the job,"* he said.

Don went on to say: *"Barry George had nothing to do with it. Scotland Yard had a fixation about him. This was the work of a trained killer. He used a custom-built weapon.*

"Jill was shot in a residential area with a single bullet that had a deliberate half-charge to deaden and muffle the sound when fired.

"O'Connor believes Ms Dando had been under surveillance before she was executed.

"It was probably two men and one watched as she left her fiance's home," said O'Connor. *"I believe that whoever was responsible had Jill under*

surveillance. She was supposedly going straight back to Gowan Avenue but got diverted with some shopping, and was late getting back."

"The TV star's neighbour Richard Hughes told police he heard a brief and sudden cry - but no gunshot. He said it was only about 20 seconds or so after she zapped her car alarm before he heard the latch of her gate as the assailant closed it behind him.

"Cops now believe it was even quicker.

"A photo-fit showed a suspect with a Mediterranean appearance, white, and well-dressed with long dark hair.

"Barry George's defence barrister Michael Mansfield QC also believes Dando was the victim of a hitman, saying it was carefully planned and executed. All my instincts tell me this was a hit from a gunman brought in to do the job."

In 2008, the conviction against Barry George was quashed on a retrial at the Old Bailey.

As an investigative journalist that left too many loose ends to believe that the helicopter crash in 1996 was just due to pilot negligence.

Then suddenly in 2019 I received an email out of the blue from a former biology student of Penny Garner at Havering College of FHE.

The man, who I will only refer to as David, told me more background to the planning conspiracy at the college and the involvement of local criminals and the Conservative Party.

"I witnessed some background on the crime and corruption in the London Borough of Havering which affected Penny and her partner John Bauldie," he said. *"I suspect that John told Matthew Harding about these issues."*

He went on to explain: *"There was a group of Irish Catholic families at the centre of a long series of criminal and corruption incidents in London Borough of Havering.*

"They all attended St Patricks Catholic Primary School next to Corpus Christi Church in Lowshoe Lane, Collier Row and later they all attended Chase Cross Comprehensive School, Romford (now renamed Bower Park Academy).

"As well as being criminals in their own right and having access to guns, they went on to join the local Conservative Party and were behind a number of "criminal fixes" in the closure of publicly owned properties for lucrative property development.

"The best-known public property closures involved such activity included closure of Romford Borough FC stadium Brooklands, the Job Centre at 61 Main Road, Romford, and the attempted closure of Havering College of FHE.

"In addition to these sites of obvious interest to property developers this criminal cabal also purchased hundreds of sold-off council flats and housing with inside information giving them time to make the first bid to the council tenant before public knowledge of the sales were allowed.

"The football stadium and Havering College were both targeted for a campaign of orchestrated criminality involving firearms, drugs, gang fights, sexual harassment, theft, vehicle sabotage with intent to cause death or injury, and malicious rumour spreading.

"One of the "problem" Catholic families had an arms cache stored in their home. "The arms and explosives were redistributed to their supporting friends of the Corpus Christi Catholic community. The machine gun sold to Havering College Physics technician Peter was test-fired on college premises causing a flood of calls to police which they ignored

"Despite my numerous reports to Romford Police Station about these events no action was ever taken."

David alleges that by campaigning to raise awareness about the criminal activities in the area he has made some high ranking enemies including Lord Lieutenants, Police Commanders, local politicians and a now deceased police Detective Inspector.

The conspiracy surrounding the deaths of John Bauldie and Matthew Harding still remains unsolved, and with Penny Garner also dead, the case seems closed.

But as someone once said: *"This can of worms only opens from the inside"* and there are still many people out there who know the truth.

- **Appendix H**

Chapter Ten
What Lies Beneath

Munitions being dumped into Beaufort's Dyke sometime in the late 1940s

SOME newspaper investigations are short-lived, others have a limited time-scale, while some take on a life of their own and run like a dog with eight legs.

And so it was for me on 12th September 1995, when a seemingly innocuous discovery quickly took over six months of my life and ended with a score of front page exclusives, a government inquiry, international attention and two major press awards.

On that day, thanks to a trusted contact in Westminster, I discovered the existence of an underwater trench in the sea channel between Galloway and Northern Ireland. A few people knew of this trench – known as Beaufort's Dyke – but generally it was not discussed. I discovered it had been used to covertly dump thousands of tonnes of the deadly Sarin gas, sealed in corroding drums at the end of World War 2.

The Beaufort's Dyke trench, which lies between the Rhins of Galloway and Northern Ireland is more than 50 km long and 3.5 km wide. The depth of the area and proximity to the coast made it an ideal location for a munitions dumping ground. It was used to dispose of ammunition and commercial explosives regularly until 1973, with a final *"emergency"* dump of 40mm Ministry of Defence (MoD) shells in 1976.

But it was only as munitions started to be washed ashore in Ireland, the Isle of Man, Cumbria and south west Scotland that a deadly secret began to unveil itself.

Irish trawler skippers had also netted munitions boxes, *"torpedo shaped containers"* and smoking canisters while fishing in this salt water channel. But no-one knew about the drums of deadly gas!

Experts and environmentalists warned that it would only be a matter of time before some of the Sarin nerve agent could be washed ashore or trawled up by unsuspecting fishermen.

The Nazis produced at least 300,000 tonnes of the substance during the war but never used it in battle.

Inhalation of just 0.5 milligrams of Sarin can kill almost instantly. The gas reduces the level of a key enzyme needed by the nervous system, causing difficulty in breathing, a decline in blood pressure, and contraction of the pupils. Survivors could still suffer nerve, brain, and liver damage.

German scientists said Sarin, 20 times as deadly as potassium cyanide, ranks as probably the world's second most lethal chemical after a related gas called Soman.

In 1995 it was already known that more than 120,000 tonnes of chemical weapons captured from Nazi Germany were dumped by the British government at sites in the North Channel, North Atlantic, the Skagerrak and the deep channel approaches to the Western Isles between 1945 and 1956. Official documents revealed that many of the dumps used to dispose of Sarin between 1945 and 1947 were considerably shallower than the 1,000 fathoms judged to be safe by 1956.

The government remained adamant that the sites posed no threat to fish stocks or human life, despite fears raised by Irish politicians in 1986 of a link with an unusual number of birth defects.

However, Dr Rune Eriksen, a Swedish expert who sat on the Helsinki Committee for Chemical Weapons, said there had been more than 400 cases of Scandinavian fishermen trawling up pieces of solid mustard gas and other chemicals in the Baltic, where weapons were dumped by the Russians.

Many fishermen have been hospitalised and there have also been fatalities.

Dr Paul Johnston, a munitions expert at Exeter University said it would only be a matter of time before Scottish fishermen suffer that same fate.

"These weapons are still active and potentially lethal," he said, *"The drums are corroding and some may have punctured."* He said chemical changes which may have occurred make Sarin *"even more corrosive and dangerous".*

"It would be a triumph of hope over experience if there was not an accident before too long," he added.

But this was just the start of my investigation which a week later revealed more sinister details about the million tonne weapons dump less than six miles from the Scottish coast.

Previously the estimated size of the dump was 120,000 tonnes of conventional munitions. But a new disclosure came as the Ministry of Defence (MoD) began answering questions from the Irish Sea Forum, a scientific watchdog group, about the presence of bio-chemical weapons in the trench. Initially the MoD denied that any chemical or biological weapons had been dumped in Beaufort's Dyke, but later admitted to the presence of Phosgene rockets, and drums of Sarin and Tabun nerve gas.

A leaked letter from the MoD's infrastructure and logistics department stated that early disposals may not have been restricted to licensed sites marked on mariners' maps. It said: *"In total we estimate that the MoD may have disposed of over one million tonnes of conventional munitions within Beaufort's Dyke."*

The MoD admitted that although most bombs and rockets had been defused, in some cases the weapons remained live. It refused to confirm or speculate on the size of the disposal of chemical weapons in the trench. But whatever that was, the MoD admission made Beaufort's Dyke the largest single underwater munitions repository in Western Europe.

But no-one saw what would happen next. As autumn moved towards winter and in high storms, more than 4,500 incendiary bombs began to be washed up on beaches around the west coast of Scotland. They were made of phosphorus, benzene and cellulose, and were designed to ignite on contact with air.

Four-year-old Gordon Baillie picked one up while playing in his uncle's garden near Campbeltown on the Mull of Kintyre. It burnt his hand and leg.

Discovery of the first phosphorus bombs on 6th October at Saltcoats on the Firth of Clyde prompted a major clean-up operation. Every day for the following two weeks, army bomb disposal teams picked up hundreds of them along the length of the Clyde coastline, round the Mull of Kintyre and on the islands of Arran, Islay, Jura and Gigha.

Children were told to keep away from the beaches, farmers advised not to gather seaweed for fertiliser, and warning signs appeared on beaches.

This was just a tip of the problem. One Kilkeel-based trawler skipper told me: *"I am picking up bombs and ammunition all the time."* He said he did not contact the naval authorities because he feared he would be forced to leave the fishing grounds. *"We just dump the stuff back over the side and say nothing about it,"* he added.

Tom Hughes, a fisherman from Portavogie, who normally fished 10 to 15 miles north of Beaufort's Dyke, said his nets had been snagged and burned by phosphorus bombs.

Simon Jack, a Girvan-based fisherman, had experienced regular catches of phosphorus in his nets and said there was an area of sea between Beaufort's Dyke and Loch Ryan which *"bubbles and steams"* on calm days.

Patrick Stewart, the secretary of the Clyde Fisherman's Association, confirmed that many of his members had trawled up bombs and other munitions in the Firth of Clyde.

At first, the Ministry of Defence insisted that the chemical bombs had no *"UK military origin"*, and that no evidence existed that these phosphorus weapons had ever been dumped at sea.

But after a cross-party group of Scottish MPs met defence secretary, Michael Portillo, the story changed. On 2nd November, the MoD admitted that the devices had come from decayed 30 pound (13.6 kilogram) incendiary bombs of a type dropped from British aircraft in the Second World War. The implication was that the bombs had been sent for dumping in the 50 kilometre long Beaufort's Dyke, rather than hundreds of miles out in the North Atlantic as had originally been claimed.

But why would these obsolete munitions suddenly start emerging from the dump? The most likely answer was a new undersea British Gas pipeline linking Scotland and Northern Ireland, just north of Beaufort's Dyke. Its contractors began ploughing a 60 centimetre deep trench for the pipeline in the seabed just three days before the phosphorus bombs started to come ashore.

Workers I spoke to immediately blamed the ploughing operation, although this was initially denied by British Gas. *"We have no evidence connecting our operations with the appearance of these munitions,"* said a British Gas spokesman.

Scientists at the Scottish Office's Marine Laboratory in Aberdeen, however, said British Gas was wrong. They said that the crew of the barge which helped to lay the pipeline submitted official reports to the coastguard describing how they had seen objects identical to the phosphorus bombs floating in the sea.

Underwater video footage taken by British Gas's contractors and studied by the scientists also clearly showed the bombs, and a host of other metallic wastes, next to the pipeline. The precise locations and nature of the munitions disposals had been poorly documented.

According to the country's top marine scientists in Aberdeen, it was *"beyond reasonable doubt"* that the phosphorus bombs were dislodged by the ploughing operation.

They floated to the surface and were blown north into the Firth of Clyde and round the Mull of Kintyre by the prevailing winds, said the scientists.

The MoD promised to carry out a full survey, adding that as long as the material remained undisturbed 263 fathoms below the waves there was *"no cause for concern"*.

Conservative Scottish environment minister Lord Lindsay said a fisheries research vessel Clupea, would carry out the survey on behalf of the government's marine laboratory in Aberdeen, in mid-November 1995, subject to the weather.

The survey would cover:

• Sampling sea bed sediment from Beaufort's Dyke and beyond its perimeter to where the gas pipeline was being laid.

• Analysis of samples from the chartered munitions dump site to check for any environmental contamination.

• An underwater television study to check that it was safe to carry out a trawl.

• A trawl survey to check the area within the dump site and to catch commercial fish and shellfish to check for any contamination.

But within his announcement there was no mention of any checks on the stability of any of the munitions.

Dr Paul Johnson said the conventional munitions would in many cases still be active and potentially explosive and any chemical drums could corrode and leak.

George Foulkes, the Labour MP for Carrick, Cumnock and Doon Valley said there had been an *"appalling cover-up"* on Beaufort's Dyke and claimed the public was being conned by the announcement of the survey.

"From discussions I have had with scientists in Aberdeen, this is just a routine survey which has been brought forward to take the sting out of public criticism," he said.

"It is also clear that the survey will not pick up anything buried in the sediment. Yet hi-tech acoustic-based sonars and laser sonars are available from North Sea installations and the governments has chosen not to use them to keep costs down."

So, in late November the Marine Laboratory began its two-week survey of the seabed around Beaufort's Dyke to determine the distribution of the munitions.

The Fisheries Research Services (FRS), an Executive Agency of the Scottish government, was also asked to establish whether dumping had contaminated seabed sediments, fish or shellfish. Their investigations were carried out in November 1995, and between March and July 1996.

Scientists confirm that bombs came from Beaufort's Dyke

EXCLUSIVE: *Pipe-laying operation dislodged phosphorus sticks*

NIC OUTTERSIDE

MORE than 4,000 phosphorus bombs washed up on Scottish beaches two months ago came from the Beaufort's Dyke munitions dump, it has been revealed.

Scientists involved in a Government survey of the dump say it is "now beyond reasonable doubt" the bombs were dislodged by British Gas pipe-laying operations.

Earlier this year, the Ministry of Defence admitted that more

No. 47,502

than one million tons of explosive and chemical weapons had been dumped at Beaufort's Dyke, a trench in the North Channel between Stranraer and Belfast.

In October, about 4,400 highly flammable phosphorus sticks were washed on to beaches in western Scotland. It was claimed that they were disturbed by British Gas contractors who had begun ploughing a 6ft deep trench for a cross-channel pipeline in the sea bed north of the dyke.

Scientists at the Scottish Office marine laboratory in Aberdeen say that the British Gas contractors submitted reports to the Coastguard describing how they had seen objects identical to the bombs floating in the sea.

Although the report of the marine laboratory survey will not be published until next

month, *The Scotsman* can reveal that the phosphorus devices did emanate from the region of Beaufort's Dyke.

Last month, the MoD said that the devices came from decayed 30lb incendiary bombs of a type dropped by British aircraft in the Second World War. But it was suggested that they could have been dredged up from another underwater explosives dump at Birch Point, two miles east of Arran.

The Aberdeen marine laboratory report into the Birch Point dump confirms, however, that it has not been used for MoD disposals. Instead, the site has been used for the disposal of commercial explosive waste from the ICI/Nobels works at Ardeer, Ayrshire.

Tens of thousands of tons of waste "fireworks-type" explosives, detonators, explosives containing TNT, nitroglycerine,

fuses and other scrap have been dumped at Birch Point.

The report says that, between July 1945 and October 1946, the site was designated for disposal of "surplus or unserviceable" military munitions, but records show it was not used for that purpose.

It adds that in addition to Birch Point, there are five other dump areas in Scottish waters: at Loch Linnhe; in the Inner Sound of Raasay, off the Aberdeen coast; off the May Island in the Firth of Forth; and at Beaufort's Dyke.

George Foulkes, Labour MP for Carrick, Cumnock and Doon Valley, has called for a halt to all commercial activity near the dyke until a detailed survey of the area has been completed.

Last night, both British Gas and the MoD said they would not comment until the marine laboratory report is published.

One of my many reports into the dumping of dangerous munitions in Beaufort's Dyke and how the gas pipe laying was dislodging them

FRV Clupea undertook four scientific cruises during this research. An acoustic survey was undertaken using RoxAnn, and munitions were detected using specialised techniques such as side-scan sonar. Seabed Contamination Samples of the seabed sediment were analysed.

None of the samples contained the chemical warfare agents Phosgene or mustard gas, or explosive or propellant residues. There was also no indication of phosphorus, which is a component of the incendiary devices.

It was concluded that dumped munitions had not resulted in contamination of seabed sediments or of commercially exploited fish or shellfish.

Underwater television cameras, used in conjunction with high quality still photography provided information on the nature of the munitions and the debris. In addition, FRS staff collected and analysed samples of seabed sediment, fish and shellfish for signs of contamination.

The survey covered a total track of over 950 km, and confirmed that munitions were distributed over a wide area which also extended outside the boundary of the officially charted dump site.

The largest concentration of dumped munitions was found in an area located within, and adjacent to, the northeast sector of the charted disposal site. The areas containing large quantities of munitions included areas crossed by the submarine gas pipeline. The findings led to a revision of the Admiralty charts for the Beaufort's Dyke area.

The survey also confirmed what British Gas discovered by accident: that many of the munitions meant for Beaufort's Dyke never got there. Instead, they were dumped in shallow waters en-route to the dyke by ships from Stranraer and Cumbria.

"There is credible evidence that a significant amount of material never made it to the site," said one scientist from the Marine Laboratory. He believed that munitions ended up in unauthorised dumps to the north and south of the dyke and possibly in the Solway Firth. *"Out of sight, out of mind was the prime criterion at the time,"* he said.

Two seamen from Stranraer who sailed on dumping expeditions in the 1940s, John Balfour and Alfie Shingleston, said that in poor weather, the ships discharged their cargoes no more than a few hundred metres off shore.

Mr Balfour (aged 61 in 1995) worked as a civilian seaman on the Malplaky, an escort ship that would accompany landing craft loaded with munitions for dumping. He claimed that many loads were not dumped into Beaufort's Dyke. *"If they were later loading up or the weather was bad or there was a swell on, they'd get to just outside the mouth of Loch Ryan and dump it there."*

He added: *"I was young at the time, but now I think it's a scandal. After what we did back then, you may as well dump the Brent Spar there too!"*

Mr Shingleston confirmed what Mr Balfour said, adding that some munitions were dumped at Milleur Point, just a few hundred yards from the mouth of the loch.

But whether the munitions were or were not dumped in the trench could be irrelevant. Dr Chris Browitt, from the British Geological Survey in Edinburgh told me that it was a mistake to think that deep channel dumping provided a safe repository for munitions.

"Deep channels are there in the first place because of the actions of strong underwater currents on the ocean floor," he explained. *"It follows that these same currents would have an effect on anything that is dumped there."*

According to a letter sent by the MoD in June 1995 to researchers at the University of Liverpool, the MoD dispatched vast amounts of old weapons to Beaufort's Dyke.

The ministry dumped some 14,000 tonnes of 5-inch artillery rockets filled with poisonous Phosgene gas in the trench between July and October 1945. Over the following three years, it consigned 135,000 tonnes of conventional munitions there, and every year into the late 1950s another 20,000 tonnes ended up in the dyke.

By the early 1970s, the discharges had reduced to about 3,000 tonnes a year, said the MoD. *"In most cases"* the dumped munitions were defused, although some weapons may still have been live.

The MoD thinks the area of Beaufort's Dyke was also *"probably"* used before 1945, *"possibly"* as early as 1920. Disposal then may not have been confined to the site defined in 1945, it said.

David Long, a marine geologist also from the British Geological Survey in Edinburgh, said that this lethal jetsam is carried by strong south easterly currents that flow from the southern end of Beaufort's Dyke. Similarly strong currents, reaching 1.5 metres a second, flow north from the Dyke's northern end.

Beaufort's Dyke is not the only military dump off Scotland's west coast. Statements from the MoD also revealed that between 1945 and 1957 it scuttled 24 ships packed with 137,000 tonnes of chemical weapons at two sites in the Atlantic. One is 1,600 kilometres southwest of Land's End, around Hurds Deep, but the other is a large area beginning 100 kilometres northwest of Northern Ireland and southeast of Rockall Deep.

Eight of the ships are sitting at depths of less than 2,000 metres, and the shallowest is in 500 metres of water. Both sites are also home to thousands of tonnes of radioactive waste from Britain's nuclear programme.

The armed forces minister Nicholas Soames told Parliament that the material dumped in the Atlantic included 17,000 tonnes of captured German bombs filled with the nerve gas Tabun. The scientists at the Marine Laboratory in Aberdeen confirmed that Sarin, together with Phosgene, tear gas and mustard gas, had also been dumped.

The MoD has always maintained that there is no scientific evidence to suggest any significant harm to human health or the marine environment from its dumps – so long as they remain undisturbed.

"The combined effects of dilution, dispersion, hydrolysis and low temperatures act to reduce the toxic potential of munition materials," said a senior MoD official.

But a scientist from the Marine Laboratory in Aberdeen rounded on this by saying: *"There is no evidence because no one has looked for any."* He said fishermen in the Baltic, another dumping site for World War 2 chemical weapons, have been severely burnt by mustard gas. *"If canisters were raised from the seabed and leaked, they could kill fishermen,"* he warned.

Although Phosgene, Tabun and Sarin should be hydrolysed in seawater into relatively harmless by-products, mustard gas is likely to persist. It is heavier than water and comparatively insoluble, so that when it leaks it tends to form an oily layer on the seabed.

In the post-war years, the MoD chose its dumping zones partly because they were far away from commercial fisheries. Since then, however, declining populations of more easily caught species combined with advances in fishing technology have driven fishermen to further and deeper waters.

Prawns are now fished just north of Beaufort's Dyke and there is a hake fishery in the dyke itself. Farther out to sea, fishermen trawl down to 1,800 metres for deep sea species such as the Orange Roughy.

Most marine scientists agreed that comprehensive surveys of the dump sites were needed to find out precisely what is in them.

If there are any doubts about the safety of a site, government experts say the most that could be done would be to ban fishing and other underwater activities in the area.

In this case, fishing could end up being banned in most of the North Channel and Irish Sea, said Dr Paul Johnston.

This would be an unacceptable curb on fishermen. *"If the weapons are removable, they should be removed as soon as possible otherwise we will end up with a series of problems,"* he said.

The phosphorus bombs are straws in the wind, said Dr Johnston. They have come ashore first because they are so buoyant, but he predicts that there could be worse to follow. It is possible, he said, that intact Phosgene containers could separate from their rockets and wash ashore. *"The effects are inherently unpredictable,"* said Dr Johnston, *"but there is a very clear risk of personal injury."*

Michael Fellows, a former Royal Navy diver, said the weapons, jettisoned in the Irish Sea, were *"liable to go bang"*. He also believes a World War 2 wreck in the Thames estuary was *"a ticking timebomb"*, which cannot be ignored. Mr Fellows said the freighter, which was carrying munitions from the US, may threaten a liquid gas terminal due to be constructed on the coast of Kent.

Mr Fellows, who had worked for 40 years in bomb and mine clearance and was decorated for his work during the Falklands War, now heads his own munitions clearance company, Fellows International.

"Most of the weapons dumped in the Beaufort's Dyke... weren't designed to go under water," he said. *"There are sporadic explosions two or three times a month, I should think, in the Irish Sea, popping off all the time."* Asked whether the oldest munitions in the Dyke were losing their ability to withstand corrosion, Mr Fellows said: *"Yes. They are getting old and they're liable to go bang."*

A local councillor in Northern Ireland, Oliver McMullan, said it was deeply worrying that the Dyke contained Sarin and Tabun, Phosgene, mustard gas and explosives. Incendiary bombs containing phosphate used to drift onto the shore each winter, he said. *"We had hundreds upon hundreds of these things getting washed up in a matter of days,"* he added.

"Out of the water, body heat will ignite them, or the heat of the sun, and then they just explode into flames.

"There's too much stuff down there that's only breaking up now. Something needs to be done. We can't just afford to leave it for another 50 years."

Then suddenly the investigation into Beaufort's Dyke took on a whole new dimension with my next discovery.

According to documents discovered at the Public Record Office approximately two tonnes of concrete-encased metal drums, filled with nuclear laboratory rubbish and luminous radioactive paint, were dumped during the 1950s into Beaufort's Dyke.

Another leaked document revealed that along with the post-war weapons dumping, the MoD and the UK Atomic Energy Authority (UKAEA) oversaw the disposal of 74,052 tonnes of low and intermediate level nuclear waste at 15 sites over a 33-year period.

The dumping began with the MoD making a single disposal of nine tonnes of atomic waste at a site in the Bay of Biscay.

In 1951 the programme was accelerated with 83 tonnes of waste sealed in concrete lined drums sunk at Rockall Deep in the North Atlantic beside a munitions dump and a further 319 tonnes at Hurd Deep and Beaufort's Dyke.

The dumping continued until 1982, with the UKAEA taking over responsibility in 1954.

Dr John Large, a leading nuclear consultant said the various dumping programmes left a deadly cocktail on the ocean floor which amounted to *"an environmental time-bomb"*.

Dr Large said his main concern was the likely chemical reaction between the atomic waste and the munitions. *"These reactions could destabilise already unstable weapons,"* he said. *"And after 40 years it is highly likely that the build-up of hydrogen inside the nuclear waste drums would have popped them open."* He said the likelihood of a weapons explosion releasing radioactivity also had to be considered.

A week later I discovered that the details of the nuclear waste dumping programme were even more sinister. UKAEA papers showed that in 1981 at least one cargo of waste had been secretly re-routed.

A written parliamentary answer by the former Scottish secretary George Younger revealed that concrete covered nuclear waste, originally scheduled for disposal in *"a deep water well to the west of Scotland"* was dumped in Beaufort's Dyke *"because of adverse weather"*. Further documents disclosed that this cargo was either whole or part of a consignment of low and intermediate level waste from the UKAEA.

The re-routing of disposals followed the pattern established with conventional and chemical munitions 30 years earlier. The UKAEA had previously denied the diversion of any nuclear waste shipments had ever taken place.

Bernard Moffat, general secretary of the Isle of Man based Celtic League said: *"We have spent 10 years asking various government departments to "come clean" about the final destinations of munitions and nuclear cargoes.*

"It should now be urgently established how many cargoes destined for Rockall Deep were diverted to Beaufort's Dyke."

Then in late December 2015, events surrounding Beaufort's Dyke took a new and unexpected turn.

The British Geological Survey (BGS) in Edinburgh, with whom I had maintained a good personal relationship for over three years, told me that they had detected through seismic monitoring *"at least eight"* unexplained blasts in the area of Beaufort's Trench between January and August.

The BGS had ruled out earthquakes as the cause of the disturbances, although a few could be attributed to the Royal Navy deliberately exploding World War 2 mines. The rest were unexplained.

Dr Chris Browitt at the BGS said the seismic network had pinpointed to within one to two kilometres that the blasts had occurred the region of Beaufort's Dyke.

George Foulkes claimed there had been *"an appalling cover-up"*, adding: *"The fact that there has been at least eight explosions this year raises the horrific prospect of the effect even one explosion could have on a gas pipeline."*

And by a weird co-incidence, the very next day the government scientists involved in the survey of Beaufort's Dyke publicly said: *"It is now beyond reasonable doubt"* that more than 4,400 phosphorus bombs washed up on beaches just six weeks earlier had been dislodged by British Gas pipe-laying operations close to the dump site.

By the start of 1996, my investigation had revealed the true size and nature of the Beaufort's Dyke dumping area, which included:

- More than one million tonnes of conventional munitions, including thousands of 4,000lb bombs, grenades, artillery shells and torpedoes.

- 14,000 tonnes of artillery rockets filled with the blistering chemical Phosgene.

- Thousands of tonnes of phosphorus incendiary bombs.

- Hundreds of 45-gallon drums of chemical weapons, believed to be the German nerve gas Tabun.

- At least two cargoes of nuclear waste, stored in concrete lined, 45-gallon steel drums.

- The wrecks of 350 ships and boats, including at least 10 military vessels.

- An unknown quantity of commercial waste from various chemical and explosives companies.

In 2015 the Celtic League published the following appraisal:

"We first started making enquiries about the Dyke in the early 1980s. We had heard reports about munitions dumping in the 1940/50s which continued up until the late 1970s.

"Over the next 15 years we engaged in an ongoing correspondence with the MoD and other agencies and by 1996 when the UK finally 'came clean' about the extent of sea dumped munitions we had amassed quite a file.

"Indeed our file was so comprehensive that eventually a copy was sought, and given to, the Irish government Department of the Marine who throughout the late 1990s pressed the UK government on the issue. The original file is now lodged in the Manx Museum Library.

"Of course we had no idea when we started our enquiries almost 40 years ago that eventually it would be revealed that a staggering one million tonnes of munitions had been dumped and in addition to Beaufort Dyke another 22 sites around the British Isles were polluted.

"Unlike Sellafield, a visible scar, the bombs of Beaufort Dyke are out of sight many fathoms under the sea. They do however still pose a danger and will do so for many decades."

Over the ensuing years since my 1995 investigation, the gas pipeline and an electricity interconnector have been completed across the North Channel.

My original investigation became the longest running of my career. The story was picked up by every British national newspaper, broadcast media and magazine publications worldwide, including New Scientist, AWE International Magazine, the BBC and CNN.

In April 1996, I was Highly Commended for *Campaigning Journalism* in the annual Scottish Press Awards and won *Daily News Journalist of the Year* in the BT sponsored national press awards.

Chapter Eleven
Nuclear Penguin

HMS Sheffield ablaze after she was hit by Exocet missiles

NO other investigation in my 28 years as a journalist was quite as explosive as this one.

Nor was it so personally life changing.

The Falklands War of April to June 1982 was the turning point in Margaret Thatcher's premiership, indeed in her whole political career.

The previous October, the Tory party conference had been alive with dissent. The so-called *"wets"* were openly conspiring against her. Bets were being taken against Mrs T surviving into the New Year. Well behind in the polls and with the new Social Democratic Party (SDP) challenging both Labour and Conservatives, few believed Thatcher would ever lead her party to another election win.

Though spring brought some relief to the battered economy, she appeared a weak, broken leader with little support even within her party. What was later called Thatcherism was still a dream, with only top-rate tax cuts in place. The ruling obsession was reducing double-digit inflation and cutting public spending. Nothing else seemed to concern the government.

In the frontline for cuts were defence and foreign affairs. Defence Minister John Nott's defence review would pull back the surface fleet to home waters. Hong Kong was to be handed over to the Chinese and a tiny colony of islands in the south Atlantic was being negotiated for *"sale and leaseback"* to neighbouring Argentina by Thatcher's trusted junior foreign minister, Nicholas Ridley. The one naval vessel in its vicinity, HMS Endurance, was to be withdrawn.

To Argentina's military junta, the British government was patently eager to dispose of the Falklands. Thus, when Ridley's initiative was mauled in the Commons and talks stalled, the invitation to the Argentinian junta to imitate India's seizure of Goa in 1961 was irresistible. The invasion was even named Operation Goa.

Even with tension mounting, Thatcher turned a deaf ear to pleas from the Foreign Office to reinforce the islands and deploy ships to the area.

While she could hardly be held directly responsible for the Argentinian invasion, it was certainly the result of her style of a one-track approach to policy. And when the invasion occurred, on the night of 31st March, Thatcher knew she faced humiliation and possible resignation.

But overnight she came into her own. In the House of Commons the next day she was able to convert a sense of national shame into one of shared purpose. The Royal Navy put to sea within two days, amid pandemonium in Portsmouth and Plymouth.

Chancellor Sir Geoffrey Howe later recalled the war as *"like being on sabbatical."* In stark contrast to her approach to domestic affairs, Thatcher scrupulously deferred to her military commanders and supported their decisions to the hilt.

During the Task Force's voyage south, Thatcher had both to maintain pressure on the enemy and keep critics and allies satisfied that she was open to a negotiated withdrawal. But this was not easy. The US opposed the war. President Reagan had backed the Buenos Aires junta and it was only Thatcher's close relations with him that secured vital logistical support of fuel and weapons as the Task Force moved south from Ascension Island. As it approached the islands and ships began to be sunk, the US even put an aircraft carrier on standby should the venture face disaster.

She believed that only total victory would salve her reputation, and any compromise that rewarded aggression could not be tolerated. Yet she knew she had to proceed by the book. She meticulously followed UN procedure, always citing its resolutions in her speeches. When told she could not shoot down enemy civilian planes on intelligence watch, she did not do so.

Thatcher admitted in her memoirs that she fell for the military cast of mind. Soldiers did not scheme and mutter against her. They stood to attention in her presence, gave her straight advice and carried out orders without question.

Had Argentinian planes bombed supply and troop ships rather than warships, a land operation could have become logistically impossible. The Task Force's heavy lift helicopters were all lost when the Atlantic Conveyor was sunk.

The most controversial British decision, the sinking of the Argentinian cruiser, Belgrano, was at the time hardly questioned. Argentina had a battle fleet at sea, including a carrier force armed with Exocet missiles. The odds were heavily on its side. To have left its navy roaming the ocean off the islands, with planes and missiles able to pick off the Task Force, would have been extraordinary. But after the Belgrano sinking, the Argentinian carrier group retreated to port and played no part in the war.

Victory was finally achieved on 14th June, when the dejected Argentinian garrison surrendered in Port Stanley.

Thatcher's reaction was one of exhausted relief. She was drained, not least by sitting up at night writing personal letters to bereaved families. The war had been no great political gamble, because she had no option, but the military gamble was huge.

An opposed landing thousands of miles from home was dangerous, and left 255 dead.

Back home the nation rejoiced in an experience it had not enjoyed since 1945: a clear military triumph. The victory dragged Thatcher's leadership from the brink of collapse. She won global celebrity, in both the United States and the Soviet Union, and 10 points were added to her poll rating. She was at last in the lead over

Labour. The emergent Social Democrats never recovered. Thatcher wrapped herself in the flag, denouncing all sceptics and crudely boasting the renaissance of the British people as a world power against dictatorship.

She received a further boost when the Argentinian dictator, General Galtieri, was overthrown.

If war had brought out Thatcher's best features, victory brought out many of her worst, in particular intolerance of those who talked back.

But it gave her the confidence and political strength to press ahead with a programme that was otherwise inert.

The Falklands changed everything. The miners were confronted, left wing local governments crushed, Europe riled and universities humbled. Most crucial of all, the patrician Tory moderates were diluted and eventually driven from power. The now-familiar Thatcher came into her own and *"the Eighties"* began.

But it was what I discovered years later in 1996 which cast the Falklands War in a totally new light.

Not only was our prized battleship cruiser HMS Sheffield sunk while carrying nuclear depth charges, but against all international treaties to keep the South Atlantic nuclear free, Thatcher had deployed a British nuclear-armed submarine into the area.

The orders were clear: if the Argentines sunk another of our flagships, a pre-emptive nuclear strike on Cordoba was to be considered. Cordoba was a financial and industrial city of one million people in 1982. It was also the production centre for the country's military aircraft.

Just think for a minute where a pre-emptive nuclear strike might have led in 1982, at the height of the Cold War. Thatcher was prepared to risk a global Armageddon to secure her political ends.

The harsh realities of modern warfare were brought home to the British Task Force during the Falklands War when destroyer HMS Sheffield sank after being hit by an Exocet missile launched from an Argentine fighter flying beneath the fleet's radar screen. The rocket's unexpended fuel set fire to the Sheffield's plastic and aluminium fittings and the ship was engulfed by fire and poisonous black fumes.

Falklands nuclear strike plan revealed

EXCLUSIVE: *Polaris submarine was within range of Argentine bases, says new report*

NIC OUTTERSIDE
Chief Investigative Reporter

BRITAIN was prepared to use nuclear weapons if a "worst case" scenario developed during the Falklands war. A Polaris submarine was deployed within range of Argentine military bases, according to evidence obtained by *The Scotsman*.

A scientific research document to be published this month by a British government-funded agency claims the Polaris vessel would have made a pre-emptive strike in the event of the British troopship Canberra or one of the Task Force aircraft carriers being destroyed by missiles.

According to the document prepared by Professor Paul Rogers, an expert on nuclear weapons, a R-class Polaris-carrying submarine armed with up to 16 nuclear missiles was diverted to patrol an area in the mid-Atlantic.

Prof Rogers claims the likely target for a threatened or demonstration attack was Cordoba, a key military base in northern Argentina.

A former senior naval officer in the Falklands Task Force has told *The Scotsman* nuclear weapons were aboard British attack vessels at the time of the conflict.

The officer yesterday also confirmed the presence of the Polaris submarine, adding: "Its presence was known to only a few.

"As for using the nuclear capability against Argentina, that was something which was talked about but probably only seriously considered as an option by the mandarins at Westminster."

The paper by Prof Rogers, of Bradford University, was prepared for the British American Security Information Council, a

London and Washington-based research organisation, and is about to be republished in extended form for the Ministry of Defence-funded Centre for Defence Studies.

The new evidence follows a report in *The Scotsman* two months ago that a classified International Energy Agency document – *Inventory of Radioactive Wastes Entering the Marine Environment: Accidents and Losses at Sea* – stated that the Royal Navy destroyer HMS Sheffield was sunk by Argentina in the South Atlantic in May 1982 with nuclear weapons aboard.

Prof Rogers said yesterday the Sheffield was armed with two WE-177 nuclear depth

bombs. Along with other Type-42 destroyers and the navy's aircraft carriers, it entered the war-zone with full nuclear arsenals.

He believes British forces hastily removed the Sheffield's nuclear depth bombs either shortly before she sank, while under tow by HMS Yarmouth, or immediately following her sinking in waters off South Georgia.

The Campaign for Nuclear Disarmament has since alleged that one of the depth bombs was damaged, recovered by divers and brought back to the Atomic Weapons Establishment at Aldermaston for examination.

Full report, Page 6

No 47,682

My revelation in 1996 about Thatcher's nuclear strike option

The battle to save her went on for five hours. Her burnt-out hulk was taken in tow towards South Georgia, but by Royal Navy accounts she rolled over and sank. Twenty of her crew were killed.

Politically, the sinking of the Sheffield – the first loss of a major British warship for 37 years – sent tremors round Westminster, with some Tory MPs demanding the bombing of Argentina.

But if it had been known that the Sheffield had sunk with nuclear weapons, it would have caused more than a tremor.

At the outbreak of the Falklands War, Britain's naval tactical nuclear weapons comprised of free-fall bombs and depth charges.

Professor Paul Rogers an expert on military uses of nuclear weapons at Bradford University and author of ***The Role of British Nuclear Weapons After the Cold War***, explained: *"At the time it was acceptable for any of the warships to carry nuclear weapons in peace time.*

"The total number of naval tactical weapons was small, perhaps 25 nuclear depth charges and a similar number of gravity bombs.

"When Argentina invaded the Falklands to the beginning of April 1982, a major naval Task Force was quickly assembled and some elements of it set sail from Britain within four days.

"Others, including HMS Sheffield, disengaged from a NATO exercise Spring Train, in the western Mediterranean and headed for Ascension Island to link with the Task Force."

Defence Minister John Nott, specifically stated that warships were being deployed with their full range of *"wartime weapons"*, which implied a nuclear capability.

The former navy minister Keith Speed, who had resigned the previous year in protest at cuts in the navy budget, later said that he *"would have been surprised if those ships from Spring Train had not been carrying nuclear weapons"*.

But there was concern in the Ministry of Defence (MoD) when it was appreciated that a very large proportion of the Royal Navy's entire stock of nuclear weapons was heading for a potential war zone. As a result, some of the nuclear weapons were lifted back by helicopter and other boats before the Task Force reached the Western Approaches.

But amid fears that two *"quiet"* German built Type 209 Argentine submarines may penetrate the Task Force defences, it was reported that *"the rest stayed on board."*

There were rumours that HMS Sheffield was carrying a couple of WE-177 nuclear depth bombs when she went down. But this was always denied by the MoD.

Following the Exocet strike against the Sheffield a cloak of secrecy surrounded her fire.

One report from a Royal Navy rating that she was deliberately scuttled as the burnt hulk was towed to South Georgia was later vigorously denied by the MoD.

Prof Rogers and others believe the scuttling may *"well have been ordered"* as the nuclear depth charges presented a real hazard on the red hot wreck.

What is also unclear is whether the Royal Navy later engineered a recovery operation to remove the nuclear depth charges. It is known that the wreck was visited some months later by a Royal Navy submarine and *"some remains"* were secretly retrieved.

This would stand with the MoD statement later that *"there has never been an instant whereby UK nuclear weapons have been "lost"."*

However, if the nuclear capability of the Sheffield and other Task Force ships had been confirmed in 1982, it would have added fuel to charges that Prime Minister Thatcher had discussed nuclear deployment against Argentina.

As I wrote at the outset of this chapter, my investigation was to prove explosive.

I discovered in the late spring 1996 an International Atomic Energy Agency (IAEA) document **Radioactive Wastes Entering the Marine Environment**, which had supposedly been *"classified"* since being presented to the government's Ministry for Agriculture Fisheries and Food in1991. But the document had been inadvertently placed in the House of Commons library in response to parliamentary questions by Labour MP George Foulkes. Mr Foulkes, the MP for Carrick, Cumnock and Doon Valley was following up on revelations I made a week earlier about an unrelated maritime nuclear incident involving a Soviet submarine in 1970.

The IAEA document only gave details of accidents that can be confirmed either by governments of respective countries or by other authoritative sources. It revealed a catalogue of more than 30 losses of nuclear weapons, reactors or cargoes at sea by Britain, the USA, France and Japan since 1950.

In one section it reported two British losses. One of these relates to the sinking of HMS Sheffield, where the IAEA reports that the destroyer was sunk in the South Atlantic with *"nuclear weapons"*.

Professor Rogers told me: *"This information sends tingles down my neck. We have been trying for years to prove that British ships in the Falklands Task Force were carrying nuclear weapons. It would also add credence to reports that an R-class Polaris nuclear submarine was stationed at a location off Argentina, ready to strike if the war escalated.*

"Extreme circumstances appeared to have justified extreme measures, but everything about this has to be seen in the context of the British nuclear establishment's long-term attitude to nuclear weapons."

He said Sheffield's weapons would have been two WE-177 nuclear depth bombs with a power rating of between 5 and 10 kilotons – slightly smaller than the 13 kiloton bomb that devastated Hiroshima.

Peace campaigner Tam Dalyell, the Labour MP for Linlithgow was horrified and said: *"At last the truth is coming out. I never had any doubt that Sheffield had gone down with nuclear depth charges. If Sheffield's arsenal had been confirmed at the time of her sinking it would have caused international outrage as Britain would have infringed the Plateloco Treaty which banned the deployment of nuclear weapons against non-nuclear South American countries."*

During the previous 14 years whenever Mr Dalyell and other MPs had asked whether HMS Sheffield was carrying nuclear weapons, they were always met by a standard reply from defence ministers: *"It would not be in the interest of national security to depart from the long-standing practice to neither confirm nor deny the presence or absence of nuclear weapons in particular locations at given times."*

The next day Mr Dalyell tabled parliamentary questions asking for the precise location of where HMS Sheffield sank and what efforts – if any – had been made to recover the ship or her weapons.

Mr Foulkes meanwhile said he was outraged by the IAEA disclosure and tabled questions calling for detailed information on any environmental damage which may have been caused by lost nuclear weapons.

Shadow defence minister David Clark immediately tabled a series of urgent questions after my investigation was first published. He asked Defence Secretary Michael Portillo to:

- Say what actions his department has taken to retrieve objects from HMS Sheffield.
- List objects removed from the ship.
- Say how the ship has been monitored since it sank.
- Say whether it was carrying WE-177 nuclear depth charges when it sank.

Meanwhile, Professor Rogers told me that the Sheffield and other Type-42 destroyers as well as the Navy's aircraft carriers entered the war-zone with their full nuclear arsenals. He believed the MoD had removed Sheffield's nuclear depth bombs either shortly before it sank or immediately after its sinking.

A week later my investigation took a much more sinister turn when I discovered that Margaret Thatcher had secretly deployed a fully nuclear armed Polaris submarine to the war zone within range of Argentine military bases and the city of Cordoba in northern Argentina.

A scientific research document by a government-funded agency the *British American Security Information Council (BASIC)* claimed the Polaris sub was ready to make a pre-emptive strike on the Argentine mainland in the event of the British troopship Canberra or one of the Task Force aircraft carriers being destroyed by missiles.

Prof Rogers claims the likely target for a threatened or demonstration attack was Cordoba.

He explained that at the time of the Falklands War, Britain had four R-class Polaris submarines - Renown, Repulse, Resolution and Revenge – sufficient to keep one on patrol in the North Atlantic at all times, with a second available for additional deployment. The R-class subs were armed with 16 Lockheed Polaris A3 nuclear missiles, each with three nuclear warheads capable of releasing 200 kilotonnes of explosive power, with a maximum guidance range of 2,500 miles.

Because the R-Class submarine was a nuclear strike/deterrent vessel, none *"would have sailed without its full nuclear arsenal".*

A former senior Royal Navy officer in the Falklands Task Force told me that nuclear weapons were aboard British attack vessels at the time of the conflict.

He also confirmed the presence of the Polaris submarine, adding: *"Its presence was known to only a few. Just because we were at war with Argentina didn't mean the Warsaw Pact had dropped its guard. Quite the opposite, they could have used the opportunity to strike while our backs were turned. As for using the nuclear capability against Argentina that was something probably only seriously considered by the Prime Minister and the mandarins back in Westminster,"* he added.

BASIC is an independent research organisation based in London and Washington which analyses international security issues and is widely recognised as a world-wide authority on defence, military strategy and nuclear policies.

Dr David Lowry, a Westminster based expert on nuclear matters said *BASIC* is one of the most conservative of research and advice groups.

"They are circumspect and would only give their backing to evidence which they feel they can support," he said.

In 1984, Labour MPs demanded a full inquiry into whether Polaris armed strike submarines had been deployed against Argentina to prepare for a nuclear strike.

The demand was never met by Thatcher's government. But when cross-examined over the Polaris deployment, Mrs Thatcher said the British fleet would have been *"seriously threatened if any of its key ships had been sunk by the Argentine navy."*

The MoD said at the same time: *"There may well have been a Polaris submarine deployed to the South Atlantic, but this was because the Navy was short of hunter-killer submarines and a Polaris submarine can fill this function."*

Prof Rogers said this claim was absolute nonsense. *"Such an explanation is little short of incredible,"* he said. *"While Polaris submarines have a limited hunter-killer capacity, this is for self-defence and they are normally escorted by dedicated hunter-killers."*

To deploy one of Britain's four strategic nuclear missile submarines in a war zone would have been a huge risk.

"Because," as Prof Rogers explained, *"since Britain needed four Polaris submarines to maintain at least one on patrol at all times, the loss of even one would have threatened the entire Polaris capacity."*

In 1984, the Ministry of Defence again denied the allegations of nuclear deployment and Laurence Freedman's authoritative ***The Official History of the Falklands Campaign: War and Diplomacy***, does the same.

The Official History describes the contorted logistical arrangements that led to the removal of the nuclear depth bombs from the frigates, following political alarm in Whitehall. Eventually at least some of the depth bombs were brought back to the UK by an RFA vessel.

In December 2003, Argentine President Néstor Kirchner demanded an apology from the British government for the *"regrettable and monstrous"* act of arming warships engaged in the conflict with nuclear depth charges·

What is also now known is that Margaret Thatcher forced French Premier François Mitterrand to give her the codes to disable Argentina's deadly French-made missiles during the Falklands war by threatening to launch a nuclear warhead against Buenos Aires, according to a book ***Rendez-vous - The Psychoanalysis of François Mitterrand***, by Ali Magoudi, who met the late French president up to twice a week in secrecy at his Paris practice from 1982 to 1984.

He also revealed that Mr Mitterrand believed he would get his *"revenge"* by building a tunnel under the Channel which would forever destroy Britain's island status.

Rendez-vous provides a series of insights into the Mitterrand's mysterious character, complicated past, paranoia and power complex, but nothing as titillating as his remarks on the former British prime minister.

"Excuse me. I had a difference to settle with the Iron Lady. That Thatcher, what an impossible woman!" the president allegedly said as he arrived, more than 45 minutes late, on 7th May 1982.

"With her four nuclear submarines in the south Atlantic, she's threatening to unleash an atomic weapon against Argentina if I don't provide her with the secret codes that will make the missiles we sold the Argentinians deaf and blind."

He reminded Mr Magoudi that on 4th May an Exocet missile had struck HMS Sheffield. *"To make matters worse, it was fired from a Super-Etendard jet,"* he said. *"All the matériel was French!"*

In words that the psychoanalyst swore to the publisher, Meren Sell, were genuine, the president continued: *"She's livid. She blames me personally for this new Trafalgar ... I was obliged to give in. She's got them now, the codes."*

Mr Mitterrand - who once described Mrs Thatcher as *"the eyes of Caligula and the mouth of Marilyn Monroe"* - went on: *"One cannot win against the insular syndrome of an unbridled Englishwoman. Provoke a nuclear war for a few islands inhabited by three sheep as hairy as they are freezing! But it's a good job I gave way. Otherwise, I assure you, the Lady's metallic finger would have hit the button."*

France, he insisted, would have the last word. *"I'll build a tunnel under the Channel. I'll succeed where Napoleon III failed. And do you know why she'll accept my tunnel? I'll flatter her shopkeeper's spirit. I'll tell her it won't cost the Crown a penny."*

Fast forward to December 2003 and the Ministry of Defence admitted for the first time that British ships carried nuclear weapons in the Falklands war.

The disclosure came as the government was forced to concede - after a long-running campaign by the *Guardian* - that seven nuclear weapons containers were damaged during a series of wartime accidents.

After the MoD had initially blocked a request for information under the Open government Code, the Parliamentary Ombudsman criticised the ministry and ordered it to publish a list of 20 accidents and mishaps involving nuclear weapons between 1960 and 1991.

But despite the Ombudsman's critical verdict, the MoD concealed the Falklands accidents, despite the now public IAEA report of 1996, and only divulged their existence after further pressure from the *Guardian*.

But the admission by the MoD failed to clear up the most controversial allegation: that the nuclear weapons were sunk along the HMS Sheffield after the ship was hit by an Exocet a month into the war. It also failed to confirm the fact that a nuclear armed Polaris first strike submarine had been deployed to the South Atlantic during the Falklands War.

Faced with the Ombudsman's refusal to support the MoD's policy of secrecy, the department opted for damage limitation, putting out a statement to all media in the traditional slot for unwelcome news: late on a Friday afternoon.

The MoD said the transfers of the WE177 depth charges took place at various times during April, May and June 1982, *"well away from other sea-going traffic, and the weapons were held in ships with the best-protected magazines before being returned to Britain"*.

The MoD insisted that the nuclear weapons never entered the territorial waters of the Falkland Islands or any South American country.

The British government has always said there was never any question of resorting to the use of nuclear weapons in the dispute.

The MoD said it was routine practice for British naval ships to carry nuclear weapons during the 1980s, but this ended in 1993.

But in her verdict on the *Guardian's* complaint, the ombudsman decided there was no danger to national security if the weapons were no longer in service. But in a bizarre twist said it was difficult to envisage that: *"The release of information about events that happened some time ago to weapons that no longer exist could cause harm if made more widely available".*

Just prior to this in 2002, Argentina's foreign minister has accused the UK of sending a nuclear-armed submarine to the South Atlantic, after making an official complaint to the UN over the Falklands dispute.

Hector Timerman then demanded that the British confirm the location of nuclear submarines in the region.

But UK officials said the accusations of militarisation were *"absurd".*

Mr Timerman told a news conference at the UN in New York that the UK was *"militarising the region",* repeating accusations made by Argentine President Cristina Fernandez de Kirchner,

"Argentina has information that, within the framework of the recent British deployment in the Falklands, they sent a nuclear submarine with the capacity to transport nuclear weapons to the South Atlantic," said Mr Timerman.

He did not elaborate on the information, but said the vessel was Vanguard-class, a group that carries Trident nuclear missiles. In that respect he was wrong, because back in 1982, Trident was yet to be bought by the UK's Ministry of Defence, let alone deployed.

Argentina's foreign minister came armed with maps and photographs to make his case to the Secretary General, the head of the Security Council, and the press. Great Britain, he claimed, was bringing new state-of-the art weapons into the South Atlantic and had sent a nuclear submarine into a nuclear-free weapons zone. *"It is a threat to regional security,"* he said.

The British ambassador Mark Lyall Grant called the accusations an escalation. He would not be drawn on the location of Britain's nuclear submarines, but said they stayed in international waters. He also spelled out in detail Britain's stance that the dispute over the Falklands was not one of sovereignty, as Argentina insisted, but one of self-determination: the islanders must be allowed to determine their own fate, he said, and they want to be British.

He added that Mr Ban had agreed to talk to the British about Argentina's complaints.

In response, Mark Lyall Grant said the government did not comment on the *"disposition of nuclear weapons, submarines etc".* And he dismissed the accusation that the UK was militarising the situation as *"manifestly absurd"*.

"Before 1982 there was a minimal defence presence in the Falkland Islands," he said.

"It is only because Argentina illegally invaded the Falkland Islands in 1982 that we had to increase our defence posture. Nothing has changed in that defence posture in recent months or recent years."

The BBC's Barbara Plett at the UN in New York said the dispute is raised every year at the UN, and usually involved both sides sending letters to the Secretary General. But this was the first time Argentina had provided such a detailed and public account of its grievances, she said.

The UN General Assembly passed non-binding resolutions urging the two to solve the dispute through negotiations.

The UK says the islanders have the right to self-determination, and London will enter into negotiations on the status of the Falklands only if the islanders request it.

The status of the islands, known in Argentina as the Malvinas, is still a highly sensitive issue for Buenos Aires. And quite why successive British governments want to retain administrative control on a group of islands almost 13,000 miles away is beyond the comprehension of most right-minded British people.

Chapter Twelve
Dead Man Hiding

Dead man hiding: IRA spy Martin McGartland

I FIRST met Martin McGartland in the reception area of the *Sunday Sun* newspaper in Newcastle upon Tyne's Groat Market in December 1997.

I was working as the Investigative Reporter for the regional weekly tabloid and Marty (as he likes to be called) became the most distinctive and unique contact I have ever had the pleasure to know during my entire career as a journalist.

Dressed in blue jeans and a zipper jacket and wearing a baseball cap, sun glasses and a scarf pulled up over his mouth Marty had a way of making *"incognito"* appear almost Hollywood.

You see, Marty was a real-life spy!

For more than four years he had risked his life working undercover as a British agent (code named Agent Carol) inside the Provisional IRA at the height of the Troubles in Northern Ireland.

Then in 1991, aged just 20, he was kidnapped by the Provos and taken to an apartment to face interrogation and torture, knowing that execution would follow. In a desperate bid to save his life, he threw himself from a third-floor window of the flats at Twinbrook and somehow, miraculously, survived the impact of falling over 40 feet.

He became known for being the only person ever to escape from the IRA's internal mole hunting unit, known as the *"headhunters"* or *"nutting squad"*.

"I was bursting for a pee and I knew they wouldn't want me peeing all over the sofa," he recalled.

"I asked a young lad to untie my hands so I could go to the toilet. As I hopped into the bathroom I noticed the bath, full to the brim with crystal-clear water. I knew exactly what this meant and my stomach churned as fear gripped me.

"At that moment I knew that if I didn't escape from the flat I would face water torture and that the interrogation unit would arrive at any minute. By the time they had finished with me they would either have a confession or I would be dead.

"The thought frightened the shit out of me."

Marty then managed to hop out of the bathroom and into the sitting room before hurling himself head first through the window to the grass below and hobbling away, made his escape.

After being resettled in the north-east of England and, thanks to his handler, given a new identity, Marty discovered that his capture by the IRA had not been the result of Provo intelligence, but he had been deliberately sacrificed by MI5.

Angry, bitter and determined to discover the truth, Marty set about challenging the mysterious government agencies who had organised his abduction. But the authorities were determined to undermine his efforts.

He found himself battling the full force of the British legal system, including the police, the Crown Prosecution Service (CPS) and senior officers of the Royal Ulster Constabulary (RUC), as well as those of MI5 and the Home Secretary himself.

During his years in hiding in the north-east, he was stopped, arrested and taken to court on scores of occasions, mostly on trumped-up offences; and often police officers lied in court in an effort to win convictions.

Eventually, the CPS, advised by MI5, ordered his trial for attempting to pervert the course of justice. But Marty was found not guilty by the jury in just ten minutes. Unbelievably, during the trial, Northumbria Police revealed Martin McGartland's real name and his new identity.

And it was at this time that Marty and I first met.

In the **Sunday Sun** offices, and before I went downstairs for this first meeting, a fellow reporter warned me: *"Marty is a bit weird and persistent, so take everything he says with a big pinch of salt."*

Another reporter interjected: *"Yeah, I reckon it's all in his head… he's definitely a head case."*

But I wanted to meet this man with my mind wide open.

So Marty and I met and we shook hands. Then in his distinctive Ulster accent he suggested we drive to a small hotel in nearby Whitley Bay to talk in *"safer"* surroundings.

As we walked out to my car his demeanour changed and he became clearly nervous, looking this way and that and lowering his head when anyone who looked at him.

When we reached my car, he carefully retrieved a hand mirror from an inside jacket pocket and kneeling down held the mirror to inspect under each wheel arch of the car.

"It's a habit," he laughed nervously.

Once ensconced in the lounge bar of the hotel, he seemed to relax and tell me his story and the events which had led up to Northumbria Police deliberately spilling his identity in a public courtroom.

Marty's story was riveting.

Born into a staunchly Irish Republican, Roman Catholic family in Belfast, Marty grew up in a council house in Moyard, Ballymurphy at the foot of the Black Mountain. His parents were separated and he had one brother, Joe, and two sisters, Elizabeth and Catherine.

As the Troubles escalated, Republican areas such as Ballymurphy increasingly came under the control of the local Provisional IRA who, in the absence of normal policing, took on their own policing functions.

One of the effects of the continuous rioting and the campaign of bombings and shootings in Belfast and across Northern Ireland was to make Marty grow up quickly. He described his childhood in West Belfast as one in which he would join with older boys in stone-throwing to goad the British Army. He also would join in with other Catholic youths to battle against Ulster Protestant boys from nearby loyalist estates; this mostly involved throwing stones at each other.

His sister Catherine was one of many children who joined the youth movement of the IRA. She was later killed after accidentally falling through a skylight at her school. Meanwhile, Marty was carving his own path in life, while bombings and punishment shootings became part of an everyday backdrop to 1980s Ulster.

After leaving school, Marty befriended a homeless man who sheltered in the disused Old Broadway cinema on the Falls Road, and provided the man with food and money. Marty's first job was working a paper round, and later delivering milk.

He became involved in petty crime, which brought him to the notice of the RUC. His activities also attracted the attention of the IRA and on several occasions he narrowly escaped local disciplinary squads. Since the beginning of the Troubles, many residents reported offences to Sinn Féin, a political party associated with the IRA, rather than the RUC. This effectively made the IRA a police force in some areas.

Marty said that he became sickened by increasing Provo violence directed at young Catholic petty lawbreakers in the form of punishment beatings (often carried out with iron bars and baseball bats) and kneecappings. So in 1986, at the age of 16 he agreed to provide information to the RUC about local IRA members, thereby preventing them from carrying out many attacks against the security forces.

At the same time, the IRA employed him as a security officer in a protection racket; his job was to guard a building site in Ballymurphy which was under the protection of the IRA.

He then worked for a local taxi firm as an unlicensed driver, paying a percentage to the IRA. This enabled him to better identify suspects who had been targeted by RUC Special Branch. While working as a taxi driver he occasionally drove IRA punishment squads around and overheard them boast about the beatings they had meted out to their victims. Many any were innocent people who had somehow incurred the wrath of a member of the IRA.

Disgusted by what he was hearing and witnessing, Marty later infiltrated the IRA in autumn 1989, having been asked to join by Davy Adams, a leading IRA member and a nephew of Sinn Féin leader Gerry Adams. This was after being recommended by a childhood friend, Harry Fitzsimmons, part of an IRA bomb team, whom Marty often drove around Belfast.

Davy Adams immediately gave Marty his first assignment, which was to check the house of a well-known Ulster Volunteer Force (UVF) figure.

Holding the rank of lieutenant in the IRA Belfast Intelligence unit, he ended up working mainly for Davy Adams, whom he drove to meetings and to survey potential IRA targets. Marty had a special tracking device attached to his car.

He was also recruited by an IRA Active Service Unit (ASU) which was headed by a man known as *"Spud"*.

Meanwhile Marty was given the code name Agent Carol by the RUC, to feed information back to them.

He convinced his IRA associates that he was a committed member of the organisation and he successfully led a double life, which was kept secret even from the mother of his two sons.

From 1989-1991, he provided information about IRA activities and planned attacks to the RUC Special Branch. During his time as a Special Branch intelligence agent, he became close to senior IRA members, having daily contact with those responsible for organizing and perpetrating the shooting attacks and bombings throughout

Northern Ireland. He also worked closely with Belfast actress Rosena Brown, a prominent and highly skilled IRA intelligence officer.

Working in the IRA Intelligence unit enabled Marty to learn about the organisation's command structure pertaining to finance, ordnance, intelligence and the detailed planning of operations.

Although Marty said he prevented the IRA from carrying out many "spectaculars", including the planned bombing of two lorries transporting British soldiers from Stranraer to Larne that could have resulted in the loss of over a dozen lives, his greatest regret was his failure in June 1991 to save the life of 21-year-old British Army Private Tony Harrison. Harrison, a soldier from London, was shot by the IRA at the home of his East Belfast fiancée where they were making wedding plans.

Marty had driven the IRA gunmen's getaway car and had been brought into the operation so late he had no time to advise his handlers, though he had previously indicated the IRA's interest in the area.

In that same year 1991, Marty provided information about a mass shooting attack planned on Charlie Heggarty's pub in Bangor, County Down, patronised by British soldiers after a football match between the prison wardens. The RUC intercepted the two couriers delivering the guns to be used to shoot the soldiers and Marty was exposed as an infiltrator.

Marty said that diaries of the late Detective Superintendent Ian Phoenix, head of the Northern Ireland Police Counter-Surveillance Unit, showed that he and other Special Branch officers had advised senior RUC officers against stopping the gun couriers' vehicles, as doing so would put Marty's life at risk and allow the actual IRA gunmen to escape. The penalty for informing on the IRA was death, often preceded by lengthy and sometimes brutal interrogations.

With his cover blown, Marty was kidnapped in August 1991 by Jim *"Boot"* McCarthy and Paul *"Chico"* Hamilton, two IRA men with previous convictions for paramilitary activities. He claimed that McCarthy and Hamilton were RUC informers based on what he had personally observed of the men during his kidnapping as he waited to be interrogated, tortured and subsequently executed. These allegations, however, were strongly denied by both men.

After his abduction by the IRA and his miraculous escape there ensued a battle of wills between senior RUC officers, MI5 and his Handler over what to do with their exposed agent.

Marty was finally relocated to the north-east coast of England, receiving nearly £100,000 (£208,500 by today's values) to buy a house and establish a new life in Whitley Bay, going by the name Martin Ashe.

But with egg on their faces the Provos were not going to give up on punishing the double agent. Three years after moving to England, the IRA sent Marty's mother a Catholic mass card with his name written on it. Mass cards are sent as tokens of sympathy to bereaved families when a member of the family has died.

Then in 1997, a few months before our first meeting, Marty's identity was revealed publicly by the Northumbria Police in court when he was caught breaking the speed limit in his car and subsequently prosecuted for holding driving licences in different names, which he explained was a means of avoiding IRA detection. He was cleared of perverting the course of justice, but his alias had been revealed and it was only a matter of time before an IRA hitman would track him down.

Over the next five years, Marty became a key and trusted contact for me for my entire time at the **Sunday Sun**, and then later when I edited the **Galloway Gazette** he gave me key information about how the IRA used the local port of Stranraer for gun running, and during my time in Aberdeen working for the daily broadsheet **The Press & Journal** gave me details about rogue Provo assassins.

Then suddenly on 17ᵗʰ June 1999, while I was sat at my desk at the Press & Journal in Aberdeen came the news I had been dreading.

Marty had been shot six times at his Whitley Bay home by two masked men, receiving serious wounds in the chest, stomach, side, upper leg and hand. He had attempted to wrestle the gun away from his assailant, but was shot in the left hand, the blast almost destroying his thumb.

170

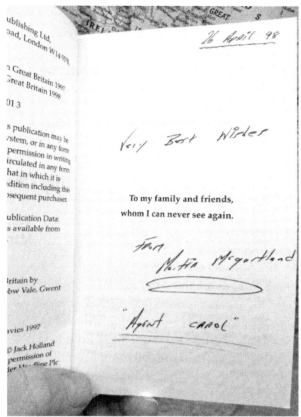

On the book's copyright page (left side, partially visible):

ublishing Ltd,
oad, London W14 9PB

n Great Britain 1997
Great Britain 1998

01 3

ublication Data:
s available from

iritain by
bw Vale, Gwent

vies 1997

© Jack Holland
permission of
der Headline Plc

Handwritten inscription on the facing page:

26 April 98

Very Best Wishes

**To my family and friends,
whom I can never see again.**

from
Martin McGartland

"Agent CAROL"

**A personal message from Martin aka Agent Carol,
in my copy of 50 Dead Men Walking**

He received assistance from his neighbours and was rushed to intensive care in hospital where he recovered from his injuries.

The Northumbria Police investigation claimed a north east criminal gang was behind the attempted murder, but Marty immediately knew who the assailants were… the IRA.

Within a few weeks of the shooting, he was on the phone to me giving me the names of the IRA operatives he believed were responsible – names widely known in the republican communities either side of the Irish border.

The day after he was shot, the incident, along with the murders of Eamon Collins, Brendan Fegan, and Paul Downey, was cited by Ulster Unionist leader David Trimble in an interview with reporters in Belfast, to question whether the IRA ceasefire was being maintained.

He reminded Mo Mowlam, Secretary of State for Northern Ireland, that this was a condition of the early release of paramilitaries under the Good Friday Agreement.

A week later, it was mentioned in the Northern Ireland Grand Committee as evidence that IRA arms decommissioning had not taken place, and in January 2000 by Robert McCartney in the Northern Ireland Assembly.

These were highly sensitive times for the Northern Ireland peace process.

Marty criticized the police for inadequate protection.

In August 2006, Ian Paisley told Peter Hain, Secretary of State for Northern Ireland: *"We have also heard how the sister of IRA informer Martin McGartland was told by police that her safety was under threat. This news broke immediately after the Secretary of State's comments that he believed the IRA had ended all of its illegal activity."*

Despite Martin McGartland being known as one of the best agents to operate during the Troubles, British Home Secretary Theresa May told a court in early 2014 that she refused to confirm or deny that he was a British agent working for MI5, offering as explanation: *"In case providing such information would endanger his life or damage national security"*.

Marty responded by lambasting May, pointing out that: *"This is one of the daftest things I have ever heard; everyone who is interested knows my past ... no current security interest is at stake."* After highlighting the two books he had written about his life as an undercover agent, one of which was made into a successful film, he also noted there have been six television documentaries on him and a number of newspaper articles. He went on to state: *"The authorities wrote to the BBC back in 1997 admitting that I have been resettled and was being protected because of my service to them. I wonder how well briefed the Home Secretary is?"*

May's department, the Home Office, oversees MI5, and she herself had signed the application in a court case brought by Marty and his partner. Marty additionally has a contract which was signed by MI5 after he was shot in England in which the representatives of the PSNI and Northumbria Police acknowledged his service in general terms.

Because he was unable to claim State benefits for security reasons MI5 had previously helped him financially; however this assistance was withdrawn after he gave an interview to the Belfast Telegraph. He commented: *"Refusing to confirm or deny my role is simply a trick to avoid the State's responsibilities toward someone who has risked his life for it."*

In the same month, May made an application using the controversial *"Closed Material Procedures"* (CMPs) which are secret courts under the recent Justice and Security Act. If these were to be used in Marty's lawsuit against the government for negligence and breach of contract, they would ensure that the public, media, as well as Marty and his lawyers, would be denied access to the hearings. Instead his case would be heard by a *Special Advocate.*

By not being present with his lawyers at the closed court, he would not be privy to anything pertaining to his case that the court submitted.

Marty pointed out that the case had nothing to do with national security or his undercover work 24 years earlier. This move by May was described by some lawyers and Human Rights' groups as *"Kafkaesque".*

Meanwhile, for 20 years Marty battled against Northumbria Police and their version that his shooting was not linked to the IRA but to local criminal gangs.

Then in September 2019, an internal report carried out by Bedfordshire, Cambridgeshire and Hertfordshire police forces cleared his name and proved Marty was right all along.

A redacted copy of their findings states that Northumbria Police should have classified the case as a *"terrorist incident"* not an attempted murder.

The report said: *"The attack on Mr McGartland is, in the professional view of the reviewing team, more than speculatively connected to Irish Republican Terrorism. This should have been acknowledged both to the victim and to the media at the time.*

"Subsequent SIO's (Senior Investigating Officers) and Chief Officers have continued to treat this as an Attempted Murder Investigation when making

decisions regarding the progress, direction and resourcing of the investigation and most importantly its priority alongside other Northumbria Police major investigations. It is an attempted murder, however the terrorist dimension cannot be overlooked."

However, the review team said it believed Northumbria detectives had been keen to progress the probe, but if this is to happen efforts needed to be made to repair the relationship between the police force and the victim.

The report added: *"Whatever decision is made as to progression, there needs to be a concerted effort to re-build the relationship with the victim. The review accepts that as the victim Mr McGartland also has his part to play in this and some independent mediation may resolve such impasse so that appropriate dialogue can be achieved."*

Marty, now aged 50, said the whole thing was covered up by the government to ensure the IRA and Sinn Fein stayed signed up to the Good Friday Agreement.

When the details of the report emerged in 2019, Marty issued a statement, saying: *"I am now urging the current chief constable of Northumbria police to immediately admit and acknowledge that the IRA had been behind my June 1999 attempted murder.*

"The Northumbria police knew the IRA had been behind my shooting and they acted in consort with MI5, the Home Office and the then Blair Labour government (and subsequent governments) who covered it up.

"This was done as part of a secret deal between police, security service and government as a result of the Good Friday peace agreement."

A Northumbria Police spokesman said in response: *"We can confirm this case has remained open since the shooting in 1999. Following a recent review, the force are investing a significant and dedicated resource into progressing the investigation.*

"The classification of the incident is currently under further review."

Over the past 23 years I have maintained a good friendship with Marty, and we still share messages through social media and the occasional phone call.

But despite the police inquiry finding in his favour, he still believes he is *"a dead man hiding"*.

"I don't live any sort of normal life. Every time I leave the house there could be someone sitting watching. I still have to check under my car every time I get in it. They are never ever going to stop targeting people like me," he says.

"I'm still with my partner. She is the only person I can 100% trust. If I didn't have her I couldn't have coped."

On Facebook, Marty gives his current secret address as: *"Timbuktu, Mali"*!

Chapter Thirteen
Green Unpleasant Land

Fluoroacetamide, one of the most deadly pesticides known to mankind

FEW people who lived through the 1990s will have escaped the decade without being affected in some way by the BSE outbreak, often called Mad Cow Disease, which impacted on both farming and our food supply.

The United Kingdom BSE outbreak was a widespread occurrence of bovine spongiform encephalopathy that affected the nation's cattle throughout the late 1980s and 1990s.

Over four million cows were destroyed in an effort to contain the outbreak, and 177 people died after contracting human variant Creutzfeldt-Jakob Disease (CJD) through eating infected beef.

A political and public health crisis resulted, and British beef was banned from export to numerous countries around the world, with some bans remaining in place until as late as 2019.

Bovine spongiform encephalopathy (BSE) is a neurodegenerative disease of cattle. Symptoms include abnormal behaviour, trouble walking, and weight loss and later in the course of the illness the cow becomes unable to move. The time between infection and onset of symptoms is generally four to five years and time from onset of symptoms to death is typically a few weeks to a few months.

BSE was thought to be due to an infection by a misfolded protein, known as a prion.

Cattle were believed to have been infected by being fed meat-and-bone meal (MBM) that contained the remains of cattle who had spontaneously developed the disease or scrapie-infected sheep products.

Cases were suspected based on symptoms and confirmed by examination of the brain and were classified as classic or atypical, with the latter divided into H- and L types.

Efforts to prevent the disease in the UK included not allowing any animal older than 30 months to enter either the human food or animal feed supply.

In Europe, all cattle over 30 months had to be tested if they were to become human food.

In the UK from 1986 to 2015, more than 184,000 cattle were diagnosed with BSE, with the peak of new cases occurring in 1993. About 4.4 million cows were killed during the eradication programme. By 2017 only four cases were reported globally and the condition was been deemed to be nearly eradicated.

British cattle were believed to have become infected in large numbers in the 1980s. The first confirmed instance in which an animal fell ill with the disease occurred in 1986, and lab tests the following year indicated the presence of BSE.

By November 1987, the British Ministry of Agriculture (MAFF) accepted it had a new disease on its hands. In 1989, high-risk foodstuffs like offal were banned for human consumption and widespread fear about beef led many British consumers to stop purchasing it.

A crucial basis for the government's assurances that British beef was safe was the belief that BSE-infected meat products would not be able to infect other animals. This was founded on their experience with scrapie-infected sheep, which had proven unable to cause any illness in humans.

However, scientists studying BSE were already questioning this assumption and, on 10th May 1990, it was widely reported that a Siamese cat named Max had become infected with BSE, providing the first confirmation outside the laboratory that it could in fact be transmitted between species through eating infected meat.

Despite this, the government maintained that British beef was safe and, later that month, the then-Secretary of State for Environment, Food and Rural Affairs, John Gummer, appeared on TV encouraging his daughter to eat a beef burger, and declared British beef to be *"completely safe"*.

Meanwhile, many more cats would go on to develop the disease, as would numerous other animals including at least one tiger in a UK zoo.

In late 1994, a number of people began to show symptoms of a neurological disease similar to CJD, a fatal disorder that occurs naturally in a small percentage of people, though usually only later in life. This new form of the disease would go on to be identified as variant CJD (vCJD), occurring primarily in younger people and caused through eating BSE-infected meat. The first known death from vCJD occurred on 21st May 1995, when 19-year-old Stephen Churchill died, although the UK government continued to emphasise the safety of British beef and, in September 1995, concluded that there was *"insufficient evidence"* to link BSE and vCJD.

It was not until 20th March 1996 that Stephen Dorrell, the Secretary of State for Health announced that vCJD *"was caused by eating BSE-infected meat"*.

A week after Dorrell's announcement, on 27th March 1996, the European Union (EU) imposed a worldwide ban on exports of British beef. The ban would go on to last for 10 years before it was finally lifted on 1st May 2006. It led to much controversy in parliament and to the incineration of over one million cattle from at least March 1996 and resulted in trade controversies between the UK and other EU states, dubbed a *'beef war'* by the media.

Restrictions remained for beef containing vertebral material and for beef sold on the bone. France continued to impose a ban on British beef illegally long after the European Court of Justice had ordered it to lift its blockade.

During the height of the crisis, as well as after cases began to decline, the UK government came under criticism for its response, and in particular for how slow it was to acknowledge the problem, to inform the public, and to take steps to deal with the outbreak.

That is the history of the BSE outbreak and the official reasons for its cause and spread.

But an investigation I undertook in 1996 cast huge doubt on what we were being told by the government and its propaganda to protect its filthy rich friends in the pharmaceutical industries. In May of that year – at the height of the BSE epidemic and thanks to a trusted contact at Westminster - I began to look at other possible reasons for this untreatable disease and a seemingly unlikely link to the UK's most serious incident of pesticide poisoning some three decades earlier.

Questions were tabled in both Houses of Parliament by Labour MPs to conduct urgent research into a poisoning incident at Smarden in Kent in 1963 and to find whether there was a link with five cases of CJD, a cluster of cancers and a higher than average incidence of BSE in the same area in 1996.

Some scientific experts had already attributed BSE and CJD to widespread use of organo-pesticides in British agriculture.

And as my own cancer in 1987-88 had confirmed a link with exposure to such pesticides I was keen to find out more.

In 1963, a herd of cattle, dozens of sheep, cats, dogs and wildlife at Smarden were killed when a factory producing organochlorine pesticides accidentally contaminated two acres of farmland with the chemical Fluoroacetamide.

The manager of the factory owned by Midox Chemicals – a government subsidised subsidiary of a Dutch multinational – reported that a *"black chemical residue"* had been dumped on the land for *"many months"*.

Cows which suffered long term poisoning displayed symptoms very similar to those affected by BSE.

The poisoning brought ruin to local farmers, held the civil population in panic, confounded veterinary surgeons and local council officials and was ascribed the status of a national emergency. The events that followed amounted to one of the first

179

environmental scandals in contemporary British history – one that would galvanise the environmental movement.

It became clear that the factory, a large shed in the middle of farmland, was manufacturing toxic chemicals and that a leak of one of these, Fluoroacetamide, led to Britain's first documented livestock mass poisoning.

The incident might have passed by as only a historical footnote, but instead the Smarden leak quickly became a national concern with international implications and has cast a long shadow across the approach to intensive agriculture in the UK in the years since.

Part of why this incident had such major repercussions is due to timing, coming as it did at the same time as American writer Rachel Carson's **Silent Spring** was first published in the UK. Seen as the first polemic of the environmental movement, Carson's book was a significant catalyst to the emergence of modern environmentalism on both sides of the Atlantic.

Local veterinarian Douglas Good had a unique knowledge of fluoride poisoning having worked with a leading expert in South Africa and on cases of animals affected by industrial fluoride poisoning in England.

Taking his cue from Carson, Dr Good disseminated what he called a **Short Story** about the incident to the press, putting across the Smarden incident as not simply a local industrial waste spill, but as deadly evidence of the pervasiveness of toxic pesticides in the environment.

Dr Good became involved after a number of animals began to die in unexplained circumstances on three farms in Smarden. He preserved the fine details of the 1963 poisoning in his published 'short story'.

Extracts from that story, which I discovered in 1996, remain poignant:

"Many meetings transpired between the Ashford veterinary practice, the factory manager and myself. Analytical test results of ground water began to come through. Fluorides were present to the extent of 5 parts per million, but bromides were a hundred times more. Testing of the ditches and ponds for bromides were carried out at intervals. But testing for fluorides was abandoned in view of the alarming quantities of bromide present.

Green unpleasant land

My exclusive revelation about the Smarden poisoning in The Scotsman

"The black chemical residue from the manufacture of Fluoroacetamide had been pumped out onto the factory land for months and the Kent River Board assured me that this could only be carried downwards into the soil.

"All ditches and ponds on Great Omenden, Kelsham and Roberts Farms were fenced off to prevent access by livestock. The remainder of the young Friesian herd on Roberts Farm was kept under close observation by the Ashford veterinary surgeons.

"Mr Lowe, the farmer at Great Omenden, also kept pigs, poultry and cattle, as well as two pet dogs, one of them a sturdy and obedient foxhound.

"But a month after the sheep deaths, and after all acid had disappeared from his ponds and ditches, a foxhound was taken ill at night.

"I will use the housekeepers words: "At 1am he jumped onto my bed, a thing he never does...his eyes staring and big...trembling a little and teeth bared as he panted and seemed mad...I was frightened...I let him out of the bedroom and he fell downstairs...he stumbled out of doors and went onto the green...there he fell over, head bent backwards and his legs kicking as he gasped for air...a horrible noise from his throat as he breathed...his eyes were very

big…then he got up, looking wildly around, then shot away and we did not see him again alive."

"The following morning he was found drowned in a pond. A post-mortem examination in the forecourt of my surgery showed only the signs of death from drowning, and the big meal he had eaten the evening before was undigested in his stomach. The owner could not accept my post-mortem certificate."

What had caused the madness before the dog bolted away in terror?

Dr Good continued: *"Mr Lowe had lost sheep, his neighbour had lost cattle, this was still poisoning! But how could it be? The water analyses for acid and bromide were almost normal, and the bromides, if responsible, would only have a sedative effect and not one of stimulation. Doubt grew in my mind. The Veterinary Investigation Centre was not so concerned with dogs, and besides they would be reluctant to intervene as litigation might be involved.*

"Meanwhile the cows at Roberts Farm were reported to be normal to the casual observer. Cyril Jull knew their milk yields had fallen, they were less alert than usual, and they were easily tired. If made to hurry, they would stop and pant like a dog. A few calves, which were born strong and healthy, died in convulsions before they were a few hours old. Mr Patterson, the Ministry Veterinary Surgeon at Wye was again pressed to come to our aid.

"Yes, he was willing to do so if we could tell him what poison to look for. The factory sold scores of pesticides, from the more complex chlorinated hydrocarbons, DDT, Lindane, Parathion, down to the simpler copper, arsenic, zinc and sulphur ones.

"The de la Warr Laboratories at Oxford offered me their help and in July a team of three visited Tenterden and took apparatus out to Roberts Farm. Within minutes of setting up their apparatus they diagnosed fluoroacetate (1080), much to the surprise of the farmer and myself.

"I hastily made use of the library at the veterinary centre, and examined all available references to fluoroacetates, both veterinary and medical, published in Australia, America and Britain.

"The action of this poison is to interfere with the supply of nourishment to the brain and other organs such as the heart and kidneys.

"The Medical Officer of Health was not aware that the fluoride in Smarden was organic, whereas the other was inorganic and much less poisonous by comparison.

"My post-mortem examination of the foxhound showed one peculiarity only to be noticed weeks later. The concrete near the drain where I carry out such work is always washed down immediately afterwards. This time, the blood stains did not wash away, and six months later the tell-tale spots are still obvious.

"The casual observer of farmer Jull's cows would see nothing amiss. However, by mid-July, two months after the first series of deaths, some of the cows developed swellings under the chest and jaw.

"Two cows were sent to the Central Veterinary Laboratory at Weybridge. One by one, they gradually died and by the end of September only 11 of the original herd of 26 young cows were alive. Every calf that had been born since May had died. There was no known treatment.

"On 30th September, the remainder of the herd were destroyed and burned. Their flesh was highly poisonous. The local horse slaughterer who collected the previous dead cows, lost two of his own dogs which accidentally ate a little of the meat. These dogs went through the same ghastly and cruel deaths suffered by the foxhound in June.

"By now, the factory undertook the emptying and cleansing of all contaminated ditches and ponds. Water was transported in a fleet of tankers to Dymchurch. Here it was to be tipped into the sea on an outgoing tide. But the harbour authorities would not permit the sludge to be tipped there, so that was transported back to the factory land from whence it came.

"A trench was dug around three sides of the sludge on instructions from the Kent River Board and to prevent further seepage of the poison.

"In mid-October the Ministry of Agriculture sent two cows from Weybridge. They were to act as guinea pigs to ensure that no further danger remained. They were allowed to graze the grass, but not permitted to drink the water, which by now, had refilled into the ditches and ponds following the high rainfall.

"Nobody would risk feeding the hay to livestock. The farmers spent their days no longer milking and caring for his Friesian herd, which had ceased to exist. They spent them scrubbing, cleaning, plastering and painting all the buildings, looking forward with hope that by spring he would be permitted to restock his farm.

"These events take no account of the wild-life, the birds, the rabbits, the nomadic cats, part owned and part lodgers. None were left. The house-martins never came this spring, and there was no bird-song in the hedgerows.

"Fluoroacetates in the form of Fluoroacetamide has been sold in Great Britain for a number of years as a pesticide against greenfly and blackfly, to both farmers and gardeners. It is also sold as a rat poison.

"Neither washing nor boiling removes the Fluoroacetamide if the crop was harvested too early after spraying. The amount permitted to spray one acre of these edible crops will kill 75,000 dogs."

Acknowledging his inspiration, Dr Good concluded his narrative by declaring that the *"subject of Rachel Carson's book* **Silent Spring** *had become a reality here in the heart of the Garden of England".*

Back in 1964, a specially convened government committee was faced with two proposals for the fate of two acres of farmland where the contamination was irreversible. The first plan was to build a concrete wall 12 feet deep into the ground surrounding the fields and cap the whole area with a concrete lid. The huge concrete dustbin would have egress points to allow the poisons to be extracted and burned off. But it was thought that local opinion would object to a huge tomb in the midst of the *Garden of England.*

A second option was favoured which would involve the clearance and dumping of 2,000 tonnes of topsoil from the farm. So the soil was sealed in 40-gallon drums and lined with concrete.

On 28th March 1964 a 1,500 tonne ship, the Halcience, sailed from Rochester with an initial 800 tonnes of Smarden soil and was bound for a *"secret Atlantic location".*

Government scientists admitted there was no way of testing how far the contamination might have spread and that: *"Nobody knows how long this poison can last in the soil."*

A year later in January 1965, the government issued strict new guidelines on the use of Fluoroacetamide labelling it *"the most toxic of all rodenticides".* It was immediately banned as a spray pesticide and until 1992 was only licensed to the pest control company Rentokil as a rat poison for use in deep sewers.

Back in Smarden the effects of the poisoning continued. The factory was closed and the farmers were compensated for the loss of stock.

But the events were then shrouded in government secrecy and an unwillingness of local people talk about it to outsiders. Details of the poisoning were subsequently kept closely guarded for years for fear of negatively affecting the economy of the area.

But within four years of the poisoning farmer Cyril Jull's wife Audrey died from cancer. Her death was followed by that of four workers at the Midox factory and a labourer on a neighbouring farm. Within 10 years of the poisoning, at least six people most closely affected by it died – most of these deaths were attributed to cancer.

"There were only four or five workers plus office staff at the Midox factory," observed Peter Grant, who lived most of his life in Smarden. *"Most of them died within 10 years of the poisoning and all were under 50.*

"We knew these people personally. They were just labourers, they didn't have any knowledge of chemistry and would handle the chemicals with bare hands. One smelt a huge cover-up," he added.

"The government didn't blame the factory until they were left with nothing else to blame."

Cyril Jull is now unwilling to talk about the so-called *'Smarden affair'*. But Gary Coomber (aged 37 in 1996) who still farms at Little Newhouse Farm at nearby Headcorn, has his own recollections. He was only four in 1963, but at the age of 33 had a heart attack, which he attributes to organophosphate sheep dip – organophosphates largely replaced organochlorine compounds in the late 1960s, because they were more short-lived in the soil.

"These poisons can take years to work and can stay in the soil and watercourses for decades," he said. *"I remember the fields round here full of rabbits. At harvest time we always carried a shotgun and couldn't reload it fast enough. Now you go out and there's not a rabbit to be seen,"* he added.

"It's no good keeping quiet anymore, or we will get to a stage when everyone is dead and there is no-one left to say: "Why didn't we tell the truth?"

Dr Ken Hunter, a toxicologist at the Scottish Agricultural Science Agency said Fluoroacetamide had never been *"formally banned"* but is simply *"no longer approved for use".*

"It is a metabolic blocker and is likely to affect a wide range of organisms," he added.

In 1985, the UK's first case of BSE was diagnosed in the Smarden area, and by 1996, Kent had a much higher than average incidence of the disease with 2,094 cases among 278 farms – many less than 15 miles from Smarden.

Then a cluster of five cases of CJD, with close connections to the village emerged. Barry Barker, then 29, a self-employed woodcutter who lived at High Halden, the family of Graham Brown, then 36, a fireman who lived at Bethersden and Betty Bottle, then 59, who lived in Ashford but whose family had long links with Egerton Forstal (four miles from Smarden) and her sister Joan Stapleton also died of CJD in 1989.

Another sister Margaret Ammon was married to a herdsman and lived on a farm hit by four cases of CJD.

I then discovered that Stephen Churchill, who died of CJD in 1995 aged 19 and who lived at Devizes in Wiltshire, spent every summer at his aunt's farm at Sissinghurst, less than seven miles from Smarden.

It was also believed that the family of 29-year-old Kent solicitor Anna Pearson, who died of CJD in February 1996, had links with Smarden, current population 1,300, and that another unconfirmed case of CJD lived in the Willesborough area of Ashford, some 11 miles from the village.

People in this area of Kent were no more likely to eat BSE-infected food than other people at most stages of the epidemic.

In 1995 there were 43 deaths of CJD in the entire UK, so to have such a cluster with a small area around Smarden was both frightening and remarkable. The only other comparable small area cluster of CJD cases was on the east coast of Yorkshire adjacent to large chemical plants.

It left scientific experts asking whether the 1963 poisoning had a more lasting legacy? CJD can take between 10 and 50 years to develop in the human body.

Scientists have also noted links between pesticides and Motor Neurone Disease (MND), Parkinson's Disease, Myalgic Encephalomyelitis (ME) and Multiple Sclerosis

Some scientists and campaigners now cited organophosphate (OP) pesticides (chemically close to organochlorines) as the most likely cause of BSE and CJD, amid claims that the chemical suppresses the victim's immune system.

Mark Purdey, a farmer who was leading the OP lobby, told me he was alarmed by the details of the Smarden incident.

"The amide link in the carbon chain of Flourocetamide is the crucial factor," he said.

"Organochlorines, like organophosphates, can switch on BSE – that's been shown in laboratory conditions, so could equally switch on CJD," he added.

The link was also supported by Japanese scientist, Professor Satoshi Ishikawa, and by other specialists in the USA.

Dr James Bridges, professor of toxicology at the Robens Institute observed: *"We know about acute poisoning and we can manage the risk. But it's so much harder to manage the risk if we don't know what it is, and that is the problem with chronic poisoning."*

In 1987 the **Medical Series** journal warned that repeated exposure to organophosphate and organochlorine even at low doses *"may cause insidious cumulative toxicity".*

Dr Goram Jamal, of the Southern General Hospital in Glasgow, reported on the effects of OPs on the peripheral nervous system. He found that typical symptoms of chronic OP poisoning included numbness and tingling in the legs, muscle twitching, forgetfulness, loss of spatial judgement, sensitivity to other chemicals, muscle spasm and loss of bodily temperature control – all symptoms of BSE and CJD!

Meanwhile, the cross-bench peer the Countess of Mar, who had campaigned against the use of organophosphate sheep dips said the Smarden poisoning *"appeared to indicate once more the toxic effects or organo-pesticides."* She immediately tabled a question in the House of Lords asking the government for details of its research into the incident and to try and establish any links to CJD and BSE.

Tom Stockdale, a retired farmer and biochemist from Dumfries, called on the government to test his own theory that organo-pesticides damage the liver's ability to fight the *"bacterial toxins"* responsible for BSE and CJD.

"One possible explanation is that the disease is caused by bacterial toxins that originate in the intestines then reach the brain," he told me.

"The important point that seems to have been overlooked is that when the liver is overloaded by the need to deactivate absorption of pesticides, its capacity to deactivate bacterial toxins is decreased. Such toxins have the capacity to

disorganise protein metabolism. It is my belief that when such bacterial toxins enter the brain they produce the symptoms known as BSE and CJD," he added.

The evidence from other farmers added to the claims of a link.

Daphne Kingsley-Lewis, who kept goats at Barton Bendish in Norfolk told me: *"A few years ago I had a herd of 51 goats and I decided to use a pour-on wormer/insecticide recommended by two veterinary practices. By accident one of the first cross triplets, bred by me, received a double dose. She became ill, staggering about, falling down and unable to eat or drink unaided. Eventually she was taken to the veterinary centre in Norwich, slaughtered and a post-mortem carried out... the verdict was BSE!"*

Subsequently Ms Kingsley-Lewis was visited by a Ministry of Agriculture vet who said no goats could be taken off the premises or sold for three years.

"None of the others were ill and needless to say I did not use that wormer again. I am still of the opinion that BSE is the result of animals exposure to such chemicals," she added.

Fast forward 23 years from 1996 to 2019, and the government is still battling claims for chronic ill health from farmers historically exposed to OP sheep dip poisoning.

Were the government to concede that organophosphates were and are indeed a serious threat to health, a huge number of costly claims for compensation would result. Survivors still hope for this since neither the NHS nor the military will recognise OP poisoning officially as a medical condition.

For decades it was denied that the Health and Safety Executive (HSE) was aware of the health risks- yet in April 2015 the **Guardian** made clear that the HSE had certainly known of such links as early as 1991.

The government was consistently reluctant to inform the public about the strong circumstantial evidence of Fluoroacetamide poisoning. Declaring it a one-off industrial accident, the government avoided discussion of the actual widespread use of these chemicals as pesticides.

In 2017, the United Nations reported that an average of about 200,000 people die from the toxic exposure of pesticides per year across the world. It called for tougher global regulation of substances meant to control pests or weeds for plant cultivation.

The UN said although pesticide use has been correlated with a rise in food production, it has had *"catastrophic impacts"* on human health and the environment.

"Equally, increased food production has not succeeded in eliminating hunger worldwide. Reliance on hazardous pesticides is a short-term solution that undermines the rights to adequate food and health for present and future generations," the UN said.

It lists an array of serious illnesses and health issues with suspected links to pesticides, including cancer, Alzheimer's and Parkinson's Disease, hormone disruption, birth defects, sterility, and neurological effects.

According to the UN report, people can be exposed to dangerous levels of pesticides in a wide variety of ways, ranging from farmers who use it on their crops to babies drinking their mother's contaminated breast milk.

"Few people are untouched by pesticide exposure. They may be exposed through food, water, air, or direct contact with pesticides or residues," it said.

The UN also highlighted profound effects on the environment: *"Pesticides sprayed on crops frequently pollute the surrounding ecosystem and beyond, with unpredictable ecological consequences. Furthermore, reductions in pest populations upset the complex balance between predator and prey species in the food chain.*

"Pesticides can also decrease biodiversity of soils and contribute to nitrogen fixation, which can lead to large declines in crop yields, posing problems for food security."

And while I was revising this book in September 2022, the reality of pesticide poisoning hit home in a shocking and personal way.

Some 35 years earlier in September 1987, following months of seemingly unrelated health problems, as a raw 31-year-old I was diagnosed with a malignant Histiocytoma (a soft tissue sarcoma) of my right shoulder muscle.

Radical surgery and seven weeks of radiotherapy removed the seat of the cancer.

But it had spread to my right lung, and in May 1988 only the removal of two thirds of that lung saved my life. None of the doctors would speculate on what caused the cancer but my own amateur detective work led me to assume it may have been linked to Lindane wood treatment fluid which I had been using while renovating our old schoolhouse. Lindane had been recently placed on a banned use of toxins, known to be carcinogens.

Then in 1996, while working on a story for *The Scotsman*, I came across a report by scientists in Sweden which made a causal link between pesticides used in forestry and soft tissue sarcomas like mine. Between 1984 and 1989 we lived on Forestry Commission land and got all our water from a bore hole on that land.

I immediately telephoned Dr Gillian Birch at the Christie Hospital in Manchester – she was a co-author of the report and oversaw my cancer treatment back in 1988. She didn't remember me but found my case files and added my details to their research. She said it was possible that our water supply may have been a cause of my cancer.

Six years later in 2002, my father (then aged 72) was diagnosed with Parkinson's Disease – we think he had the disease for a few years prior to diagnosis. Dad died from Parkinson's in 2008.

As a family we never linked dad's illness with my cancer.

Then in September 2022, while researching causes of Parkinson's Disease, following my own recent diagnosis of the same condition, I read of new evidence linking it with exposure to pesticides used in forestry.

The words hit me like a runaway steam train!

For three years between 1984 and 1988 dad and I drank the same water from the same bore hole!

Parkinson's Disease is only rarely hereditary.

But exposure to deadly pesticides is often life threatening or fatal.

Dad and I had endured multiple exposures!

Meanwhile, the legacy of Smarden still lives on.

- **Appendix J**

Chapter Fourteen
VI Paedos

VIP nonces and paedophiles: Cyril Smith MP, Greville Janner MP and TV celebrity Jimmy Savile

JIMMY Savile, Gary Glitter, Greville Janner, Cyril Smith, Rolf Harris, Stuart Hall, Jonathan King, Oliver Reed and Chris Denning are just a few of the UK's high profile child sex offenders to have been convicted or outed since 2010.

But there are many more.

In 2014, the Metropolitan Police began investigating paedophile and sexual abuse claims against 76 British politicians, 178 TV and movie celebrities and seven sports stars.

Peter McKelvie, a former child protection officer who first raised the alarm about high profile individuals engaged in child sex abuse, claimed senior politicians, military figures and even people linked to the Royal Family were among the alleged abusers.

Mr McKelvie said that their campaign of abuse may have been going on for as long as 65 years, but *"there has always been the block and the cover-up and the collusion to prevent an investigation."*

His claims led to Scotland Yard's 2013 **Operation Fernbridge** investigation into allegations of a paedophile network linked to Downing Street and beyond.

"*For the last 30 years and longer than that, there have been a number of allegations made by survivors that people at the top of very powerful institutions in this country - which include politicians, judges, senior military figures and even people that have links with the Royal Family - have been involved in the abuse of children,*" claimed Mr McKelvie.

Describing the child abusers as making up a "*small percentage*" of the British Establishment at the time, Mr McKelvie admitted there was "*a slightly larger percentage*" of people who knew about the abuse but did not report it to the police.

He said these people: "*felt that in terms of their own self-interest and self-preservation and for political party reasons, it has been safer for them to cover it up than deal with it.*"

Meanwhile, a former Metropolitan Police officer said he was told a member of the Royal household and an MP had both been identified as part of a major child abuse inquiry.

But the operation was shut down by the Crown Prosecution Service (CPS) for "*national security reasons*".

The ex-officer explained how a named detective sergeant based at London's Marylebone Police Station in the late 1980s spoke to him about the investigation and the fact it had been axed.

The former officer said: "*I was in a car with two other vice squad officers. They were discussing a madam who had provided a girl of about 15 to the film actor Oliver Reed. The detective sergeant said he had just had a major child abuse investigation shut down by the CPS regarding an MP. He said the CPS had said it was not in the public's interest because it 'could destabilise national security'.*"

Reed was never prosecuted over underage sex, despite a raft of evidence against him.

The Metropolitan Police Deputy Assistant Commissioner Steve Rodhouse said: "*We have seen lots of allegations of cover-ups, and I think it's helpful that people are coming forward. We will go where the evidence takes us, without fear or favour, I think that is what the public expect.*"

In 2016, it was announced that the Independent Police Complaints Commission was investigating 14 separate referrals spanning four decades, amid cover-up claims.

The claims - referred to the IPCC by the Met – allege the force suppressed evidence, hindered or halted investigations and covered up offences because of the involvement of MPs and police officers.

Former Met Deputy Commissioner Albert Laugharne said that, while head of Lancashire Police, he had been asked by a DPP officer to lie about allegations involving the late Lib Dem MP Cyril Smith, later unmasked as a paedophile. A surveillance operation that unmasked government minister Leon Brittan's links to child sex abuse was also said to have been shut down by Met detectives.

The Sunday Mirror revealed in 2014 how the former Home Secretary was snapped by officers during a 1986 investigation into rent boy orgies run in North London buildings.

But the day before swoops on alleged suspects were due to be carried out, officers on Operation Orchid were told it had been disbanded.

Smith and top judges were also believed to have been photographed entering the underage sex dens. Sources claim up to 16 high profile figures were due to be arrested.

Leon Brittan was under investigation by the Met over sex abuse allegations at the time of his death in January 2015. But the CPS said they had not found enough evidence to prosecute and his family subsequently demanded apologies for the *"damage to his reputation"*.

In 2013, police investigating allegations of a child paedophile network seized a list naming top politicians, a member of MI5 and a famous pop star. They were allegedly visitors to a bed and breakfast guest house which operated as a brothel where youngsters were abused at gay sex parties.

The names were recorded on a handwritten note found by police at the North London home of child protection worker Mary Moss during a raid. She had initially declined to co-operate with the investigation. Documents and a laptop were seized and Ms Moss later handed over other 19 files she had put in a neighbour's shed.

The papers include a list of men who went to sex parties in the 1980s at the Elm Guest House, in Barnes, south west London.

Among them were two former Conservative cabinet ministers, four other senior Tories, a Labour MP, a prominent Irish republican and a leading National Front member. The note also allegedly named two members of the royal household – one a former Buckingham Palace employee – plus the owner of a multinational company and two pop stars.

In confidential government documents Leon Brittan was one of four senior Westminster figures named in connection to child sexual abuse.

Along with Leon Brittan, the former British diplomat Sir Peter Hayman, and former ministers William van Straubenzee and Peter Morrison were named in secret government files. It was reported that Brittan and Hayman were among the suspects who were involved in an alleged Westminster paedophile ring operating in the 1980s, according to an investigation by the Australian current affairs programme *60 Minutes* entitled *Spies, Lords and Predators.*

The fact that a paedophile ring had been operating within the British Establishment first emerged in an investigation by campaigning Tory politician Geoffrey Dickens. In November 1983, the MP for Littleborough and Saddleworth sent a 40-page document to then Home Secretary Leon Brittan detailing alleged VIP child abusers, including Cyril Smith and other senior politicians. In a newspaper interview at the time, Mr Dickens claimed his dossier contained the names of eight *"really important public figures"* that he planned to expose, and whose crimes are believed to have stretched back to the 1960s.

But in March 1984 Home Secretary Brittan told Mr Dickens that his dossier had been assessed by prosecutors and passed on to the police, but no further action was taken.

In 1989, Brittan was suddenly made Commissioner for Competition at the European Commission, resigning as an MP to take the position. He accepted the post as European Commissioner reluctantly, as it meant giving up his British parliamentary ambitions.

I found this revelation both rather poignant.

In late 1990, while I was working as the editor of a weekly newspaper in Argyll, I was told by a leading Scottish Conservative politician that Brittan had been moved to Europe, because *"he has an unnatural fascination for young boys".*

In May 1995, Geoffrey Dickens died. A short time later his wife destroyed his copy of the paedophile dossier. The only other copies

- one received by Mr Brittan and another allegedly sent to the Director of Public Prosecutions - are believed to have been lost or destroyed.

In September 2010, Cyril Smith died aged 82 without ever being charged with sex offences. In November 2012, the CPS admitted that Smith should have been charged with crimes of abuse more than 40 years earlier. The CPS also admitted Smith had been investigated in 1970, 1974, 1998, and 1999, but they had rejected every opportunity to prosecute him.

A former special branch officer, Tony Robinson, said a historic dossier *"packed"* with information about Smith's sex crimes was actually in the hands of MI5 - despite officially having been lost decades earlier.

Then in June 2014, former Labour MP Simon Danczuk called on Leon Brittan to say what he knew about the Dickens dossier.

A month later Home Office permanent secretary Mark Sedwill revealed that 114 files relating to historic allegations of child sex abuse, from between 1979 and 1999, had disappeared from the Home Office.

I squirmed with anger when I heard this news as it suddenly seemed personal.

I had suffered systematic sexual abuse as a young teenager in the early 1970s. The abuser was the District Commissioner for Scouts in my home town and a locally well-known man.

The abuse had begun soon after my 14th birthday and over the course of 15 months, it became regular, routine and progressively invasive. I had been sworn to secrecy by my abuser. After all, I was the one he had caught *'playing with'* himself and I would be totally humiliated if anyone found out.

I did eventually escape in the June of 1971. But drowning in guilt, fear, shame and embarrassment I could not tell anyone.

Many years later in 1990, I moved to Scotland and found a geographical escape from my past. One year after moving north I met a young woman who told me of the sexual abuse she had suffered as a 14-year-old, adding that I was the first person she had confided in. This was an epiphany and I saw a possible way out.

A colleague at work was married to a police officer and I used him to help me lodge a formal complaint against my abuser via the Inspector at the local police station. He, in turn, passed on the complaint to the police force in my childhood home town.

Two weeks passed before I was asked to attend the local police station to talk with the Inspector again. He invited me into an interview room at the back of the station, where he told me something I was not ready for... my abuser was dead.

How could my abuser be dead? How could he not face justice for what he had done?

Then some 14 years later in January 2006 I moved to Wales to begin again, both at work and at home. Work had a purpose as I edited a small weekly newspaper. It was treading water, but allowed stability for a full seven years.

Stories came and went and along the way and I also wasted no opportunity to expose convicted child sex offenders whenever their cases came to light. Ironically the so-called *'paedo files'* in North Wales seemed more expansive than anywhere else I had lived or worked previously.

Among paedophiles and child abusers we exposed were a British Army sergeant major, a North Wales man who ran an orphanage in Africa, a children's play park designer, a head teacher and many more.

My empathy with the victims was immense and we made sure we named, photographed and shamed the guilty – often on the front page of my paper.

Then in June 2013, while researching online for more information about another North Wales' child sex abuse case we were carrying in the paper, I decided to look for any lasting details about my own abuser.

It didn't take long and the moment will stay with me forever. I discovered that my abuser was indeed dead. But he had died in 1996, aged 64... some five years AFTER the police told me he was already dead! I double and triple checked my facts.

Had the police in 1991 cocked up? Had they identified the wrong man? Or worse still was it a conspiracy to protect someone of importance in the local community? How many people in power were entangled in this paedophile network? I guess I will never know, but I had been denied the justice and closure I had wanted all those years earlier.

Six years later as I write this chapter I believe one thing is certain… paedophiles and child abusers were and are immersed in the highest levels of British society.

But how do they operate without recrimination and above the arms of the law?

It has been a long and sorry story.

Back in the 1970s, at the time of my own abuse, paedophiles even tried to go mainstream.

PIE (the Paedophile Information Exchange) was formed in 1974. It campaigned for *"children's sexuality"*. It wanted the government to axe or lower the age of consent. It offered support to adults *"in legal difficulties concerning sexual acts with consenting under age partners"*. The real aim was to normalise sex with children.

It's an ideology that seems chilling now. But PIE managed to gain support from some professional bodies and progressive groups. It received invitations from student unions, won sympathetic media coverage and found academics willing to push its message.

One of PIE's key tactics was to try to conflate its cause with gay rights.

Homosexuality had only been decriminalised in 1967. There was still prejudice and inequality. The age of consent was 16 for heterosexuals but 21 for homosexual men.

It was easy to join PIE. According to a ***Times*** legal report on a blackmail case from February 1977, there was no need for subterfuge, just an application and a cheque for £4.

In the report, the prosecutor in the case stated: *"He said on the form that he was a paedophile, male, married, 29 years old and attracted to girls between the ages of seven and 13 years."*

Unsettlingly for a modern audience, the PIE member received anonymity (as is typical in blackmail cases) and there is no mention of any prosecution of him. Meanwhile, the blackmailer was jailed for three years.

The brazenness could be shocking. Keith Hose, one of PIE's leaders during the 1970s, was quoted by a newspaper saying: *"I am a paedophile. I am attracted to boys from about 10, 11, and 12 years of age. I may have had sexual relations with children, but it would be unwise to say."*

When Peter Hain, then president of the Young Liberals, described paedophilia as *"a wholly undesirable abnormality"*, a fellow activist hit back. *"It is sad that Peter has joined the hang 'em and flog 'em brigade. His views are not the views of most Young Liberals."* And when a columnist supported Hain in the **Guardian** he was inundated with mail from people - many willing to give their name - who defended sex with children.

A **Guardian** article in 1977 noted with dismay how the group was growing. By its second birthday in October 1976, it had 200 members. There was a London group, a Middlesex group being planned, and with regional branches to follow. The article speaks of PIE's hopes to widen the membership to include women and heterosexual men.

But during the 1980s, PIE came a cropper. Its notoriety grew in 1982 with the trial of Geoffrey Prime, who was both a KGB spy and a member of PIE. He was jailed for 32 years for passing on secrets from his job at GCHQ to the Soviet Union, and for a series of sex attacks on young girls.

A short article from the **Daily Mail** in June 1983 records how a Scout Master in Castle Bromwich, Birmingham, resigned after being exposed as a member of PIE.

In August 1983, a Scottish headmaster, Charles Oxley, handed over a dossier about PIE to Scotland Yard after infiltrating the group. He said the group had about 1,000 members.

PIE was eventually disbanded in 1984.

And the story moves on...

In November 2016, former England and Tottenham footballer Paul Stewart said he had been sexually abused at a similar age to me. His statement at last opened up the doors for many others to speak out.

Former Crewe players Andy Woodward and Steve Walters, ex-Manchester City player David White, as well as Mr Stewart all spoke out about abuse in the game.

Mr Stewart, now 58, a former England international who started his career at Blackpool and also played for Tottenham Hotspur,

Manchester City and Liverpool, said an unnamed coach abused him daily for four years up to the age of 15.

Mr Stewart said he believed there were *"hundreds of victims"* of sexual abuse who could come forward.

The NSPCC said callers to a new abuse hotline had raised concerns about children now and in the past, and it expected *"many more"* to come forward.

But paedophilia goes right to the top of British society.

And in 2019 leaked FBI files revealed that the late Lord Mountbatten had *"a perversion for young boys"*.

Lord Louis Mountbatten, was an uncle of Prince Philip, Duke of Edinburgh, and second cousin once removed of Queen Elizabeth II.

The decorated war hero – who was a valued mentor to his great-nephew Prince Charles and was said to have counselled him on his love life – was under US surveillance for more than three decades.

Ron Perks, who was the Earl's driver in Malta in 1948, also broke his silence to claim one of his favourite places was the Red House near Rabat, *"an upmarket gay brothel used by naval officers"*.

And Anthony Daly, a rent boy to the rich and famous in the 1970s, claims he was told *"Mountbatten had something of a fetish for uniforms and beautiful boys in school uniform"*.

The first FBI files on the Earl date to February 1944 – soon after he was made supreme allied commander in south-east Asia during the Second World War.

After the war, he was the last Viceroy of India, then chief of defence until 1965. He was killed in an IRA bomb attack in 1979.

Homosexual acts were banned until 1967 and it is believed many FBI memos on Mountbatten's sexuality have been edited or destroyed.

But one file references a 1944 interview with Elizabeth de la Poer Beresford, Baroness Decies.

The memo says: *"She states that in these circles Lord Louis Mountbatten and his wife are considered persons of extremely low morals.*

"She stated Lord Louis Mountbatten was known to be a homosexual with a perversion for young boys. In Lady Decies' opinion he is an unfit man to direct

any sort of military operations because of this condition. She stated further his wife was considered equally erratic."

In early 2020, it was revealed in MI5 files disclosed to a public inquiry that former Prime Minister Margaret Thatcher had personally supported one of her MPs who had an alleged *"penchant for small boys"*. An MI5 lawyer told the Independent Inquiry into Child Sexual Abuse (IICSA) that the service considered only the national security implications of allegations of possible child abuse by Peter Morrison, Conservative MP for Chester, and did not pass information to the police.

The lawyer said MI5's review of its files uncovered no evidence to indicate the existence of a Westminster paedophile network and nothing to suggest any attempt to cover up a child abuse ring in parliament.

But the witness, who gave evidence anonymously, admitted that memos and a letter from 1986 had discussed claims that Morrison had a *"penchant for small boys",* and there was nothing to indicate MI5 passed the information in its possession to police.

The inquiry heard that two 1986 memos were written by Eliza Manningham-Buller, who went on to be the director general of MI5 between 2002 and 2007.

Her role, the inquiry was told, would have been confined to passing on information, rather than making decisions on what to do about the MP, who had been one of the first backbenchers to urge Thatcher to stand for the Tory leadership in 1975 and was her parliamentary private secretary in 1990.

In one 1986 memo, the future Dame Eliza stated Morrison had told her he was being door-stepped by reporters seeking comments about five-year-old allegations that the press had become keen to publish.

The inquiry heard Ms Manningham-Buller wrote that Morrison did not tell her what the allegations involved, adding: *"Peter hoped the press would publish something so that he could sue and nail the lies that were being spread about him.*

"The prime minister was aware of it and was supporting Peter."

Admitting that in the 1980s the service considered the allegations only in national security terms, the MI5 lawyer said: *"It's a matter of regret that no consideration was given at the time to the criminal aspects of the matter.*

"The knowledge and understanding of child sexual abuse at the time was much, much lower than it is now. So I'm to some extent unsurprised that wider consideration wasn't given in 1986. With hindsight, it's a matter of real regret."

Brian Altman QC, lead counsel to the inquiry, also quoted from the 2014 independent Wanless-Whittam review of information held in connection with child abuse between 1979 and 1999, which had summarised MI5's handling of the Morrison allegations by saying: *"In response to claims from two sources that a named member of parliament has 'a penchant for small boys' ... Matters conclude with acceptance of his word that he does not, and the observation that 'at the present stage ... the risks of political embarrassment to the government is rather greater than the security danger'."*

Mr Altman said: *"The risk to children is not considered at all."*

The witness said that if the same information came into MI5's possession today, it would be referred to the police.

Mr Morrison, who between September 1986 and June 1987 was deputy to Conservative Party chairman Norman Tebbit, was knighted in 1991 and died in 1995 aged 51.

The inquiry was told by Mr Altman that there will be exploration of *"whether there was a culture whereby people of public prominence were shielded from investigation at the expense of their victims"*.

Mr Morrison was one of three case studies, along with Cyril Smith and Green Party member David Challenor - who was jailed for 22 years in August 2019 after being convicted of sexual assault against a 10-year-old girl - considered by the inquiry.

Mr Altman said a question by Labour deputy leader Tom Watson in the House of Commons in 2012, in which he said there was *"clear intelligence suggesting a powerful paedophile network linked to parliament and No 10"*, could be seen as the *"catalyst for the establishment of this inquiry"*.

In late February 2020, an official inquiry found that political institutions in the UK failed to respond to historical claims of child sexual abuse but there was no evidence of an organised paedophile network at Westminster.

The Independent Inquiry into Child Sexual Abuse said there had been a *"significant problem"* of deference towards people of public prominence. Its report said political parties and police had turned a *"blind eye"*.

Former Liberal Party leader Lord Steel, one of those it criticised, was forced to quit his party as a result of the inquiry's findings. It found that institutions *"regularly put their own reputations or political interests before child protection"*.

It cited as an example Lord Steel, who was criticised for not acting on information that the late MP Cyril Smith had abused children.

Lord Steel earlier told the inquiry how in 1979 he failed to pass on allegations against the then MP for Rochdale - even though he believed them to be true - because it was *"past history"*.

He subsequently recommended Smith for his knighthood.

Professor Alexis Jay, who chaired the inquiry, said: *"It is clear to see that Westminster institutions have repeatedly failed to deal with allegations of child sexual abuse, from turning a blind eye to actively shielding abusers."*

However, the report found no evidence of a co-ordinated *"paedophile ring"* in Westminster, following claims by Carl Beech, who was jailed in 2019 for making false allegations.

It stated there was also no evidence such a network was covered up by security services or police.

It highlighted how former Prime Minister Margaret Thatcher and ex-Conservative party chairman Norman Tebbit were aware in the 1980s of rumours about Tory MP Peter Morrison's paedophile tendencies, but did nothing about it.

The allegations *"should have rung alarm bells in government"*, it said. It found there had been a *"consistent culture for years"* in the Tory whips' offices to protect the image of their party by *"playing down rumours and protecting politicians from gossip or scandal at all costs"*.

The report said that at that time *"nobody seemed to care about the fate of the children involved, with status and political concerns overriding all else"*.

"Even though we did not find evidence of a Westminster network, the lasting effect on those who suffered as children from being sexually abused by individuals linked to Westminster has been just as profound," it added.

The report identified Peter McKelvie and said while his concerns were genuine, there was simply no evidence to support them.

In its conclusions, the report states: *"There is ample evidence that individual perpetrators of child sexual abuse have been linked to Westminster.*

"However the inquiry has found no evidence to support the most sensational of the various allegations of child sexual abuse made over recent years that there has been a powerful paedophile network operating within Westminster."

The report goes on: *"Similarly no evidence of any attempts to cover up or suppress information about the existence of such a ring was found at M15, SIS, GCHQ or in the Metropolitan Police Special Branch records now held by Metropolitan Police Counter Terrorism Command."*

The IICSA inquiry was launched by Theresa May in July 2014 and is split into 15 separate strands, looking at alleged abuse and subsequent cover ups in various institutions including the Roman Catholic and Anglican churches and children's homes.

Just as this book was going to press, it was revealed that a computer hard drive belonging to a sex offender couldn't be used as evidence against him because it had been kept in a police chief's safe for 14 years. The storage device containing indecent images of children belonged to ex-Lord Mayor of Leeds Neil Taggart. But the West Yorkshire Police and Crime Commissioner's (PCC) office did not disclose its existence until after Taggart admitted child sex offences.

PCC Mark Burns-Williamson said he was unaware the images existed until then. He apologised for the *"embarrassing"* mistake but added: *"There's been no intentional cover-up with this."*

An employee at the PCC's office, who had previously been employed by the West Yorkshire Police Authority, remembered the storage device on 6th June 2017.

Taggart, who was a former police authority chairman, was jailed in July 2017 for making and distributing indecent photographs of children. When officers had searched his home in September 2016 they discovered 36,003 indecent images and videos of children on his computer equipment.

When Taggart left the police authority in May 2003 his hard drive was *"retained and stored"*.

A police whistle-blower said: *"I can't think of any reason why they would have kept the hard drive. It was expensive equipment. On a high-profile investigation for very serious offences of child sexual imagery, why have they not brought it forward?*

"I don't know if he (Mr Burns-Williamson) withheld evidence, but given that it took so long to disclose this evidence, it does seem suspicious."

Mr Burns-Williamson said: *"As soon as the member of staff recalled that something had been stored, West Yorkshire Police were immediately notified. It's embarrassing, yes. There have been errors made, so, yes, I absolutely do apologise for that."*

The paedophile network is at last beginning to unravel.

Chapter Fifteen
Russian Roulette

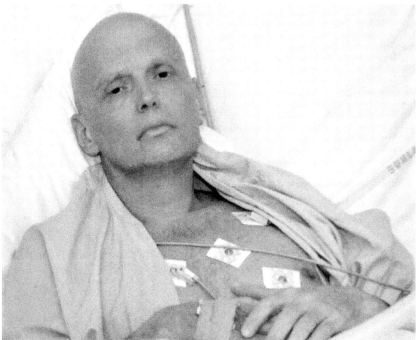

Alexander Litvinenko on his deathbed in 2006 after being allegedly poisoned with radioactive Polonium

I GUESS it was my 12th birthday when my father took me to the cinema to see my first so-called *adult* movie.

He had asked me to choose which film I would like to see from a *What's On* guide in our local evening newspaper. And as an enquiring boy devoted to James Bond movies I plumped for Martin Ritt's film adaptation of John Le Carre's spy novel ***The Spy Who Came in From the Cold***, starring Richard Burton and Claire Bloom. Dad warned me that this BAFTA winning film was a *"serious"* movie and might be too grown-up for me, but after pestering he agreed to take me to the local ABC cinema in Hove for my birthday treat.

The movie was indeed dark – the fact it was filmed in black and white made it seem even more sombre – and told the grim story of real spies, double agents and double crosses set against the Soviet Union and the Berlin Wall. The movie was full of intrigue and ends as both Burton's character, double agent Alex Leamus, and his co-worker Nan Perry, a young member of the Communist Party are both shot dead while scaling the Berlin Wall.

I recall gasping in shock... surely this isn't how James Bond movies end.

This was my very first glimpse of the world of real spies.

Years later some lines said by the Burton character Leamas still haunt me: *"What the hell do you think spies are? Moral philosophers measuring everything they do against the word of God or Karl Marx? They're not. They're just a bunch of seedy squalid bastards like me, little men, drunkards, queers, henpecked husbands, civil servants playing Cowboys and Indians to brighten their rotten little lives."*

As the years passed I became increasingly engrossed in books and movies which cast a glimmer of light onto the unseen world of spies and counter spies.

The Whistle Blower, a 1986 British made film starring Nigel Havers, James Fox and Michael Caine gave me an even more fascinating insight... this time into the dirty workings of British Intelligence.

Caine plays Frank Jones a retired British naval officer. His bright and idealistic son, Robert (Havers), works as a linguist at GCHQ, the secret British intelligence listening station, using his love of Russian to listen to various pieces of communication on the other side of the Iron Curtain.

Robert tells his father that strange things are happening at GCHQ, and he's planning on leaving the service.

He tells his dad: *"We live in an unseen world of shadows. Then there are the lies. They start on the very first day. Nobody is as they seem, nothing is what it is made out to be. The truth recedes. Our secret world is beyond the law"*.

Those lines were to stay with me for all my years as an investigative newspaper journalist.

But however well written and acted they were, these movies were, after all, sanitised entertainment for the masses. They provided just small glimpses into the real world of shadows, of murders, phone tapping, burglaries, propaganda, downright lies and dirty tricks.

Then in 1995, while working as an off-diary reporter for *The Herald* daily newspaper in Glasgow I was asked to investigate and write a lengthy series of news features on the 10th anniversary of the suspicious death of Scottish nationalist politician Willie McRae.

It became one of the most intriguing investigations I had ever undertaken.

At the time of his death on a bleak Highland road in 1985, close friends of Mr McRae claimed he was carrying secret documents relating to the nuclear industry and may have been the victim of a government secret services assassination.

Mr McRae, a lawyer and leading figure in the SNP, set off from Glasgow on Friday, 5th April 1985, to spend the weekend at his cottage in Kintail in north west Scotland.

At 10am the next day he was found in his crashed Volvo by an Australian tourist, about 35 yards off the A87 near Loch Loyne. The car was upright across a small burn and believed to have been there since midnight.

The Australian waved down a car in which by sheer chance Dundee SNP councillor, David Coutts, was travelling to Skye with his wife Alison and two friends.

Mr Coutts, who immediately recognised Mr McRae, summoned an ambulance and the police. He also discovered that Mr McRae's cheque cards and papers were strewn some way from the car, the papers meticulously torn up.

PC Kenny Crawford, a young constable on relief duty from Inverness, quickly gathered personal items from the scene of the crash and placed them in a holdall.

Mr Coutts told me that it seemed to him that the young policeman was keen to get off the hillside quickly. *"He didn't even ask for my name, but just bundled everything up,"* he said.

The injured Mr McRae was taken first to Raigmore Hospital in Inverness and later to Aberdeen Royal Infirmary, where he died at 3am on the Sunday. However, it was only when a nurse washed his head on his arrival at Aberdeen that a gunshot wound in his right temple was discovered and the police informed.

Officers from the Northern Constabulary revisited the scene of the crash, but by then it was impossible to conduct the level of rigorous, on-site investigation which might have produced crucial answers.

During the search PC Crawford found a Smith and Wesson .22 pistol beyond where the car was found. It had been fired twice.

Mr Crawford, who had since left the force, told me in 1995 that the gun was *"some yards"* downstream, but he believed it had been knocked from a ledge in the car when they had retrieved Mr McCrae's body. He also believed the gun had fallen into a small waterfall and the fast running burn had transported the weapon from the site of the vehicle.

However, Mr Coutts said that while removing Mr McCrae's body from the car, PC Crawford's cap had fallen into the burn. He said he bent down and retrieved it yet saw no sign of a gun.

The evidence contradicted statements made by former Solicitor General Peter Fraser that the gun had been found directly under the door of the car.

The case was closed formally by Thomas Aitchison, the procurator-fiscal in Inverness, who decided the death was not suspicious. Mr Fraser made the personal decision not to order a Fatal Accident Inquiry into the death.

When I interviewed him in 1995, Mr Aitchison said the case came under the Official Secrets Act and he had been reminded at his retirement four years earlier that he was still bound by the Act.

"I was told not to talk about this case to anyone," he added.

Some aspects of Mr McRae's lifestyle had been used by the Crown over the years to indicate he was potentially suicidal. Yet on Friday 5th April 1985, he showed little sign of being a man about to take his own life. His diary was full and he remarked to a number of people that he was close to completing some important project. *"I've got them, I've got them!"* the 61-year-old told friends excitedly, but he also expressed fears that Special Branch was closing in on him.

Sources I spoke with in 1995 believed he was carrying secret documents relating to the Dounreay experimental nuclear facility at the time of his death.

Mr McRae had won a notable victory against the UK Atomic Energy Authority in 1980 when he presented the principal legal opposition to plans to dump nuclear waste in the Mullwharcher hills, Ayrshire. He was planning to repeat the performance at the inquiry to reprocess nuclear waste at Dounreay: his legal firm was named on the list of objectors.

A close colleague of Mr McRae claimed that on the night of his death he was carrying vital and confidential reports which showed glaring holes in Dounreay's health and safety record.

I was shown copies of these reports, which revealed problems with various parts of the nuclear facility including areas of weakness in Highly Active Analytical Cells and the discovery of a radiation field from gamma particles hidden within a reprocessing plant.

Peter Roche was a former activist for the *Scottish Campaign to Resist the Atomic Menace (Scram)* who later worked for Greenpeace. He said it had been long believed that Dounreay was being used as an unlicensed emergency store for high quality plutonium for military purposes, and Mr McRae may also have had evidence of this. In either case McRae was seen as a liability to Britain's controversial nuclear industry.

A copy of the Mullwharcher report that he was also said to have been carrying was nowhere to be found after the incident. His other copy went missing after a break-in and fire three years earlier at the Edinburgh headquarters of *Scram*. McRae's home had often been broken into, he believed by British secret services.

A year before his death, an elderly rose-grower and nuclear protester, Hilda Murrell, was found murdered after important files had been stolen from her home in Shrewsbury.

John Conway, a retired police officer with the Northern Constabulary said: *"Because of who and what he was, William McRae for years had been a 'known person' not only to the security service MI5, but also to Special Branch officers of Strathclyde Police and the Northern Constabulary."*

Mr Coutts later added: *"Until the powers that be can prove Willie's death was a suicide I am convinced there has been a massive cover-up.*

"I hope that as a result of your investigations we may now get a proper inquiry into the circumstances surrounding his death."

A spokesman for the Celtic League said my evidence had made the case for an open inquiry into Willie McCrae's death *"irresistible"*.

At the time of writing this chapter – some 25 years later – no formal inquiry has ever been called into McCrae's death.

But soon after I had concluded this investigation for **The Herald** I was handed a book by friendly source working for a prominent Labour MP, who had particular interest in the *"dirty tricks"* of the British secret services.

The book **Open Verdict** by Tony Collins, first published in 1990, was a true eye-opener.

Collins' heavily researched 260 page account details 25 mysterious deaths of people – mostly computer programmers – working in Britain's defence industries. Despite the range of projects, their work essentially concerned different facets of the same problem: electronic warfare.

The case histories collated by Collins suggest that the people involved in electronic warfare had an unfortunate habit of dying under the strangest circumstances. They go to Bristol and either jump off a bridge or drive off in a car with nylon rope tied to a tree and looped round their neck. They apply the handbrake while driving down a motorway, ending up in a U-turn and hit the brick wall of a disused cafe with extra cans of petrol in the car boot to ensure incineration. They tie their hands, and put a plastic bag over their head, or in the case of one woman, hop in high heels into a lake. They connect their teeth to the mains supply or they jump out of a hotel window. And so it goes on.

A particularly popular method of suicide for those working in the defence industry seems to be gassing with carbon monoxide. Someone even went to the lengths of lying under a car in a garage with their face near the exhaust pipe. They stab themselves to death, too!

Yet coroners, police chiefs and defence spokespeople all seem confident that there are no suspicious linkages.

As an exception to this rule, Collins quotes the coroner in one case as admitting: *"I can't say where the pressure is coming from. Please don't ask. I will lose my job. So much pressure has been put on me from all quarters."*

Collins readily admits that at least some of the deaths were innocent suicides. But the sum total of coincidence remains just too hard to swallow and stacks up as a firm pointer to some unknown common factor… the work of British Secret Services.

But as in real life, there is no neat explanation. The best Collins can do is run through the possible explanations and add an epilogue. This tells the story of an engineer who believed he was the victim of psychological warfare that nearly drove him to an accident, which a coroner would probably have interpreted as suicide.

Collins offers no solutions to the puzzles he has documented. But the finger of suspicion ends up pointing firmly at psychological pressure, perhaps with the assistance of chemical hallucinogens, brought to bear on workers in the defence industry who are party to the most valuable secrets and who have become potential security risks either because of personal peccadillos that leave them open to blackmail, or because they simply wanted to change their job.

At the time Randall Heather, a counter-intelligence researcher at St Edmund's College, Cambridge, entertained the possibility that hostile Secret Service agencies – or even our own - were capable of a sophisticated attack on defence scientists.

"It is possibly an attempt to intimidate the small group of scientists who work in these fields," he said. *"These are not normal types of accidents and suicides. These are not normal types of people who are dying."*

I refer back to my chapter about Depleted Uranium and the most peculiar death of Stephen Milligan MP who was found dead in his London flat in 1994. He was naked except for a pair of stockings and suspenders, with an electrical flex tied around his neck and a black bin liner over his head, with a whole orange stuffed in his mouth.

Now fast forward to 2006 and the very public murder of FSB turned MI6 agent Alexander Litvinenko. It took 10 years until British judge Robert Owen's 300 page report into the death of Litvinenko, alleged that Russia's President Vladimir Putin *"probably"* ordered his killing.

And then like a John Le Carre scripted double cross, it emerged that our own British secret service MI5 were the more likely murderers of the double agent.

Litvinenko, a former agent of Russia's FSB, the successor to the KGB, defected to Britain in 2000 and worked for MI6. In November 2006, the spy died of acute radiation syndrome in a London hospital. Ever since, his death has been used as political football in UK-Russia diplomacy.

So, after a judicial inquiry held during a period of unprecedented anti-Russian feeling in the UK, we finally arrived at Judge Owen's verdict.

Interestingly, much of the evidence presented to him was kept private for *"security reasons."*

Judge Owen stated: *"There can be no doubt that Alexander Litvinenko was poisoned by Mr Lugovoi and Mr Kovtun (two former KGB agents) in the Pine Bar of London's luxury Millennium Hotel on 1st November, 2006.*

"I have further concluded that the FSB operation to kill Mr Litvinenko was probably approved by Mr Patrushev, then head of the FSB, and also by President Putin," he added.

But Judge Owen had no actual evidence that Putin ordered Litvinenko's murder.

That didn't stop our right-wing press launching into hysterical overdrive when the judgement was announced. The **Daily Mail**, not known for restraint, decided there was a *"new cold war."*

"Images reveal how Russian spy was poisoned with Polonium in London hotel - as bombshell report reveals Putin DID order his assassination," it claimed.

The paper centred its coverage on Litvinenko's claims that Putin was a *"paedophile"*.

The Sun, also couldn't grasp the meaning of *"probably"*.

Their headline screamed: *Alexander Litvinenko was murdered because he accused Putin of being a Paedo.*

Russia's government responded angrily to the accusations.

Foreign Ministry spokeswoman Marina Zakharova said: *"It is no surprise that the launch of a public inquiry into Litvinenko's death coincided with the flaring of tensions in Ukraine. The UK authorities created a dangerous precedent where they used their domestic legal system in a politically laden investigation."*

It is an interesting political paradox.

While our government and judiciary only took 10 years to complete their Litvinenko probe, it's been 26 years since our own agents *"probably"* murdered Irish civil rights lawyer, Pat Finucane.

It is suspected that former PM Margaret Thatcher *"probably"* ordered the killing.

So, why in 2016 did David Cameron believe that Marina Litvinenko, a Russian, had more right to an investigation into her husband's murder than UK citizen Geraldine Finucane? The hypocrisy is shameful.

We pride ourselves on our justice system. But we have many examples where fairness is selective and can be influenced by the political issues of the day. The Hillsborough Disaster, Cyril Smith and Greville Janner's paedophile activities, The Lockerbie Disaster, The Guildford Four and The Birmingham Six all bear testament to that.

So, let's look at the Litvinenko case from a less jaundiced position

Litvinenko defected from Russia to Britain after he was sacked from the Russian FSB for unprofessional misconduct. He became a British citizen and worked for extensively for MI6. He was a valuable asset to the British owing to the very public allegations he made and they were able to broadcast through the media for smearing Putin and other Russian government officials with corruption claims.

As a former *"Kremlin spy",* the propaganda value that our government and its media allies exploited through Litvinenko was considerable.

But then came an even more valuable propaganda opportunity for the British – Litvinenko's death.

Who is to say that his British handlers did not bump off the Russian former spy with their own supply of radioactive Polonium?

And given Litvinenko's personal umbrage with the Russian government for being sacked from the FSB, he could be relied on by the British to give a plausible-sounding death bed statement imputing Putin for his demise.

Litvinenko's own father Walter Litvinenko now admits he pursued a smear campaign against the Russian government out of grief, but changed his mind after Aleksandr's widow revealed his son had been working for British intelligence.

"If I knew back then that my son worked for the MI6, I would not speculate about his death. It would be none of my business," he said.

"He might as well have been killed by Russian secret services. They had a right to do it because traitors are to be killed," he added.

He called his son a victim of a grand spy game. But he doubts that Andrey Lugovoy, who British police named their chief suspect, had a hand in his death or acted as a government agent.

"The FSB wouldn't send some dumbhead to spill Polonium on himself, to leave traces all over my son. It appears that someone left traces of Polonium on Lugovoy intentionally. Polonium traces were found at the stadium, on the road and even on a plane. It's strange to think that Lugovoy would be such an idiot," he said.

He says he regrets his participation in the smear campaign against Russia in general and Putin in particular.

Andrey Lugovoy, the businessman Scotland Yard accused of killing the double agent, also spoke about Litvinenko's father's change of heart.

"Litvinenko's father's comments reflect what I've been saying for more than five years are that Britain's accusations don't stand up," he said.

Lugovoy reiterated sentiments that the British Secret Services had embarked on a slander campaign in an attempt to *"discredit Russia."*

He also drew a connection between the death of Litvinenko and the British Intelligence Services. *"Litvinenko died in November 2006. In March-April, I was openly offered cooperation by MI6 and in order to motivate me somehow, I was denied a visa. That was in May 2006. And after I called Litvinenko, I was granted a visa all of a sudden. I have always connected these two events,"* Lugovoy recalled.

Litvinenko's younger brother also believes that MI5 probably committed the murder. Maxim Litvinenko rejects the findings of Judge Owen's inquiry into his brother's death, saying that to blame the Kremlin is *"ridiculous."* He says the report was an obvious attempt to put pressure on Russia and that British Secret Services had more reason to want Litvinenko dead than Putin.

Maxim said: *"I don't believe for a second that the Russian authorities were involved. The Russians had no reason to want Alexander dead. My brother was not a Russian spy, he was more like a policeman. He was in the FSB, but he worked against organised crime, murders, arms trafficking, stuff like that. He did not know any state secrets or go on any special missions. It is the Western media that have called him a spy."*

His relations with Russia were so stable that Alexander planned to return, his brother claimed, because he didn't have enough work in London.

"He had already started to get in touch with old friends and would have gone back in due course," he said. *"My father and I are sure that the Russian authorities are not involved. It's all a set-up to put pressure on the Russian government."*

He claimed that British authorities had not collaborated with Russian investigators on his brother's case and cast doubt on whether Polonium was really the murder weapon saying he believes it could have been planted to frame the Russians.

"I believe he could have been killed by another poison maybe thallium, which killed him slowly and the Polonium was planted afterwards," he claimed. *"We have always asked for his body to be exhumed so that we can verify the presence of Polonium in the body but we have been ignored. Now after 10 years any trace would have disappeared anyway so we will never know."*

He also claimed that several other deaths, including the suicide of Boris Berezovsky, the dissident who had initially supported Litvinenko financially, and the murder of the owner of a nightclub where traces of Polonium were found, could be linked to his brother's death.

Judge Owen's inquiry report is also based on forged evidence, claimed Kovtun, one of the two Russians suspected of poisoning Litvinenko.

"There had been no doubts Judge Robert Owen would arrive at such conclusions. These rely on forged evidence and the open hearings exposed that. There were no doubts that when the proceedings continue behind closed doors, forged evidence will be used again," he said.

Kovtun described the pieces of evidence presented to the inquiry as *"insane and easily refutable."*

"The witness was giving conflicting testimonies all the time. The case is extremely politicized," he said. *"Yet I'd hoped for the common sense and courage of Judge Owen. May this decision remain on his conscience?"*

Fast forward once again and in 2018, we witnessed the copycat of all copycats of attempted spy killings with the Salisbury chemical attack.

And within hours the British government was again holding Moscow responsible for the attempted assassination of Sergei Skripal and his daughter Julia in the quiet Wiltshire town… just eight miles from its own chemical and biological warfare laboratory at Porton Down!

It was widely publicised that the real identities of the suspects Alexander Petrov and Ruslan Boshirov had been established by British security agencies and this proved that they were serving officers in the GRU, the Russian military intelligence service

These details as well as other information, gathered through a variety of methods of intelligence, were passed on to allied countries, with one instalment delivered just before the issue was addressed at a highly charged session of the United Nations Security Council.

It was the contents of this intelligence which, according to diplomatic sources, led to the US and other Western states joining the UK in a vociferous condemnation of Russia. This support would not necessarily have been automatic, the diplomats pointed out, had the information provided not been strong and persuasive. It should be noted, however, that Italy's populist government did not join in with denouncing Moscow.

Yet Emmanuel Macron stressed to French diplomats that the Cold War must not restart and there needed to be dialogue with Moscow on a range of issues from chemical weapons, cybersecurity, missile proliferation and polar region environment. A swathe of central European countries –
Hungary, Austria, and the Czech Republic – had been vocal about closer ties with Russia.

The site in Salisbury where the Skirpals were found collapsed on a public bench – the bench has now been removed

Was the Salisbury attack a useful club to beat Russia into negotiations? There has been endless theorising in the media about the nature of the attack – that Novichok was inadvertently brought in by Julia Skripal on her clothing or, in another version, a bag of sweets; that Julia was the real target after *"a bust-up with her boyfriend's mum because he said they were starting a family"* (the woman was supposedly a high-ranking Russian official); that the Novichok was put into the Skripals' drinks in a pub; that the breakthrough in identifying suspects came after the *"chilling"* content of an electronic message to Moscow that was picked up by a junior personnel at an RAF station in Cyprus saying: *"The package has been delivered"* and so on.

Then, after Salisbury resident Dawn Sturgess sadly died after coming into contact with Novichok remnants from the Skripal attack, came the tale that teams of Russian agents had been making *"dead drops"* of the nerve agent all over the city in preparation for the attack; and that there was a new lead of *"a giant crop circle"* showing *"the symbol of chemical weapons"* spotted just hours before the death.

The Russian ambassador in London, Alexander Yakovenko, then accused MI5, MI6 and the CIA of deliberately planting these stories.

Yet almost five years later the UK government has failed to provide a direct motive for the attack on the Skripals.

Sergei Skripal had been released in a spy swap in 2010 and had been living openly under his own name in this country since then. Other Russians who were part of that exchange continue to live similarly openly, in this country or elsewhere, without facing any threats.

The only explanation – one arrived at by default – is that the attempt on Sergei Skripal's life was in revenge for comrades he had betrayed to MI6, for money, after becoming a double agent.

But there is no explanation why this should happen so many years later, breaking in the process the traditional rules of a spy swap. The timing of the act, with all the adverse publicity it would attract, with a Presidential election looming and just weeks before Russia was due to host the FIFA World Cup makes no sense.

The narrative reads straight out of a badly written spy novel:

- The GU, Russia's military intelligence unit, dispatched two of their elite officers, who proceeded to fly direct from Moscow under aliases they had allegedly already employed and using Russian passports. These alleged assassins carried with them two perfume bottles full of Novichok, one of the deadliest nerve agents ever devised. This would be enough to kill around 800,000 people.

- On arriving in the UK these highly-trained covert agents book a hotel with a CCTV camera on the front door, and the next day, 3rd March, they travel to Salisbury by train, allegedly to recon the area, then return to London. They are apparently observed by CCTV cameras the entire time.

- The day following, on 4th March, they again travel to Salisbury, this time the master assassins walk to Skripal's house and somehow *"smear"* the liquid Novichok on the handle of his front door. No eye-witness, photograph or piece of CCTV footage has ever been made available to show either of these two men anywhere in the area of Skripal's house. The whereabouts of the opened bottle of poison has never been established.

- Having applied the poison, the two highly trained assassins do two things before returning to London: They drop their second, unopened, bottle of Novichok (presumably enough to kill 400,000 people) in a charity donation bin, rather than destroying it or taking it back to Russia. They stop by an antiques store to browse.

- The two assassins leave the country that afternoon, flying direct to Moscow, without knowing if their alleged target is dead, and again making no effort to conceal their origins.

- Despite both handling the poison, and somehow carrying enough of it back to contaminate their hotel room, neither of the men – nor any of the staff, train passengers or passers-by who come into contact with them – ever become sick, even though only 0.2mg of Novichok is a lethal dose.

- Later that afternoon, Sergei and Julia Skripal are found *"almost unconscious"* on a park bench in Salisbury town centre. It is claimed this was due to contact with the Novichok smeared on Sergei's door handle, though reports originally stated neither he nor his daughter had returned to the house, and the timing makes it unlikely they did.

- The person who found them was the most senior nurse in the British Army (likely in the area as part of Toxic Dagger, the British Military's landmark chemical weapons training exercise which began on 20th February). The nurse and her family administer *"emergency aid"* to the two alleged poisoning victims. Neither she nor anyone else on the scene, nor any of the first responders, ever experience any symptoms of nerve agent poisoning. Neither do any of the other people the Skripal's came into contact with that day.

• DS Nick Bailey, a CID officer who was in contact with the Skripals or their home at this time subsequently becomes ill. It has never been stated how exactly he was exposed. It was initially reported he was a first responder to the scene, but that story was changed and it was later claimed he visited the Skripal house. Despite the alleged lethality of Novichok in even very minute doses, Bailey is fit to return home after 18 days.

• Porton Down, the British government's chemical weapons research centre, is brought in to help identify what chemical – if any – the Skripals/Bailey were exposed to. Within a month they release a statement claiming the poison was *"a Novichok like agent"*, but that they could not pinpoint its origin. How they were able to test for a theoretical chemical without having a sample to test against has never been explained.

• In late June of 2018, Charlie Rowley finds the unopened perfume bottle a full of Novichok (whether he bought it from a charity shop or found it in a bin is unclear, both stories have been reported). Upon using the perfume Rowley's partner, Dawn Sturgess, falls ill. Later that day Rowley also falls ill. Sturgess dies in hospital two weeks later. But Rowley survives, making him the fourth person in this narrative to survive exposure to an agent lethal in doses as small as 0.2mg.

• Sergei Skripal and Julia both recovered and allegedly chose to live secluded lives. Sergei has not appeared in public at all since allegedly being found on that park bench. Julia made one brief press statement. Their current whereabouts are totally unknown.

This is the UK government's version of what happened. Unvarnished and unsanitised. None of it is disputed, exaggerated or speculative.

There have been claims that Skripal may have continued in the spying game. It is true that he had been giving talks, in this country and abroad, for a while. But one person who went to one of his lectures at a British military facility on the south coast described it as *"generally historic and anecdotal."*

Skripal's travels had taken him to the Czech Republic and Estonia, where he had been involved in seminars with intelligence officials. There are conflicting reports about what he was able to tell them; but the general consensus is that it was not anything earth-shattering, certainly nothing important enough to sign a death warrant. Skripal had also been visiting Spain, where he was recruited by MI6, with reports that he had been helping the country's CNI intelligence services.

Alexander Litvinenko had been helping the Spanish authorities look into alleged links between Russian organised crime and the Kremlin, before he was murdered.

This is one of a number of parallels between the Litvinenko and Skripal cases. Others include the use of highly unusual materials (Polonium and Novichok); two-man teams flying in to carry out the attack; as well as trails of radioactive isotopes and nerve agents found in the respective investigations. These similarities would seem to indicate real links between the two cases.

The Metropolitan police assistant commissioner Neil Basu, the head of UK counter-terrorism policing, said the investigation into the Salisbury attack was continuing.

Basu said the issues involved in bringing charges over the attack were complex. *"You'd have to prove he [Putin] was directly involved,"* he said.

"In order to get a European Arrest Warrant (EAW), you have to have a case capable of being charged in this country. We haven't got a case capable of being charged.

"We're police officers, so we have to go for evidence. There has been a huge amount of speculation about who is responsible, who gave the orders, all based on people's expert knowledge of Russia. I have to go with evidence."

The two Russian intelligence agents charged are still in Russia and liable to arrest if they leave. British prosecutors claim there is enough evidence to charge the Russian pair with conspiracy to murder Skripal, who sold Russian secrets to Britain before settling in the UK.

They have also been charged with conspiracy to murder his daughter, Julia, and DS Nick Bailey, who fell ill after going to the Skripals' home.

Basu said: *"The two that we announced in the press conference are wanted by us for extradition to be charged in this country. The whole of the investigation is still a live criminal investigation."*

The two Russians were further charged with the use and possession of Novichok, contrary to the Chemical Weapons Act.

Highly regarded US author Caitlin Johnstone summed it all up in a piece she wrote in November 2019.

"It's important to avoid fake news," she said. *"The difference between state media and western media is that in state media the government controls what information the public is given about what's going on in the world in order to prevent political dissent, whereas in western media this is instead done by billionaires.*

"Any attempt to understand the world which fails to take into account the fact that extremely powerful people are pouring massive amounts of money and resources into manipulating your understanding of the world will necessarily result in a distorted worldview.

"Whenever news media reports unsubstantiated assertions from anonymous sources in government agencies, just mentally insert "Here is something the government told us to tell you:" into the beginning of the report, because that's all they're doing.

"Sometimes all I can do is stare in awe at the power and efficiency of the propaganda machine," she added.

Or to quote again from **The Whistle Blower**: *"Then there are the lies. They start on the very first day. Nobody is as they seem, nothing is what it is made out to be. Our secret world is beyond the law".*

- **Appendix K**

Appendices

Appendix A:
Nuclear leaks in the UK

Windscale, Cumbria, 1957: Fire at a military plutonium reactor spread radioactive contamination over large parts of England and Western Europe

Dounreay, Caithness, 1963-2019: Hundreds of thousands of radioactive particles from old reactors contaminated the shoreline and the seabed

Sellafield, Cumbria, 1983: The government advised people not to swim or use beaches along 10 miles of coastline after a radioactive leak from a reprocessing plant

Chapelcross, Dumfriesshire, 2000-05: 126 radioactive particles from defunct reactors found on the shore of the Solway Firth

Thorp Reprocessing Plant, Sellafield, Cumbria, 2005: A leak of nuclear fuel dissolved in concentrated nitric acid, enough to half fill an Olympic-size swimming pool. The mixture, contained about 20 tonnes of uranium and plutonium fuel.

Hinkley Point A, Somerset, 2006: A leak of fission products from a containment facility. Five years earlier in 2001, Magnox Electric Ltd was fined £100,000 for safety offences at the Hinkley Point.

Bradwell, Essex, 2009: Magnox Electric Ltd was found guilty of breaching laws on the disposal of radioactive waste by failing to inspect a holding tank that had been leaking radioactive liquid from the nuclear power station for 14 years.

Sellafield, Cumbria, 2006-11: 1,233 radioactive particles and pebbles contaminated by historic leaks found and removed from nearby beaches

Dungeness B, Kent, 2013: The Environment Agency revealed that the nuclear power station had been leaking radioactive waste for many months. Routine tests on boreholes drilled close to the plant found traces of radioactive tritium measuring more than seven times the agreed level.

Appendix B:
MPs and Lords - Freemasons

Sir Tony Baldry
Conservative MP for Banbury (1983-2015)
Brian Binley
Conservative MP for Northampton South (2005-2015)
Bob Blackman

Conservative MP for Harrow East (2010-2019)
Ian Bruce
Conservative MP for South Dorset (1987-2001)
Sir Peter Emery
Conservative MP for East Devon (1959-2001)
Phil Gallie
Conservative MP for Ayr (1992-97) (also an MSP)
Keith Harding
Conservative MSP for Mid Scotland and Fife (1999-2003)
Joseph Hiley
Conservative MP for Pudsey (1959-1974)
Greville Ewan Janner
Labour MP for Leicester West (1970-1997)
David Jones
Conservative MP for Clwyd West (2005-2019
Gwilym Jones
Conservative MP for Cardiff North (1983-1997)
Sir Keith Joseph
Conservative MP for Leeds North East (1956-87)
Sir Edwin Leather
Conservative MP for North Somerset (1950-64)
Jack Lopresti
Conservative MP for Filton and Bradley Stoke (2010-2019)
Niall MacDermot
Labour MP for Derby North (1957-1970)
Angus MacDonald
SNP MSP for Falkirk East (2011-2019)
Jamie McGrigor
Conservative MSP for the Highlands and Islands (1999-2016)
David McLetchie
MSP and former leader of the Scottish Conservative Party (1999-2005)
Reginald Maudling
Conservative MP for Chipping Barnet (1950-1979)
Brian Monteith
Conservative MSP for Mid Scotland and Fife (1999-2007)
Robert Neill
Conservative MP for Bromley and Chislehurst (2006-2019)
Anthony Nelson
Conservative MP for Chichester (1974-1997)
Sir Ian Percival

Conservative MP for Southport (1959-1987)
Peter Rost
Conservative MP for Erewash (1970-1992)
Michael Russell
SNP MSP for South of Scotland (1999-2003 and 2007-2011) Argyll and Bute (2011-2019)
Cyril Smith
Liberal MP for Rochdale (1972-1992)
David Sumberg
Conservative MP for Bury South (1983-1997) and an MEP
Sir Charles S. Taylor
Conservative MP for Eastbourne (1935-1974)
Stefan Terlezki
Conservative MP for Cardiff West (1983-1997)
Sir Neil Thorne
Conservative MP for Ilford South (1979-1992)
Sir David Trippier
Conservative MP for Rossendale and Darwen (1979-1992)
Sir Peter Vanneck
Conservative MEP for Cleveland and Yorkshire North (1979-1989)
Sir Gerard Vaughan
Conservative MP for Reading East (1983-1997)
Sir Alfred Cecil Walker
Democratic Unionist MP for Belfast North (1983-2001)
Gary Waller
Conservative MP for Keighley (1979-97)
Sir John Wells
Conservative MP for Maidstone (1959-87)
Clement Atlee
Earl Attlee Labour Prime Minister (1945-1951)
Michael Baillie- Baron Burton
John Balcombe - Lord Justice Balcombe
Christopher Bathurst - Viscount Bledisloe
Conrad Black - Lord Black of Crossharbour
Adam Bligh - Earl of Darnley
Andrew Bruce - Earl of Elgin and Kincardine and head of the Royal Arch in Scotland
Edward Bulwer-Lytton - Baron Lytton
Hugh J F Lawson - 6th Baron Burnham
Charles Cadogan - Earl Cadogan

Ian Campbell - 12th Duke of Argyll
Angus Campbell-Gray - Lord Gray
Andrew Cavendish - Duke of Devonshire
John Murray Chadwick - Lord Justice Chadwick
William Clark - Baron Clark of Kempston and former Conservative MP
Spencer Compton - Marquess of Northampton
Charles Cornwall-Legh - Baron Grey of Codnor
David Dalrymple - Lord Hailes Scottish Judge
Edmund Davies - Judge and Baron Edmund-Davies
Mark Dundas - Marquess of Zetland
Sir Joseph Duveen - Baron Duveen
David Erskine - Earl of Buchan
Thomas Erskine - Earl of Kellie
Sir Edward Eveleigh - Lord Justice Eveleigh
Sir Henry Wemyss Feilden – Baronet Feilden
Prince Edward, Duke of Kent - Grand Master of United Grand Lodge of England
Prince Michael of Kent - Grand Master of the Grand Lodge of Mark Master Masons
Edmond W FitzMaurice - 7th Earl of Orkney
Henry James Fitzroy - Earl of Euston
Sir William Forbes - Baron Forbes
John Ganzoni - Baron Belstead; former leader of the House of Lords
Shane Gough - Viscount Shane Hugh Maryon Gough
George St Vincent Harris - Baron Harris
George Hay - Marquess of Tweeddale
Malcolm Hilbery - Lord Justice Hilbery
Arthur Hill - 4th Marquess of Downshire
Egerton Hubbard - 2nd Baron Addington
Donald Kaberry - Baron Kaberry of Adel and former Conservative MP
Henry George Charles Lascelles - Earl of Harewood
Alexander Lindsay - Earl of Balcarres
Richard Long - Viscount Long and former Conservative MP
Roger Lumley - Earl of Scarborough
George Makgill - Viscount of Oxfuird and Senior Rose Croix Mason
Barry Maxwell - Lord Farnham
Peter Millett - Lord Justice Millett
Archibald Montgomerie - Earl of Eglinton and Winton
Alexander Mountbatten - Marquess of Carisbrooke
Alexander Murray - Earl of Dunmore

Christopher John Norton - Lord Rathcreedan
Cecil Parkinson - Lord Parkinson and former Conservative Minister
Thomas Boothby Pasrkyns - Baron Rancliffe
James Prior - Baron Prior and former Conservative Cabinet Minister
Francis Pym - Baron Pym; Former Conservative Foreign Secretary
George Ramsay - Earl of Dalhousie
Matthew White Ridley - Viscount Ridley
Geoffrey Alexander Rowley-Conwy - Baron Langford
Edward Short - Baron Glenamara of Glenridding and former Labour MP
Sir David Steel - Lord Steel of Aikwood and former leader of the Liberals
Charles John Chetwynd Talbot - Earl of Shrewsbury and Earl of Talbot
Geoffrey Taylour - Marquess of Headfort
Sydney Templeman - Lord Justice Templeman
Charles Townshend - Marquess Townshend
Lloyd Tyrell-Kenyon - Lord Kenyon
John Vane - Baron Barnard
John Vivian - Baron Swansea
Sir George Waller - Lord Justice Waller
Richard Walter - Earl of Donoughmore
William Whitelaw - Viscount Whitelaw former Deputy Prime Minister
John Widgery - Baron Widgery Former Lord Chief Justice
Edward Bootle-Wilbraham - 2nd Earl of Lathom
Francis Vernon Willey - Lord Barnby and former Conservative MP
Fiennes Wykham - Baron Cornwallis

Appendix C:
Countries Bombed or Invaded by the USA since 1945
2014 - present
Iraq and Syria
Claimed to be against ISIS. Hundreds of thousands killed or injured.
2011 - present
Somalia
Ongoing drone strikes.
2011
Libya
Early US attacks under UNSC 1973 were followed by NATO's *Operation Unified Protector,* leading to regime change and death of Gaddafi.
2004 - present
Yemen
Ongoing drone strikes, allegedly targeting terror suspects.
2004 - present
Pakistan
Ongoing drone strikes, allegedly targeting militants.
2003 - 2011
Iraq
Invasion, bombing and regime change against Saddam Hussein.
2001 - present
Afghanistan
Regime change and boosting the opium trade under the pretext of pursuing Osama Bin Laden.
1999
Yugoslavia, Serbia
Allegedly to stop ethnic cleansing.
1998
Afghanistan
Cruise missile attacks on Osama Bin Laden's compounds.
1998
Sudan
Cruise missile attack on an antibiotic factory wrongly alleged to be producing WMD.
1995
Bosnia
Bombed Serbian forces and used Depleted Uranium artillery.
1993
Somalia

Up to 10,000 more Somalians were killed by US troops during America's so-called *humanitarian mission*.

1991

Iraq

Bombing devastated Baghdad. 177 million pounds of bombs fell in the most concentrated aerial onslaught in the history of the world.

1989 - 1990

Panama

More than 4,000 innocent civilians were killed in Panama during the US invasion. 15,000 people left homeless.

1987 - 1988

Iran

Operation Prime Chance, nominally to protect US flagged oil tankers in the Gulf

1986

Libya

Attempt to kill Gaddafi, Tripoli bombed. Operation El Dorado Canyon, one of more than 50 attempts to assassinate foreign leaders.

1979 - 1989

Nicaragua

30,000 lives were killed by the US contras in Nicaragua from 1979 to 1989. Ronald Reagan's *"freedom fighters"*.

1981 -1992

El Salvador

About 20 Americans were killed or wounded in crashes while flying reconnaissance missions. Evidence surfaced of a US role in the ground fighting. 75,000 civilian deaths at a cost of six billion dollars.

1983 - 1984

Grenada

Operation Urgent Fury, termed by the UN General Assembly termed it *"a flagrant violation of international law"* Hundreds of civilians were killed.

1969 - 1970

Cambodia

600,000 civilians were killed in Cambodia by US bombing between 1969 and 1975. More bombs dropped than the whole of WW2.

1961 - 1973

Vietnam

South Vietnam devastated and tens of thousands killed.

1964 - 1975

Laos

Over 500,000 people were killed in Laos when America subjected civilians to *"secret bombing"* from 1964 to 1973, dropping over two million tonnes of bombs on the country.

1965
Indonesia
700,000 Indonesian civilians were murdered in 1965 when the US armed and supported General Suharto.

1965
Peru
Bombing and assistance to counter-insurgency operations.

1964
Belgian Congo

1959 - 2000
Cuba
40 years of attacks, bombings, full-scale military invasion, sanctions, embargoes, assassinations, and the Bay of Pigs invasion in 1961.

1958
Indonesia
Large scale killings

1954
Guatemala
A CIA-organised coup overthrew the democratically-elected government of Jacobo Arbenz, initiating over 35 years of death squads, torture, disappearances, mass murder, totalling over 100,000 victims.

1948 - 1953
China
23,000 people were slaughtered in Taiwan by US-backed, trained, equipped, and funded forces (Chiang's Nationalist army) during the late 1940s.

1950 - 1953
Korea
Up to one third of the population (4.5 million) killed in order to prevent re-unification.

Appendix D:
UK outbreaks of Foot and Mouth Disease:
1922-1924
This outbreak had its origins in Ireland and first showed itself on the UK mainland on the north-west Lancashire coast. It first appeared among a shipment of cattle from Belfast which were landed at Fleetwood docks in

August 1922. 40 cattle were slaughtered at Fleetwood, but the disease had already spread to Cheshire and other neighbouring counties.

In November 1923 Hansard reported costs on the basis of the number of cases was £599,100. By this time 245 farms had been infected in 25 counties. The epidemic continued into 1924 by which time there were 1,929 outbreaks and 69,000 cattle, 26,000 sheep and 33,000 pigs were culled.

1952-1953

This major outbreak initially centred on Cumbria and southern Scotland which included 500 individual outbreaks and compensation costs of £2.5million (a huge figure at the time)

By 1953 the disease had spread to Aberdeenshire in North East Scotland and progressed to South Wales where in 11 outbreaks 112 cattle, 261 sheep and 63 pigs were slaughtered.

1967–68

The UK experienced the worst Foot and Mouth Disease epidemic of the 20th century.

It was attributed to pig swill containing infected Argentine lamb at a farm in Shropshire. 2,364 outbreaks were recorded during a nine-month period, resulting in the slaughter of nearly 450,000 animals.

Ninety-four percent of the cases occurred in North-West Midlands and North Wales. The average number of animals that were slaughtered in each confirmed case was around 200.

2001

The most severe outbreak of Foot and Mouth Disease occurred in the UK during 2001 causing a crisis in British agriculture and tourism. Over six million cows and sheep were killed in an eventually successful attempt to halt the disease. Cumbria was the worst affected area of the country, with 893 cases. Officially, there were 2,000 cases of Foot and Mouth in the 2001 UK outbreak.

2007

Foot and Mouth virus escaped from a government vaccine facility at Pirbright in Surrey causing disease on adjacent farms. Movement restrictions had a severe economic impact on the farming industry.

Appendix E:
UK national newspapers circulation (November 2019)

Metro (free)	1.420 million
The Sun	1.223 million
The Daily Mail	1.136 million

The Sun on Sunday	1.042 million
The Mail on Sunday	959,671
The Sunday Times	665,618
The Daily Mirror	463,256
The Times	367,074
The Sunday Mirror	378,239
The Daily Telegraph	308,015
The Daily Express	302,690
The Sunday Telegraph	246,797
The i	221,083
The Daily Star	183,127
The Financial Times	168,958
The Observer	160,068
The People	144,832
The Guardian	128,492

Appendix F:
Books by John Bauldie

The Telegraph, 56 issues from 1981-1996

Bob Dylan and Desire, Wanted Man Study Series 1983

The Ghost of Electricity, Romford UK, self-published 1988

Wanted Man: In Search of Bob Dylan, London, Black Spring Press, 1990

The Bootleg Series Volumes 1-3, liner-notes Columbia Legacy, New York, 1991

Diary of a Bobcat, Romford, Wanted Man, 1995

All Across The Telegraph: A Bob Dylan Handbook, London, WH Allen, 1987

Oh No! Not Another Bob Dylan Book, UK: Square One Books, 1991 aka *Absolutely Dylan: An Illustrated Biography*, Viking Studio Books, 1991

Appendix G:
Deaths from pesticide poisoning in England and Wales: 1945-1989, by Casey P, Vale JA

Deaths from pesticide poisoning occurring in England and Wales between 1945 and 1989 (no data available for 1954).

Pesticides were responsible for 1012 (1.1%) of the 87,385 deaths from poisoning occurring over this 44-year period.

At least 73% of all pesticide fatalities were due to suicide and overall there was a predominance of males (male:female ratio 2.4:1).

No deaths from pesticide poisoning in children under 10 years have been reported since 1974 although almost 50% of suspected pesticide poisoning incidents involve this age group.

Herbicides were responsible for 787 (78%) fatal poisonings, 110 (11%) were caused by insecticides, 69 (6.8%) by rodenticides, 30 (3.0%) by wood preservatives and 16 (1.6%) by other pesticides.

The herbicide, Paraquat, was responsible for 570 of 1012 (56%) deaths and, although there has been a progressive decline in the annual number of deaths from Paraquat poisoning since 1982, Paraquat remains the most common cause of fatal pesticide poisoning in England and Wales.

Sodium chlorate caused 113 (11.2%) deaths, most of these fatalities occurring between 1965 and 1983; only one death has been recorded since 1984. The phenoxyacetate herbicides resulted in 50 deaths; 2.4-D was implicated most commonly.

Sixty-eight deaths were due to organophosphorus insecticides; demeton-S-methyl, malathion and mevinphos were involved most frequently. Only eight deaths resulted from organochlorine insecticides and two of these also involved an organophosphorus insecticide.

Appendix H:

Famous British Spies:

Mark Allen
Denis Donaldson
Kevin Fulton
Peter Lunn
Oleg Lyalin
Howard Marks
Martin McGartland
Omar Nasiri
Michael Oatley
Sergei Skripal
Stakeknife
Richard Tomlinson
Jenna Ferguson

Famous British/Russian Double Agents:

Len Beurton
George Blake
Anthony Blunt
Frank Bossard
Guy Burgess
John Cairncross
David Crook
Tom Driberg
Raymond Fletcher
Alexander Foote
Guy Liddell
Donald Maclean
Melita Norwood
Ernest Holloway Oldham
John Peet
Kim Philby
Goronwy Rees
Dave Springhall
Bob Stewart
John Alexander Symonds
Edith Tudor-Hart
Arthur Wynn

Bibliography

Chapter 1
1. J Smith, Clouds of Deceit (1985)
2. T Wheldon, Committee on Medical Aspects of Radiation in the Environment (COMARE) 14th Report (1989)
3. C Caulfield, Multiple Exposures (1990)
4. I Sutherland, Dounreay: An Experimental Reactor Establishment (1990)
5. D Sumner, T Wheldon, W Watson, Radiation Risks (1991)
6. C Busby, Low level radiation from the nuclear industry: the biological consequences. (Aberystwyth: Green Audit) (1992)
7. C Busby, Radiation and Cancer in Wales (Aberystwyth: Green Audit) (1994)
8. C Busby, Wings of Death: Nuclear Pollution and Human Health (Aberystwyth: Green Audit) (1995)
9. UKAEA, Dounreay Background Brief (1996)
10. C Busby, Jacobs Journal of Epidemiology and Preventive Medicine (1996)
11. Health and Safety Executive Great Britain and Scottish Environment Protection Agency, Safety Audit of Dounreay (1998)
12. UKAEA, Restoring Our Environment (2004)
13. C Busby and AV Yablokov, Chernobyl 20 years on… the health effects of the Chernobyl Accident (2006)
14. C Busby, Wolves of Water. A Study Constructed from Atomic Radiation, Morality, Epidemiology, Science, Bias, Philosophy and Death (2006)

Chapter 2
1. S Knight, The Brotherhood (1984)
2. M Short, Inside the Brotherhood (1989)
3. M Baigent & R Leigh, The Temple and the Lodge (1989)
4. Secretary of State for Scotland & The Home Office, Evidence Submitted to Lord Cullen's Inquiry into the Circumstances Leading up to and Surrounding the Events at Dunblane Primary School on Wednesday 13 March 1996 (1996)
5. M North, Dunblane: Never Forget (2000)
6. K Bowers, Hiding in Plain Sight (2000)
7. S Uttley, Dunblane Unburied (2006)
8. D Harrison, The Transformation of Freemasonry (2010)
9. P Aylward, Understanding Dunblane and other Massacres: Forensic Studies of Homicide, Paedophilia, and Anorexia (2012)
10. R Berman, The Foundations of Modern Freemasonry: The Grand Architects, Political Change and the Scientific Enlightenment (2014)
11. The Guardian, Freemasonry Explained: a guide to the secretive society (2018)

Chapter3

1. R Chambers, To Send or Not: Cases and materials on extradition and rendition (1988)
2. J Pilger, Distant Voices (1992)
3. G James, In the Public Interest (1995)
4. J Mayer, The Maher Arar case (The New Yorker) (2005)
5. B Davies, Terrorism: Inside a World Phenomenon (2005)
6. S Grey, Ghost Plane: The Untold Story of the CIA's Secret Rendition Programme (2006)
7. C Calderwood, A Brief History of the Middle East (2006)
8. T Paglen, Torture Taxi: On the Trail of the CIA's Rendition Flights (2007)
9. CS Smith, Bad Men: Guantanamo Bay and The Secret Prisons (2008)
10. House Hearing, 110th Congress, Diplomatic Assurances and Rendition to Torture: The Perspective of the State Department's Legal Driver (2013)
11. J Bravin, The Terror Courts: America's Experiment with Rough Justice at Guantanamo Bay (2013)
12. S Ivey, Delta Green: Extraordinary Renditions (2015)
13. The Senate Intelligence Committee, Report on Torture (2015)
14. L Siems, Guantánamo Diary (2017)
15. D McCarthy, Selling the CIA: Public Relations and the Culture of Secrecy (2018)

Chapter 4

1. M Dando, Biological Warfare in the 21st Century (1994)
2. J Freedland, A catalogue of failures that discredits the whole system (The Guardian) (2001)
3. DEFRA, Origin of the UK Foot and Mouth Disease Epidemic 2001 (2002)
4. A Woods, A Manufactured Plague: The History of Foot-and-mouth Disease in Britain (2004)
5. M Mort, I Convery, C Bailey & J Baxter, The Health and Social Consequences of the 2001 Foot & Mouth Disease Epidemic in North Cumbria (Institute for Health Research, Lancaster University) (2004)
6. DEFRA, Foot and Mouth Disease - Applying the Lessons (2005)
7. M Mort, I Convery, C Bailey & J Baxter, Animal disease and human trauma : emotional geographies of disaster. (2008)
8. M Doring & B Nerlich, The Social and Cultural Impact of Foot and Mouth Disease in the UK in 2001: Experiences and Analyses (2009)
9. TJ Knight-Jones & J Rushton, The economic impacts of foot and mouth disease – What are they, how big are they and where do they occur? (Preventive Veterinary Medicine) (2013)
10. A Donaldson, Foot and Mouth Disease (Veterinary Times) (2016)

Chapter 5
1. G Orwell, Nineteen Eighty-Four (1949)
2. J Bamford, Body Of Secrets: How America's NSA & Britain's GCHQ Eavesdrop On The World (2001)
3. D Anderson, A Question of Trust (2015)
4. O Jones, The Establishment (2015)
5. D Anderson, Bulk Powers Review (2016)
6. A Toben, Surveillance Zone: The Hidden World of Corporate Surveillance Detection & Covert Special Operations (2017)
7. D Lyon, The Culture of Surveillance: Watching as a Way of Life (2108)
8. E Snowden, Permanent Record (2019)
9. S Zuboff & N Zanzarella, The Age of Surveillance Capitalism: The Fight for a Human Future at the New Frontier of Power (2019)
10. J Bruder & D Maharidge, Snowden's Box: Trust in the Age of Surveillance (2020)

Chapter 6
1. RW Rowland, A Hero From Zero (1988)
2. S McCleod & T Sancton, Death of a Princess (Diana Princess of Wales) (1998)
3. R Tomlinson, The Big Breach (2001)
4. N Botham, The Murder of Princess Diana - The Truth Behind the Assassination of the People's Princess (2004)
5. J Morgan, Cover-up of a Royal Murder (2008)
6. J Morgan, Diana Inquest: The Untold Story (2009)
7. J Morgan, Paris-London Connection (2012)
8. A Power, The Princess Diana Conspiracy: The Evidence of Murder (2013)
9. J Morgan, How They Murdered Princess Diana: The Shocking Truth (2014)
10. D Howard & C McLaren, Diana: Case Solved: The Definitive Account That Proves What Really Happened (2019)

Chapter 7
1. D Flintham & N Herbert, Press Freedom in Britain (1991)
2. M Leapman, Treacherous Estate (1992)
3. K Williams, Read All About It! A History of the British Newspaper (2009)
4. BH Leveson, An inquiry into the culture, practices and ethics of the press: executive summary and recommendations [Leveson Report] (2012)
5. S Barnett & Townend, And What Good Came of it at Last? Press – Politician Relations Post?Leveson (2014)
6. R Cohen-Almagor, After Leveson Recommendations for Instituting the Public and Press Council (2014)
7. RJ Thomas & T Finneman, Who watches the watchdogs? British newspaper metadiscourse on the Leveson Inquiry (2014)

8. N Davies, Hack Attack: How the truth caught up with Rupert Murdoch (2015)
9. S Barnett, The Tragic Downfall of British Media (2016)
10. O Jones, We Can No Longer Pretend the British Press is Impartial (2017)
11. C Frost, Privacy and the News Media (2019)

Chapter 8
1. Red Act, Depleted Uranium, Sick Soldiers and Dead Children (1993)
2. EG Dixon, Assessment of the Risks from Imbedded Fragments of Depleted Uranium (1993)
3. Felicity Arbuthnot, A Poisoned Legacy (1999)
4. D Fahey, Don't Look, Don't Find: Gulf War veterans, the US government and depleted uranium, 1990-2000 (2000)
5. FF Hahn, Carcinogenesis of Depleted Uranium Fragments (2000)
6. Royal Society Great Britain, The Health Hazards of Depleted Uranium munitions (2002)
7. A Gutt & B Vitale, Depleted Uranium - Deadly, Dangerous and Indiscriminate: The Full Picture (2003)
8. Felicity Arbuthnot, Depleted Uranium - an untold story (2007)
9. Francis Boyle, The Criminality of Nuclear Deterrence (2012)
10. RA Fathi, Medicine, Conflict and Survival (2013)

Chapter 9
1. Robert Shelton, No Direction Home (1986)
2. John Bauldie, All Across The Telegraph (1987)
3. The Independent, John Bauldie an Obituary (1996)
4. Expecting Rain, Devoted to Dylan and the Wanderers (1996)
Bolton News, Pilot Error Killed Chelsea Boss Harding (1997)
5. Bolton News, Harding Crash, Fans Partner Sues for £m (1998)
6. Don Hale, Heli Death Link to Dando (2008)
7. Don Hale, Police: Hitman Did kill Crimewatch presenter Jill Dando (2014)

Chapter 10
1. M Dando, Biological Warfare in the 21st Century (1994)
2. R Edwards, The WW2 bombs dumped off western Scotland washing up on beaches (New Scientist) (1995)
3. Fisheries Research Services, Survey of the Beaufort's Dyke Explosives Disposal Site – November 1995 (1996)
4. C Arthur, Ministers admit nuclear waste was dumped in sea (The Independent) (1997)
5. G Ford, L Ottemoller, B Baptie, Analysis of Explosions in the BGS Seismic Database in the Area of Beaufort's Dyke, 1992–2004 (2005)

6. Noblis, A Short History of the Development of Nerve Gases (2011)
7. V Bael & Bellis, EU Anti-Dumping and Other Trade Defence Instruments (2011)
8. Center for Disease Control and Prevention, Facts About Sarin (2017)
9. The Admiralty, British Munitions 1944: Recognition and Disposal (2018)
10. Chemsea, Chemical Munitions Search and Assessment (2018)

Chapter 11
1. P Rogers, As Lambs to the Slaughter: Facts About Nuclear War (1981)
2. P Eddy, P Gillman, M Linklater, The Falklands War (1982)
3. A Barnett, Iron Britannia: Why Parliament Waged Its Falklands War (1982)
4. T Dalyell, One Man's Falklands (1982)
5. T Dalyell, Thatcher's Torpedo (1983)
6. D Brown, The Royal Navy and the Falklands War (1987)
7. P Rogers, Guide to Nuclear Weapons (1988)
8. RC Thornton, The Falklands Sting: Reagan, Thatcher, and Argentina's bomb (1998)
9. S Gregory, The Hidden Cost of Deterrence: Nuclear Weapons Accidents (1990)
10. P Rogers & M Dando, Directory of Nuclear, Biological and Chemical Arms and Disarmament (1990)
11. D Blakeway, The Falklands War (1992)
12. P Rogers, *The Role of British Nuclear Weapons After the Cold War* (1995)
13. IAEA, *Radioactive Wastes Entering the Marine Environment* (1996)
13. RC Thornton, The Falklands Sting: Reagan, Thatcher, and Argentina's bomb (1998)
14. A Magoudi, *Rendez-vous - The Psychoanalysis of François Mitterrand* (2005)
15. H Bicheno, Razor's Edge: the unofficial history of the Falklands War (2006)
16. L Freedman, *The Official History of the Falklands Campaign: War and Diplomacy* (2007)

Chapter 12
1. M McGartland, Fifty Dead Men Walking (1997)
2. M McGartland, Dead Man Running (1998)
3. P Foot, Who Framed Colin Wallace? (1989)
4. Belfast Telegraph, Dark World of Agents is Not Black and White (2012)
5. K Fulton, Double Agent: My Secret Life Undercover in the IRA (2019)
6. PR Keefe, Say Nothing: A True Story Of Murder and Memory In Northern Ireland (2019)
7. T Leahy, The Intelligence War against the IRA (2020)

Chapter 13

R Carson, Silent Spring (1962)

D Good, A Short Story (1963)

2. HM government, Use of fluoroacetamide and sodium fluoroacetate as rodenticides: Precautionary measures (1970)

3. J Pattison, The emergence of bovine spongiform encephalopathy and related diseases (1998)

4. RM Ridley & H Baker, Fatal Protein: The Story of CJD, BSE and Other Prion Diseases (1998)

5. C Ainsworth & D Carrington, BSE disaster: the history (2000)

6. P Van Zwanenberg & E Millstone, Policy-Making Under Conditions of Uncertainty and Controversy: BSE Policy in the UK, France, the Netherlands, Portugal and the European Commission (2001)

7. P Van Zwanenberg & E Millstone, BSE: Risk, Science, and Governance (2005)

8. M & N Purdey, Animal Pharm: One Man's Struggle to Discover the Truth About Mad Cow Disease and Variant CJD (2007)

9. JFM Clarke, Pesticides, pollution and the UK's silent spring, 1963–1964: Poison in the Garden of England (2017)

10. Ground Sure, Sheep dip – has the wool been pulled over our eyes? (2019)

Chapter 14

1. G Wilson, Child-Lovers, The Study of Paedophiles in Society (1981)

2. M Farrell, Understanding the paedophile (1989)

3. A Meyer, The Child at Risk: Paedophiles, Media Responses and Public Opinion (2007)

4. S Goode, Paedophiles in Society (2011)

5. S Danczuk, Smile for the Camera: The Double Life of Cyril Smith (2014)

6. L Delap, Child welfare, child protection and sexual abuse, 1918-1990 (2015)

7. The Guardian, The Number of British Paedophiles May Be Far Higher Than Thought (2017)

8. V Wolfe, Child Sex Offenders: What makes a Paedophile? (2017)

Chapter 15

1. C Pincher, Inside Story (1978)

2. P Wright, Spy Catcher (1987)

3. C Pincher, A Web of Deception (1987)

4. A Cavendish, Inside Intelligence (1987)

5. D Charters & M Tugwell, Deception Operations (1989)

6. T Collins, Open Verdict (1990)

7. E Volkman, Espionage (1995)

8. C Andrew & V Mitrokhin, The Mitrokhin Archive (2000)

9. G Thomas, Secrets and Lies (2007)

10. M Sixsmith, The Litvinenko File (2007)

11. A Goldfarb & M Litvinenko, Death of a Dissident: The Poisoning of Alexander Litvinenko and the Return of the KGB (2008)

12. L Harding, A Very Expensive Poison: The Definitive Story of the Murder of Litvinenko and Russia's War with the West (2016)

13. M Urban, The Skripal Files (2018)

14. R Shepherd, Unnatural Causes (2018)

15. N Kollerstrom, The Great British Skripal Hoax (2019)

16. C Andrew, The Secret World: A History of Intelligence (2019)

Glossary of Abbreviations

ASU	Active Service Unit
BAFTA	British Academy of Film and Television Awards
BBC	British Broadcasting Corporation
BGS	British Geological Survey
BNFL	British Nuclear Fuels Ltd
Bq	Becquerel (measurement of radioactivity)
BSE	Bovine Spongiform Encephalopathy
CBI	Confederation of British Industry
CCTV	Closed Circuit Television
CEO	Chief Executive Officer
CFA	Clyde Fisherman's Association
CIA	Central Intelligence Agency
CJD	Creutzfeldt-Jakob Disease
COINTELPRO	Counter Intelligence Program
CO2	Carbon Dioxide
COMARE	Committee on Medical Aspects of Radiation in the Environment
CPS	Crown Prosecution Service
CMPs	Closed Material Procedures
CRCE	Centre for Radiation, Chemical and Environmental Hazards
DEFRA	Department for Environment, Food and Rural Affairs
DFR	Dual Fluid Reactor
DofH	Department of Health
DfE	Department for Education
DRIPA	Data Retention and Investigatory Powers Act
DSRL	Dounreay Site Restoration Ltd
DU	Depleted Uranium
EAW	European Arrest Warrant
EDM	Early Day Motion
EU	European Union
ECHR	European Court of Human Rights
FBI	Federal Bureau of Investigation
FHE	Further and Higher Education
FMD	Foot and Mouth Disease
FRS	Fisheries Research Services
FRV	Fisheries Research Vessel
FSB	Russian Security Services
FTSE	Financial Times Stock Exchange
GCSE	General Certificate of Secondary Education
GM	Genetically Modified
GCHQ	Government Communications Headquarters
GU	Russian Military Intelligence Unit

HMP	Her Majesty's Prison
HMS	Her Majesty's Ship
HSE	Health and Safety Executive
IBV	Avian infectious Bronchitis Virus
IICSA	Independent Inquiry into Child Sexual Abuse
IPCC	Independent Police Complaints Commission
ISAM	International Standard Asset Management
OFQUAL	Office of Qualifications and Examinations Regulation
IAEA	International Atomic Energy Agency
ILS	Instrument Landing System
IRA	Irish Republican Army
ISIS	Islamic State of Iraq and Syria
ISOF	Iraqi Special Operations Forces
KGB	Soviet Secret Service
KIPP	Knowledge Is Power Program
MAFF	Ministry of Agriculture Fisheries and Food
MBM	Meat-and-Bone Meal
Met	Metropolitan Police
MI5	Military Intelligence Section 5
MI6	Military Intelligence Section 6
MND	Motor Neurone Disease
MoD	Ministry of Defence
MOSSAD	Israel Intelligence Agency
MP	Member of Parliament
ME	Myalgic Encephalomyelitis
NATO	North Atlantic Treaty Organization
NCB	National Coal Board
NGVFA	National Gulf Veterans and Families Association
NHS	National Health Service
NPA	National Pig Association
NPR	Number Plate Recognition
NSA	National Security Agency
NUF	National Union of Farmers
NUM	National Union of Mineworkers
OP	Organo Phosphate
OSA	Official Secrets Act
PA	Press Association
PAC	Public Accounts Committee
PCC	Police and Crime Commissioner
PIE	Paedophile Information Exchange
PM	Prime Minister
PMQs	Prime Minister's Questions
PPS	Parliamentary Private Secretary
PSNI	Police Service of Northern Ireland

QC	Queen's Counsel
RFID	Radio-Frequency Identification
RIPA	Regulation of Investigatory Powers Act
RUC	Royal Ulster Constabulary
RWMAC	Radioactive Waste Management Advisory Committee
SAS	Special Air Service
SAT	Scholastic Aptitude Test
SBS	Special Boat Service
SCRAM	Scottish Campaign to Resist the Atomic Menace
SDP	Social Democratic Party
SEPA	Scottish Environment Protection Agency
SIO	Senior Investigating Officer
SIS	Secret Intelligence Service
SNP	Scottish National Party
SOV/OPS	Special Spying Operations
TB	Tuberculosis
UKAEA	UK Atomic Energy Authority
UKIP	United Kingdom Independence Party
UN	United Nations
VAT	Value Added Tax
WHO	World Health Organisation

Picture Credits

About the Author

Deep Throat is written and edited by Nic Outterside, and published by *Time is an Ocean Publications*.
Nic is an award-winning journalist and creative author, who over 38 years has worked across all forms of media, including radio, magazines, newspapers, books and online.
Among more than a dozen awards to his name are *North of England Daily Journalist of the Year, Scottish Daily Journalist of the Year, Scottish Weekly Journalist of the Year* and a special award for investigative journalism.
In 1994, 53 MPs signed an Early Day Motion in the UK House of Commons praising Nic's research and writing.
In 2016 Nic was awarded an honorary doctorate in written journalism.

Printed in Great Britain
by Amazon

15908544R00150